T0156775

REVISED AND EXPANDED EDITION

MAKE A SCENE

Writing a Powerful Story One Scene at a Time

JORDAN ROSENFELD

REVISED AND EXPANDED EDITION

MAKE

Ⓐ

SCENE

JORDAN ROSENFELD

**WRITER'S
DIGEST
BOOKS**

WRITER'S DIGEST BOOKS

An imprint of Penguin Random House LLC
penguinrandomhouse.com

Copyright © 2017 by Jordan Rosenfeld
Penguin supports copyright. Copyright fuels creativity, encourages diverse voices, promotes free speech, and creates a vibrant culture. Thank you for buying an authorized edition of this book and for complying with copyright laws by not reproducing, scanning, or distributing any part of it in any form without permission. You are supporting writers and allowing Penguin to continue to publish books for every reader.

ISBN 978-1-4403-5141-9

Edited by Karen Krumpak
Designed by Alexis Estoye

146122990

DEDICATION

This second edition is dedicated to all the writers who toil in near obscurity, wondering if anyone ever reads their words. Your words matter!

ACKNOWLEDGMENTS

Make a Scene's first incarnation was a labor of love and a leap of faith from a new writer with little "platform" and even less publishing experience. When I first wrote this book back in 2006, there was no social media—not even Facebook, if you can imagine such a time. I let my readers know of its existence by an email newsletter and hand-mailed postcards. I've been amazed and rewarded by my many readers over the ten years of this book's existence, and recently I felt I owed it to them to update some things that have needed expanding over the years as my own writing knowledge has grown. This second chance, however, would not exist without the faith and guidance of Rachel Randall and Phil Sexton at Writer's Digest Books. As always, I would not have been able to complete it without the support of my many friends, notably Amy McElroy, who keeps me honest as a writer. And there is no greater support than my husband, Erik, and my son, Ben, who wasn't even a twinkle in my eye when I first dreamed up this book. In an age where they say that print is dead, I thank everyone who keeps proving "them" wrong.

ABOUT THE AUTHOR

Jordan is the author of the writing guides *Writing the Intimate Character: Create Unique, Compelling Characters Through Mastery of Point of View*; *Writing Deep Scenes: Plotting Your Story Through Action, Emotion & Theme* with Martha Alderson; *A Writer's Guide to Persistence: How to Create a Lasting & Productive Writing Practice* with Rebecca Lawton; and *Write Free: Attracting the Creative Life*. She is also the author of suspense novels *Women in Red*, *Forged in Grace*, and *Night Oracle*.

Jordan's articles and essays have been published in such places as *The Atlantic*, *mental_floss*, *the New York Times*, *New York Magazine*, *Pacific Standard*, *Quartz*, *Scientific American*, *Writer's Digest magazine*, *The Writer*, and more. Visit her website: www.jordanrosenfeld.net or follow her on twitter: @JordanRosenfeld.

TABLE OF CONTENTS

PART I

ARCHITECTURE OF A SCENE

PART II

CORE ELEMENTS OF THE SCENE

PART III

SCENE TYPES

PART IV

OTHER SCENE CONSIDERATIONS

PREFACE

....
2017

A bit more than ten short years ago (they went by fast!), I joined a friend
on a self-made writing retreat in Mendocino, California, in the middle of
winter. Rain doused our log cabins all weekend and steam rose from the
moss-covered roofs, providing the perfect ambience, and motivation, to
keep writing. We kept warm by making our own fires in the wood-burn-
ing stove while sharing writerly shoptalk on our breaks, and I wrote the
proposal for the first edition of *Make a Scene* by hand, with pen and paper.
This was before all the technology we now take for granted, and I didn't
even own a laptop. Back then, my cell phone was twice as big as my wal-
let and definitely not smart, there were no iPads or electric cars, and we
didn't even have social media yet (unless you count Myspace)! No Twitter or Facebook—and we sure as heck couldn't have imagined Snapchat.
When I sent the good news to friends about selling *Make a Scene* to Writer's Digest Books, I did it by e-mail, inputting one person's name at a time.

A lot has changed since that day, but very little when it comes to good
writing. Ten years later, I can still say with confidence that learning how
to write strong scenes remains the single most important element of the
craft that you can learn. If anything, I'd argue it's even more relevant to
fiction in the modern publishing marketplace, where books now compete
with streaming video clips, immediate access to movies in your pocket,
high-quality TV, and an addiction to instant gratification.

I've had the good fortune to watch my editing clients pursue publication of their books, and those who can craft compelling scenes have seen the most success. To my new readers, I hope you will join the many others who have found the magic of scenes and learn to employ them in your own work. To all of my dedicated readers over the years who have contacted me to say that this book made them a better writer, I thank you. Let's keep making a scene.

INTRODUCTION

Just as you are not a *singular* thing, but a *sum* of blood and flesh and organs and neurons working together, a scene contains all the elements of great fiction. Many writers understand that they must "show, not tell," but don't necessarily understand that this requires all the elements of fiction to work together, to inform each other, in order to create a narrative that is compelling and capable of maintaining a reader's attention.

I feel confident when I say that if you can understand what a scene is, how all its elements collaborate to create a vivid and compelling piece in the larger puzzle of your story, and how those moments add up to a satisfying sense of completion, you'll write your drafts differently and become a more self-assured writer with a page-turner on your hands.

To make scene construction clear, start with the basic function and structure of a scene. Even if you can identify a scene in someone else's work, you may not be able to do so when it comes to your own writing (I have worked with plenty of writers who struggled with this). Where does a scene stop and start? Can too much or not enough of one element ruin the whole story? I want you to know why you should bother to write scenes and how a single scene is built before you try to build a house out of them.

The bulk of this book explores different kinds of scenes that compose a narrative, from suspense scenes to contemplative scenes. The different types of scenes are like notes in a symphony: Individually they may be intense or mild, contemplative or dramatic, but when used in combination with other scenes, they form a fantastic narrative that feels rich and complex.

By the book's end, you should be able to build vivid scenes and link them together in a way that creates a compelling narrative that engages the reader and makes you proud.

Throughout this book I've included sidebars in which published authors share their insights on all aspects and techniques of scene writing. These exclusive thoughts prove that even best-selling authors can be inspired and moved by a well-written scene.

To help you avoid tactics that could bore the reader, I leave you with this caveat: *The audience is watching.* The first draft is your one shot to tell yourself the story without anyone breathing down your neck. After that, you must write (and especially revise) as if the reader is sitting behind your desk, awaiting your finished pages. What this means is that it is your job to entertain and inform the reader through clear writing and powerful scenes; if you are using fancy prose or showy strategies to amuse yourself or prove something to yourself, you aren't keeping your audience in mind.

Though it's not wise to write *first* drafts with the superego breathing its foul, critical breath down your neck, your readers should be the most precious people imaginable (second in line only to your characters). You see, most readers are not writers; they don't know how hard it is to write. They have very little patience or empathy for your struggles. They just want a good story, and they will abandon one that doesn't hold their interest in a heartbeat. It's up to you to ensure that they don't lose interest in *your* story.

PART I

ARCHITECTURE OF A SCENE

" You climb a long ladder until you can see over the roof, or over the clouds. You are writing a book. You watch your shod feet step on each round rung, one at a time; you do not hurry and do not rest. Your feet feel the steep ladder's balance … you climb steadily, doing your job in the dark. "

—ANNIE DILLARD

FUNCTIONS OF A SCENE

You've felt the pulse-pounding drama of a good story, caught up in a book so real you felt as though it were happening to you and turning pages at a furious clip. What makes that story, book, or essay come to life? Strong, powerful scenes.

Writing is a wildly creative act, and therefore writers often wish to defy rules and formulas. Just when a rule is agreed upon, it seems, some writer comes along to break it. The good news is that, while there *is* a formula to scene writing, it's not straightforward. It's not like a paint-by-numbers kit, where you fill in the listed colors and voilà, you have a perfect painting of dogs playing poker, in all the right proportions. The scene-writing formula is more like the creative spontaneity of cooking: You start with the ingredients the recipe calls for; you work within the guidelines, using pans, heat, and time; but variations on the main ingredients yield different, even surprising, results.

The only certain result you want is to snare readers' attention with your very first sentence and never let them go. Since writing competes with the fast-paced, seductive intensity of online streaming and social media, your challenge is to write scenes with the power to rivet readers right where they read.

THE SCENE DEFINED

So what is a scene, exactly? Scenes are the essential DNA of story: They are the individual "cells" of information that shape the essence of the story in which sympathetic characters undertake significant actions in a vivid and memorable way on the journey toward a compelling plot goal. When strung together, individual scenes add up to build fully developed plots and storylines.

The recipe for a scene includes the following basic ingredients:

- **PROTAGONIST:** The main character, who has goals and is complex and nuanced, and who undergoes change throughout your narrative, demonstrated in "words and deeds"
- **ANTAGONIST AND ALLIES:** The characters who thwart and support your protagonist
- **A POINT OF VIEW:** The lens through which the scenes are seen (either a limited, internal POV or some form of omniscient POV)
- **MOMENTUM:** Beat-by-beat action that allows the story to feel as if it is unfolding in real time
- **NEW PLOT INFORMATION:** Events, discussions, discoveries, epiphanies, etc., that advance your story and deepen characters, usually as consequences of prior scenes, so that scenes weave together
- **TENSION:** Conflict, suspense, and drama that test your characters and ultimately reveal their personalities, and line-by-line intensity that keeps readers reading
- **SETTING AND TIME PERIOD:** A rich physical setting that calls on all the senses and enables the reader to see and enter the world you've created
- **THEMATIC IMAGERY:** Also called "sensory imagery," details evoking the five senses and often symbolic visual analogies and metaphors that reveal themes, emotion, and subtext
- **NARRATIVE SUMMARY:** A spare amount of narrative summary or exposition, "telling" language that cuts to the chase when needed

Arguably, the one thing in this list that truly makes a scene a scene is momentum—events happening and people acting out behaviors in a simulation of real time—but well-balanced scenes include a little bit of everything. Mixing those ingredients together in varying amounts will yield drama, emotion, passion, power, and energy: In short, a page-turner. Some scenes need more physical action, while others may require a lot of dialogue. Some scenes will take place with barely a word spoken or with very small actions; other scenes may require vivid interaction with the setting. As you make your way through this book, you will get a better grasp of the power of the scene and how to use it to achieve your desired effects.

In part two, we'll discuss all of the above ingredients, as well as these more complex scene considerations:

- Dramatic tension, which creates the potential for conflict in scenes
- Scene subtext, which deepens and enriches your scenes
- Scene intentions, which ensure characters' actions are purposeful
- Pacing and scene length, which influence the mood and tone of individual scenes

These latter ingredients deepen your scenes and help you take them beyond the perfunctory. Dramatic tension will make the reader care about your characters and keep her glued to the page. Subtext can build imagery and emotion into the deeper layers of scenes so that your writing feels rich and complex. Scene intentions help guide your characters and take them through changes in as dramatic a way as possible. By pacing your scenes well and choosing the proper length for each scene, you can control the kinds of emotional effects your scenes have, leaving the reader with the feeling of having taken a satisfying journey.

ANATOMY OF A SCENE

To help clarify how all of the components I've just discussed function within a scene, here is a complex snippet of a scene from Erika Swyler's novel, *The Book of Speculation*, about a librarian named Simon trying to understand the mystery of his family—why the women have all drowned on the same day for generations—to stop it from happening to his sister, Enola. I have labeled the scene to show its parts.

> What makes a curse isn't the words themselves, but the will bound to them, intention married to ink and tragedy. [*Narrative summary.*] A blis-

ter bursts in the cradle between my thumb and forefinger, a stinging drop of lymph falls, smearing a word. [*Sensory imagery.*] I can break the curse but preserve the history. [*First Person Point of View, Simon.*]

A car pulls into the driveway, followed by an insistent pounding recognizable by its annoyance. [*Momentum, creating a sense of real-time passing.*]

"It's open."

Enola stomps in with Doyle behind her, a languorous presence. "I told you to come back. Where the hell have you been? I tried your cell but it's going to voice mail." [*Dialogue that conveys emotion: Enola's mad.*]

"It got shut off. Watch the floor." I gesture to the hole.

"Was that there the other night? What the hell happened?"

"Pothole," Doyle says, grinning.

Enola edges around the living room, eyes roaming the floor and walls. "I thought you didn't want to come back here. That's what we agreed. Thom said he's good to take you on when you're ready." She pauses by the picture of her and Mom, the picture Frank took. [*Setting details that also reveal backstory.*] "You can't be here anymore. Get your stuff and come with us for a while. It'll be fun."

"Little Bird, what's a day's difference going to make? He can catch up to us." To me Doyle says, "We're heading to Croton for some of August before we swing down south again. Atlantic City for part of the fall, then down south." He leans up against the door and props his feet on the frame, worn boot heels showing this to be his favorite position. [*Visual imagery that reveals character information.*]

She shoots him a look.

"I'll come with you," I say. "There's a curator job in Savannah I'm looking into. I just need to take care of something first." [*New plot information. Simon has some kind of plan.*]

"If it's about the book, it has to stop, Simon. You're scaring me. If it's about Frank and Mom—let it go. She's dead and there's nothing he can do to take it back." [*Dialogue that adds tension.*] As if on cue, Frank's truck starts up. We watch it roll out of the driveway and down the street— to the marina, to the bar, to wherever sad men who've fu**ed their best friends' wives go.

"I think we should have a last bonfire before we go." The idea is so quick, so natural, it's almost brilliant. "Remember when we were little and we used to cook out?"

"No," she says. Doyle is up from his post at the door, rubbing his hands against her shoulders. [*Tension. Enola and Simon are always on opposite sides of any topic.*]

"It was great. Corn and hot dogs, burgers, lobsters, too. Dad and Frank would make a bonfire and let us toast marshmallows." The us who toasted marshmallows was Alice and me. Even then we had our shared and parallel lives, watching each other while flakes of charred sugar and cornstarch flew into the sky. [*New character information.*] "I want a last bonfire. I want one good memory here. We deserve a good memory."

"As if one bonfire could fix it," she says. [*Tension. Enola isn't convinced that things will get better.*]

Think of the elements illustrated in the marked sections above as crucial ingredients that you want to employ in your own writing. Swyler's novel is an example of how unique each scene will be, even when you're using the same essential ingredients. While any scene may rely on these same components, only *this* scene has the components arranged in this particular way around these particular details. You might choose a different method of creating dramatic tension—like writing in the third-person point of view, opting for more or less dialogue (or none), evoking the setting or interior monologue, or using very different actions to create a sense of real time—but you can see that Swyler did, in fact, use all the foundational ingredients of a scene and, by doing so, she held your attention. This is exactly what your scenes need to do for your readers.

THE OLE "SHOW, DON'T TELL" DILEMMA

What exactly does it mean to show and not tell? Should your characters be doing wild stripteases or crying, "Look, nothing up my sleeve," before pulling out a rabbit? If you want them to, sure, but in this case *show* means "don't overexplain; trust your reader." Or, as I'm fond of saying, "demonstrate, don't lecture." Let your characters do the storytelling through their words and deeds while you take a back seat.

Telling, also referred to in this book as narrating or narrative summary, is a form of *explaining*. And while every story has some necessary summary, it must be used judiciously. Imagine yourself as the storyteller with a group of enthralled children gathered around and hanging on your every word. Say that, right at the climax, when Snow White bites into the poisoned apple (a juicy bit of action), you go off on a tangent like this: "Snow White thought about taking a bite of the apple, but she had been having trust issues since her stepmother had hired the woodcutter to kill her. Remembering her stepmother's betrayal sent her into a whirlwind of doubt. ..." Bored yet? You can bet those kids would be bouncing in their chairs asking, "But what happened to Snow White after she bit into the poisoned apple?!" Grown-up readers respond the same way to telling.

Think about it another way: Most people read with their physical eyes and a handy little part of the brain known as the visual cortex. The brain is, in fact, considered more important in the function of sight than the eyes are, and in the act of reading it plays an even bigger role. The brain helps the reader with the most important organ used for reading: the inner eye, or the eye of the imagination (not some mystical link to spiritual realms). This eye is responsible for constructing in the mind the visual images that are rendered only in text on a page. You want the reader to see what you describe as vividly as you see your dreams at night; therefore, you must give the reader as much opportunity as possible to do so. You must be detailed, specific, and provide enough sensory and visual clues to make the task of seeing easy.

Narrative summary, on the other hand, offers words only to the reader's inner ear, as if someone were standing off to the side, whispering to him. While the eye allows the reader to become emotionally involved, activating the heart and the viscera, the inner ear seems to be linked more closely to the function of sound alone. Too much stimulation on the inner ear can temporarily lull your reader into apathy or even put him to sleep. This is one of the reasons that narrative passages should be kept to a minimum.

Scenes use the ingredients mentioned earlier to construct a powerful, vivifying experience that mimics life for the reader. At its best, powerful scene writing allows a reader to feel as if he has entered the narrative and is participating in it, rather than sitting passively by and receiving a lecture. You know you're in a scene when your own heart is pumping and you're white-knuckling the pages, waiting to see what happens next. When you fall into the story and forget the world around you, the author has done a good job of immersing you in scenes.

Narrative summaries, when used in place of scene work or when used in excess, cause the reader to feel that the writing is boring, condescending, or lecturing—which can be a turnoff for readers. That said, narrative summaries, when used correctly, do have a place and a function in scenes, and we'll take a closer look at those functions throughout this book.

SCENE LENGTH

Before we wrap up this chapter, let's talk about another issue that's sure to rise in your mind: scene length. One of the benefits of writing in scene form is that the ending of a scene provides a place for the reader to take a pause—not necessarily a comfortable pause, but a place to stop, if they must. You may wonder when to use a short scene versus a long scene. Once again, the decision rests with you, but we'll take a quick look at the benefits of each one.

Long Scenes

Generally speaking, if a scene runs to more than fifteen pages, it's on the long side. While it's not the final word, I think a scene should be something you can read in a sitting, on a lunch break, between other tasks, and put back down (though never too easily). Even the most avid reader wants to pause eventually, and scene and chapter breaks offer them chances to do so.

Long scenes don't need to be avoided, but they should be peppered into the book sparingly. Too many long scenes in a row will cause your narrative to drag.

Use long scenes in the novel when you want to do the following:

- Intentionally slow the pace after intense action or dialogue to allow the protagonist and the reader to digest what has happened and to build new tension and suspense

- Include a lot of big action in a given scene (fights, chases, explosions) so the scene doesn't hinge on action alone
- Add a dialogue scene that, to feel realistic, needs to run long

Short Scenes

A scene that takes place in ten or fewer pages is considered short. Some scenes are as short as a couple of pages. Short scenes often make readers hungry for more. But remember that too many short scenes in a row can make the flow of the plot feel choppy and disrupt the continuity that author John Gardner said creates "a dream" for the reader.

A short scene has to achieve the same goals as a longer scene, and in less time. It must still contain main characters engaging in actions based upon scene intentions. New information that drives the plot forward must be revealed. The setting must be clear. In the short scene, you have even less room for narrative summary.

Short scenes are most effective when you want to do the following:

- Differentiate one character from another (a secretive, shy, or withdrawn character, for instance, might only get short scenes, while an outspoken character may get longer scenes)
- Pick up the pace right after a long scene
- Leave the reader hungry for more or breathless with suspense
- Include multiple scenes within a chapter
- Create a sense of urgency by dropping bits of information one by one, forcing the reader to keep reading

Whether you go long or short depends on your own stylistic preferences. Just keep in mind as you decide what kind of flow you want for your manuscript that length affects pacing.

SCENE BEGINNINGS, MIDDLES, AND ENDINGS

Scene structure mimics plot structure, so, with a few exceptions, each scene needs to have its own beginning (or launch, as I'll call it later), middle, and end. The following three chapters will pare down the scene to these three basic sections. The beginning should be vivid, memorable, and help immediately draw your reader into the scene. Scene middles are the vast territory where the stakes must be raised and characters get caught in conflict, resulting in consequences that drive your plot ever forward. Scene endings, of course, set the stage for the scenes that follow and leave a feeling or taste with the reader that should be unforgettable. When all three sections of a scene are handled well, the result is an incredibly vivid reading experience. The remaining chapters of part one will help you address these important structural elements of a scene.

STRONG SCENE LAUNCHES

All great novels and stories start out with a mere idea. Maybe it's a large idea that spans centuries and crosses continents, like Patrick Rothfuss's first book in The Kingkiller Chronicles series, *The Name of the Wind*; or maybe it's magic realism manifest into stories, like Aimee Bender's books. No matter how grand or ordinary, strange or beguiling your idea, you must take it through an alchemical process that transforms it into a story. How do you do that? This is the function of the scene; it is your story maker. Inside each scene, the vivid details, information, and action breathe life into your flat idea and round it out into something in which a reader participates.

Any story or novel is, in essence, a series of scenes strung together like beads on a wire, with narrative summary adding texture and color between. A work of fiction will comprise many scenes, the number of which varies for each individual project. And each one of these individual scenes must be built with a structure most easily described as *beginning, middle*, and *end*. The beginning of each scene is the focus of this chapter.

The word *beginning* is a bit confusing, since some scenes pick up in the midst of an action or continue where other actions left off; so I prefer to use the term *launch*, which more clearly suggests the place where the reader's attention is engaged anew.

In a manuscript, a new scene is usually signified visually by a break of four lines (called a "soft hiatus") between the last paragraph of the previous scene and the first paragraph of the next one, or sometimes by a symbol such as an asterisk or a dingbat, to let the reader know that time has passed and a new scene is beginning.

Each new scene is a spoke in the wheel of the plot you started with, and the spoke must be revealed in a way that is vivifying for the reader and provides an experience, not a lecture. Scene launches, therefore, pave the way for all the robust consequences of the idea or plot to unfurl. Each scene launch is a reintroduction to your character and the situation she is embroiled in, capturing your reader's attention all over again.

You want to start each scene by asking yourself the following questions:

- Where are my characters in the plot? Where did I leave them in the last scene, and what are they doing now?
- What is the most important piece of information that needs to be revealed in this scene?
- What is my protagonist's goal for this scene?
- How will that goal be achieved or thwarted?

Only you and the course of your narrative can determine which kinds of launches will work best for each scene, and choosing the right launch often takes some experimentation. This section will provide you with techniques for launching with characters, actions, narrative summary, and setting.

CHARACTER LAUNCHES

It's generally a good idea to get your characters on the page sooner rather than later. And, depending on how many points of view you use, the majority of scenes should involve your *main* character(s) (although there may be scenes from which your main character needs to be excluded, for the sake of your plot). If you write fantasy or science fiction, your characters may not be people, but dragons, elves, robots, or any of a vast miscellany of other life forms. The edict is still the same—bring your character into the scene as soon as possible. (Part three will elaborate on how to do this.)

Remember, if your scene launch goes on for too many paragraphs in passive description or narrated ideas without characters coming into play, the reader begins to feel unmoored in time and space, impatient for something to happen and someone for it to happen to. If your character isn't present by the second paragraph in any given scene, you're in danger of losing the reader.

SET SCENE INTENTIONS FOR CHARACTERS

While the hallmark of a scene may be the momentum that generates the feeling of real time, a scene feels purposeful when you give the character that stars in it an intention, or a goal to pursue. Scene intention is discussed in detail in chapter eleven, but it's worth mentioning here because you need to know your characters' intentions at the launch of every scene so you can reveal, follow, build upon, and even thwart that intention. To set scene intentions, you must make the following decisions:

- What the most immediate desires of the characters are
- When your characters will achieve their intention or encounter some type of opposition
- Whether the intention makes sense to your plot
- Who will help your characters achieve their goal, and who will oppose them

Scene intentions ought to be intricately tied to the plot, i.e., your character's goal—and the unfolding of that goal through actions, discoveries, and explorations your character undertakes that drive the story continually forward. You don't want free-floating intentions or vignettes that leave the reader wondering why your character has set out to do something.

ACTION LAUNCHES

Many writers believe they must explain every bit of action that is going on right from the start of a scene, but narrative summary defeats action. The sooner you start the action in a scene, the more momentum is available to carry the reader forward. If you find yourself explaining an action, then you're not *demonstrating* the action any longer; you're floating in a distant star system known as Nebulous Intellectulus—more commonly known as your head—and so is the reader.

Keep in mind the key elements of action: time and momentum. It takes *time* to plan a murder over late-night whispers; for a drunk character to drop a jar at the grocery; to blackmail a betraying spouse; or to kick a wall in anger. These things don't happen spontaneously; they happen over a period of time. They are sometimes quick, sometimes slow, but once started they unfold until finished.

The key to creating strong momentum is to start an action without explaining anything. A scene from M.R. Carey's *The Girl With All the Gifts* does just that:

> When the key turns in the door, she stops counting and opens her eyes. Sergeant comes in with his gun and points it at her. Then two of Sergeant's people come in and tighten and buckle the straps of the chair around Melanie's wrists and ankles. There's also a strap for her neck; they tighten that one last of all, when her hands and feet are fastened up all the way, and they always do it from behind. The strap is designed so they never have to put their hands in front of Melanie's face. Melanie sometimes says, "I won't bite." She says it as a joke, but Sergeant's people never laugh. Sergeant did once, the first time she said it, but it was a nasty laugh. And then he said, "Like we'd ever give you the chance, sugar plum."

M.R. Carey plunges his reader into the scene in this novel. For a significant portion of the early scenes, the reader doesn't know why Melanie, a ten-year-old child, is restrained in this way. The lack of explanation for what is happening forces the reader to press on to learn more. The action here gives the reader clues: Something about Melanie is either threatening or dangerous, though, based on her internal narration, we don't yet know what. We want to know what grown men, including a Sergeant, no less, would have to fear from a child so much that he would have to strap her into a chair and point a gun at her the whole time. Clearly something more is going to happen in this environment, and judging from the tone of the paragraph, we can probably expect something intense and thrilling. Action launches tend to energize the reader's physical senses.

Here's how to create an action launch:

- **GET STRAIGHT TO THE ACTION.** Don't drag your feet here. "Jimmy jumped off the cliff"; not "Jimmy stared at the water, imagining how cold it would feel when he jumped."
- **HOOK THE READER WITH BIG OR SURPRISING ACTIONS.** A big or surprising action—outburst, car crash, violent heart attack, public fight—at the launch of a scene can then be the stage for a bunch of consequences to unfold. One caveat: You'll be unlikely to pull this off in every scene.
- **BE SURE THAT THE ACTION IS TRUE TO YOUR CHARACTER.** Don't have a shy character choose to become suddenly uninhibited at the launch of a scene—save that for scene middles. Do have a bossy character belittle another character in a way that creates conflict.
- **ACT FIRST, THINK LATER.** If a character is going to think in your action opening, let the action come first and the thought be a reaction. "Elizabeth slapped the Prince. When his face turned pink, horror filled her. *What have I done?* she thought."

NARRATIVE LAUNCHES

Writers often try to include narrative summary, such as descriptions of the history of a place or the backstory of characters, right at the launch of a scene, believing that the reader will not be patient enough to allow actions and dialogue to tell the story. In large doses, narrative summary is to scenes what voice-overs are to movies—a distraction and an interruption.

Yet a scene launch is actually one of the easier places to use a judicious amount of narrative summary (since you've only just gotten the reader's attention), so long as you don't hold the reader captive too long.

Take the opening of an early scene in Gina Frangello's novel *Every Kind of Wanting*.

> You think you know our story, Nick, but that would imply that I was capable of honesty. You think our stories are some joint thing, a common narrative on which we, the coconspirators, would agree, but you don't know anything yet.
>
> One thing you taught me is that all empathy involves a kind of method acting. You used to say I was a natural actress, but with bipolar as

rapid-cycling and tidal as mine, maybe inhabiting alternate states isn't particularly foreign.

The above bit is almost entirely narrative summary, all set inside the narrator's mind. However, we do get a sense of a complicated tale about to unfold, one with secrets and lies—the best kind of story. We get the sense that this will be a story in which things are not as simple as they seem, and that there may be multiple perspectives that need to be accounted for. Indeed, the narrator, Lina, goes on to offer this startling bit of information:

> The first time I told you I wanted you to hit me, I asked, "Do you have a problem with that?" You laughed and said, "I'm guessing you haven't met many people who had a problem with that." But you'd be surprised. You said, "The thing is, I don't know how to hurt someone without hurting them," then caught me off guard by offering, "You could show me first, on me, what you like."

This little bit of dialogue acts as a kind of mini-scene, breaking up the slow pace of the narrative summary and bringing back a feeling of momentum just as the scene threatens to dissolve in the slow pace of the summary.

Narrative launches should be reserved for the following occasions:

- **WHEN NARRATIVE SUMMARY CAN SAVE TIME.** Sometimes actions will simply take up more time and space in the scene than you would like. A scene beginning needs to move fairly quickly and, on occasion, summary will get the reader there faster.
- **WHEN INFORMATION NEEDS TO BE COMMUNICATED BEFORE AN ACTION.** Sometimes information needs to be imparted simply to set action in motion later in the scene. Consider the following sentences, which could easily lead to actions: "My mother was dead before I arrived." "The war had begun." "The storm left half of the city under water."
- **WHEN A CHARACTER'S THOUGHTS OR INTENTIONS CANNOT BE REVEALED IN ACTION.** Coma victims, elderly characters, small children, and other characters sometimes cannot speak or act for physical, mental, or emotional reasons; therefore the scene may need to launch with narration to let the reader know what they think and feel.

SETTING LAUNCHES

Sometimes setting details—like a jungle on fire, or moonlight sparkling on a lake—are so important to plot or character development that visual setting must be included at the launch of a scene. This is often the case in books set in unusual, exotic, or challenging locations, such as snowy Himalayan mountains, lush islands, or brutal desert climes. If the setting is going to bear dramatically on the characters and the plot, then there is every reason to launch with it.

John Fowles's novel *The Magus* is set mostly on a Greek island that leaves an indelible imprint on the main character, Nicholas. He becomes involved with an eccentric man whose isolated villa in the Greek countryside becomes the stage upon which the major drama of the novel unfolds. Therefore, it makes sense for him to launch a scene in this manner:

> It was a Sunday in late May, blue as a bird's wing. I climbed up the goat-paths to the island's ridge-back, from where the green froth of the pine-tops rolled two miles across to the shadowy wall of mountains on the mainland to the west, a wall that reverberated away south, fifty or sixty miles to the horizon, under the vast bell of the empyrean. It was an azure world, stupendously pure, and always when I stood on the central ridge of the island, and saw it before me, I forgot most of my troubles.

The reader needs to be able to see in detail the empty Greek countryside in which Nicholas becomes so isolated. It sets the scene for something beautiful and strange to happen, and Fowles does not disappoint.

Here's how to create an effective scenic launch:

- **USE SPECIFIC VISUAL DETAILS.** If your character is deserted on an island, the reader needs to know the lay of the land. Any fruit trees in sight? What color sand? Are there rocks, shelter, or wild, roaming beasts?
- **ALLOW SCENERY TO SET THE TONE OF THE SCENE.** Say your scene opens in a jungle where your character is going to face danger; you can describe the scenery in language (simile, metaphors) that conveys darkness, fear, and mystery.
- **USE SCENERY TO REFLECT A CHARACTER'S FEELINGS.** Say you have a sad character walking through a residential neighborhood. The de-

scriptions of the homes can reflect that sadness; houses can be in disrepair, with rotting wood and untended yards. You can use weather in the same way. A bright, powerfully sunny day can reflect a mood of great cheer in a character.

- **SHOW THE IMPACT OF THE SETTING ON THE CHARACTER.** Say your character is in a prison cell; use the description of the surroundings to show how they shape the character's feelings. "He gazed at his cell: the uncomfortable, flat bed, the walls that squeezed around him, the dull gray color that pervaded everything."

The scene launch happens so quickly and is so soon forgotten that it's easy to rush through it, figuring it doesn't really matter how you get it started. Don't fall prey to that kind of thinking. Take your time with a scene launch. Craft each one as carefully and strategically as you would any other aspect of your scene. Remember that a scene launch is an *invitation* to the reader, beckoning him to come further along with you. Make your invitations as alluring as possible.

3

POWERFUL SCENE MIDDLES

Where, exactly, *is* the middle of a scene? The term *middle* is misleading because scenes vary in length and have no precise midpoint. The best explanation is to think of each scene's middle as a realm of possibility between the scene opening and its ending, where the major drama and conflict of the scene unfolds. It's also crucial that you keep action, tension, and conflict alive to avoid losing your reader at this precarious point.

Be wary, because the middle has a seductive power to tempt writers into narrative side roads and pretty flower beds of words which, like those poppies in *The Wizard of Oz*, make the reader want to drift off to sleep.

If you grabbed the reader's attention with an evocative scene launch, the middle of your scene is the proving ground, the Olympic opportunity to hook the reader and never let her go.

UP THE ANTE: COMPLICATIONS

You are probably a very nice person who loathes the idea of even accidentally causing harm to another person. While this kindness is noble in life, in fiction writing it's a liability. You *must* complicate your characters' lives, and you must do it where the reader can see it—in scenes. Doing so is known as "upping the ante." That phrase is most often heard in gambling circles when the initial bet goes up, making the potential win greater along with the risk. What you must ante up in your scenes are those things your characters stand to lose (or even gain), whether it's pride, or a home, or deep love. It also means that at some point you're going to have to take those things away from your character (at least temporarily), which evokes conflict in your characters. When you up the ante, you build the anticipation, significance, and suspense that drive the narrative forward and bring the reader along for the ride.

This process is both terrible and wonderful. Terrible, because you must hurt your characters—you must take beloved people and possessions away from them, withhold desires, and sometimes even kill them for the sake of drama or tension. Yet it is also wonderful, because mucking about in your characters' lives will make the reader more emotionally invested in them.

In its simplest form, a traditional fictional narrative, whether story or novel, should address a problem that needs to be resolved or a situation that needs to be understood: A young girl finds herself pregnant and abandoned by her family and her lover, so she falls into a life of prostitution on her road to spiritual redemption; a relative dies and leaves all his money to one family member, which launches a family feud; parents turn around at the mall and discover their child is gone. The problem or situation must also include or encompass smaller problems (often called subplot points) with consequences, which is where scenes come in.

Earlier, I mentioned the need to set scene intentions. An intention is your direction to the character as to what aspect of the larger plot problem will be set into play in a given scene (see chapter eleven for more on scene intentions). Remember, your scenes transform flat ideas into vivid experiences for the reader.

Let's walk through the nebulous middle of a scene, complicating as we go, using one of the examples above—that of the pregnant girl abandoned and left without resources.

Let's call your pregnant protagonist Britney. Resist the easy way out, which would be to narrate in flat prose that "Britney did some difficult and compromising things to take care of herself." Just get right to the work of revealing her plight in vivid scenes.

Start in a logical place—bereft Britney needs to obtain food and shelter so she can figure out what to do next. This will be her scene intention, her motivation. Therefore, she will need to go somewhere and do something to get that need met. Now, remember your ingredients from chapter one: Britney, your character, stumbles into a physical setting—a dive bar, which you will be sure to describe in all its grimy, low-lit glory. You will be sure to reveal through her point of view—probably the first or third person—that she has chosen this location because she knows she can garner the attention of men, whom she feels are most likely to help her out. You will hopefully show the surprised responses of the men and the bartender, some parrying dialogue, some catcalling and other general reactions to her presence—all of which is action. Then, as she stands there huddled against a barstool, frightened and unsure, a seedy-looking man approaches her—and so your drama begins.

Perhaps this man makes her an indecent proposal to do something she does not find palatable in return for money, and she is desperate enough to consider it. This is a complication. You have just upped the ante, and she now has something to lose—possibly her health, integrity, or her morality—in order to gain what she needs—money, food, and shelter. The reader will worry for her, which creates suspense and anticipation. The reader will not be able leave this poor girl's side; he will have to know what happens next.

And what will happen next? First, remember that the reader is your omnipresent witness. Don't draw the curtain between yourself and him and then report back passively later. Don't stop the complications, either. Though you may want the bar fellow to turn out sweet and help Britney out of the kindness of his heart (because you love your character), the middle of your scene is no place for him to turn out to be a saint. Save that for a surprise ending. Scenes need dramatic tension to enact their tugging power on a reader. If he turns out nice, the reader can put down your narrative and sleep easy, and you don't want that!

Consider using a handy graph that one of my editing clients found useful for working out complications in her scene middles. Make four columns and rows on a page, like so (the rows can be longer if necessary):

PROTAGONIST	SCENE INTENTION(S)	COMPLICATION	RESULT
Britney	To get food/shelter	She goes to a seedy bar	Meets "savior" who wants to help
Britney	To take man's help	Man is really a criminal	Hits man with beer bottle and runs
Britney	To get away from man	She has no car and no $$	Hitchhikes

A scene can unfold in a couple of paragraphs or over two dozen pages. As long as Britney is engaged in the same essential resulting action with this seedy stranger in fictional real time—a streamlined series of events without a break in time—and in a single location (the interior of a moving car or other vehicle counts as a single location), your scene can be as long as it needs to be.

You need to make whatever happens to Britney in this scene complicated enough that it compels the reader to go on to the next scene or chapter. And you have the same task ahead of you for future scenes.

TECHNIQUES TO UP THE ANTE

Learning how to torture your characters and complicate their lives takes practice and a bit of a thick skin, which you can build through practice. A note of warning: While complications build anticipation and drama, you should not make things difficult on characters "just because." Complications have to reveal character and push your plot forward; you shouldn't be needlessly cruel *or* too easy on your characters. Even when adding necessary complications, it's hard to strike that balance, so here are some specific techniques to add plot-relevant complications to your characters' lives in the middle of scenes.

The Withhold

Your characters need goals, desires, and ambitions to appeal to the reader's sensibilities. But to create the juicy tension that keeps a reader turning pages, at times you must dangle the objects of desire just out of reach, using a technique known as withholding.

There are many things you can withhold in scenes, such as emotions, information, and objects. Let's take a closer look at each.

Emotional withholding comes in many forms: A father withholds his approval of his son, no matter what the son does to win him over; a woman withholds her love for her abusive husband, and he abuses her more in the hopes of securing it.

One of literature's most controversial and yet powerful illustrations of emotional withholding is found in the novel *Lolita* by Vladimir Nabokov. Even after protagonist Humbert Humbert, who has a perverse predilection for young girls, "possesses" young Lolita by becoming her legal guardian after the death of her mother, Lolita gives him her body but withholds the one thing he truly wants: her love and respect. The entire novel is a series of intense, often-difficult scenes that show Humbert's desperate attempt to finagle the perfect circumstances for Lolita to love him. The act of withholding, which Nabokov employs in one form or another in nearly every scene of the book, makes it possible for the reader to tolerate and even empathize with Humbert and nearly forget what he is: a pedophile.

Here Humbert writes of a time when he merely wanted to hold her, to be loved by Lolita, and of her ultimate denial

> Sometimes ... I would shed all my pedagogic restraint, dismiss all our quarrels, forget all my masculine pride—and literally crawl on my knees to your chair, my Lolita! You would give me one look—a gray furry question mark of a look: "Oh no, not again" (incredulity, exasperation); for you never deigned to believe that I could, without any specific designs, ever crave to bury my face in your plaid skirt, my darling! ... "Pulease, leave me alone; will you," you would say ...

Emotional withholding is a great way to elicit sympathy, empathy, and concern for otherwise unlikable characters, as well as to build concern and drama around sympathetic characters. (Though please note: I don't recommend you follow in Nabokov's footsteps to make a pedophile sympathetic. Many people believe his novel is a metaphor for other things, and one can only hope they're right.)

Withholding information is the most common type of withholding you'll find in scenes. Many things can be withheld: the whereabouts of a kidnap victim; the location of a stolen treasure; the address of the apartment where a Jewish person is hiding from the Nazis. Withheld information usually sets up a power struggle, as the person who has the information holds power over the person who wants it. (That is, unless you decide to bring in a torturer, which shifts the power back again.) Every scene should contain some plot information that is withheld, or else you might conclude your narrative too early on and fall into the bad habit of repeating information the reader already knows.

Withholding objects is also an option. You might remember a game from childhood known as monkey in the middle, in which two children toss an object back and forth over the head of a third child, who tries desperately to grab for it. While it looks like a game, it's also a form of torture for the third child. A person witnessing this scene would want to intervene on behalf of the poor child and grab the coveted item out from the hands of those tossing it.

You can play a form of monkey in the middle with your characters if there is an important object that your character wants, but that he must not gain too soon. This is a great technique when two characters want the same object, whether they are fighting for their lives over a gun on the floor, plotting to steal a precious piece of jewelry, or seeking a locked-up teddy bear that represents comfort. The longer you withhold the object from the person or people who want it, especially during the middle of the scene, the more tension you can build.

THE ELEMENT OF DANGER

A fantastic way to up the ante in the middle of the scene is to put your protagonist or someone he loves in danger. This can be physical danger—the maiden tied to the railroad tracks—like in Annie Proulx's novel *The Shipping News*. The main character, Quoyle, is a doormat of a man who has terrible self-esteem and can't swim. His inability to swim is a metaphor for how he navigates the world. When he sees a body bobbing in the harbor, he takes it upon himself to rescue it, capsizing his boat in the process and nearly drowning himself. While clinging to a floating ice chest, Quoyle's life flashes before his eyes, and for the first time, the reader sees that he wants to become a stronger man.

Putting your character in danger is one of the most immediate ways to capture the reader. How your character reacts to danger also reveals something about his true nature. Perhaps your timid character suddenly shows some bravery or, conversely, a macho character turns out to be quite terrified when his life is at stake.

Then there is emotional danger, such as an encounter with a psychotic person, blackmail that threatens a character's livelihood, or mental abuse such as in this bit of a scene from Jane Smiley's Pulitzer Prize–winning novel *A Thousand Acres*. Here, an abusive father suddenly rages at one of his grown daughters, Ginny, whom he considers disloyal:

> He leaned his face toward mine. "You don't have to drive me around any more or cook the goddamned breakfast or clean the goddamned house." His voice modulated into a scream. "Or tell me what I can do and what I can't do. I know all about you, you slut! You've been creeping here and there all your life, making up to this one and that one. But you're not really a woman are you? I don't know what you are."

Those offensive and abusive words are strong enough in their own right, but with the characters' history added into the mix—this man physically abused his daughters when they were young—they are all the more horrifying. It's a painful but brilliant stroke of emotional danger that keeps the reader riveted.

Don't be afraid to invoke emotional danger in your character's lives; they can take it, and it actually builds both reader empathy and dramatic tension.

In truth, the essence of any conflict involves a little danger. While in life people tend to avoid arguments and conflict, in fiction, conflict is a great drama builder. I recommend that in every story or novel your characters get into at least one heated argument—this is a great way to create a sense of emotional danger without having to give your characters bleak childhoods and painful tragedies.

SCENE STEALER

Noria Jablonski, author of *Human Oddities*, discusses delaying anticipation in Vladimir Nabokov's *Lolita*.

The magic of Lolita is that Nabokov seduces the reader into a kind of complicity with Humbert Humbert, and when the scene arises where they are about to consummate their relationship at the Enchanted Hunters hotel, I was guiltily rooting for him. Never mind that he has drugged Lolita and intends to violate her, however lovingly. Never mind the fact that he has neglected to tell Lolita that her mother is dead.

Part of why I wave my foam finger for Humbert is simply the fact that I've known all along that this scene was coming, but it's been delayed for a hundred and thirty pages. [Nabokov] delays the anticipated moment, letting the thrill build and build. What sweet relief—Humbert's and mine—that it is Lolita who ultimately seduces him.

The Unexpected Revelation

Scene middles are a great place for a character to learn that he was adopted, that his wife has cheated on him with his best friend, or that he has been wrongly accused of a crime. Revelations can come via letters found in a dead relative's old chest of drawers, from another character's mouth, from an overheard conversation, or even through a device such as dreams. However they manifest, revelations are transformative pieces of plot information that drive your narrative forward and offer huge potential for drama in the scenes where they are revealed.

The power of a revelation is immense. Who can forget the moment in Star Wars when Luke hears those terrible words from Darth Vader—"I am your father"—and how they change everything he knows and believes; or the moment when the title character in Charlotte Brontë's novel *Jane Eyre* learns the terrible truth about the secret past of her love, Mr. Rochester, a truth that forces them to cancel their planned wedding. These revelations come with devastating emphasis.

Revelations can also provide relief and comfort, returning fortune and identity and offering a character a chance where before there was none—

like Cinderella learning she has a fairy godmother, or Harry Potter discovering he's a wizard destined for a great wizardry school beyond the oppressive confines of his aunt and uncle's home—and if you have tested your characters already, withholding from them and putting them in danger, then you might find it useful to provide a revelation that changes their fate in an instant.

SUCCESSFUL SCENE ENDINGS

Are you more inclined to remember the moment you first fell in love, or the moment when your lover broke your heart and walked out your door for the last time? Most of us tend to remember what happened more recently and what had the greater emotional impact on us. Scene endings carry dynamic emotional weight, when done right, and should leave the reader wanting more. Endings are by their nature conclusive. Sometimes they conclude simple things like conversations or dates. In other cases, they end livelihoods and lives. But some endings are unresolved and leave the reader with more questions. Both kinds are acceptable in scene endings. (See chapter twenty-one for my advice on final scenes.)

Another use for the end of a scene is to make space for readers to take a breath and digest all that they have just finished reading. Endings linger in memory because they are the moments when things finally begin to add up and make sense. At the end of a scene, if it has been done well, the reader will have more knowledge of, and a greater investment in, the plot and characters, and feel more compelled to find out what happens next. In fact, you know you've done your work when the reader reaches the end of a scene and absolutely must press on. For novels, often each chapter is one long scene, but sometimes a chapter is a collection of shorter scenes.

It is helpful to put scene endings in one of two categories: zoom-in endings and zoom-out endings. Just like a camera can zoom in or out on an image captured in its lens, endings should either bring the reader up close or pull back and provide a wider perspective.

ZOOM-IN ENDINGS

Anything that invites intimacy or emotional contact with the characters and their plight at the end of a scene has a zoom-in effect on readers, drawing readers closer, even uncomfortably close, to ensure that they have a powerful emotional or "aha" moment.

Character Summaries

Looking back on the events that have come before, characters can summarize, in the form of interior monologues or simple dialogue, what has just happened in the scene at hand.

"Wow," Snow White might say to one of her bluebird friends, "I can't believe the Queen actually sent the woodcutter to cut out my heart! I was so naïve to trust her!" This summary device is useful when your plot is complex, you have multiple main characters, or there is a mystery involved. The more pieces there are to put together, the more useful end summaries can be. A character summary also helps to show readers where your character is at this final moment before you launch into the next scene.

For instance, in Michael Cunningham's novel *The Hours*, a character named Laura has been debating leaving her family because she feels suffocated. At the end of an important scene, she comes to this decision (told in limited third-person point of view):

> She will not lose hope. She will not mourn her lost possibilities, her unexplored talents (what if she has no talents, after all?). She will remain devoted to her son, her husband, her home and duties, all her gifts. She will want this second child.

This kind of ending gives the reader a way of measuring the character's emotional pulse at the end of the scene. Up until this point, Cunningham has built a great deal of anxiety into Laura's storyline, and for this tiny moment, the readers can rest, feeling sure they know what Laura has decided to do. Of course, this is not the end of this character's story, or her dilemma; that is saved for the end of the book.

You do want to be careful not to provide too many summaries—you'll know if you have done so because the action will start to disappear. If you're getting feedback as you write, too much summary will likely cause your reader to report getting twitchy and bored. Use summary endings for character development, to reveal something more about a character that the reader didn't know before.

Revelatory Dialogue

Revelations create drama and tension in your scenes. In chapter three we discussed how revelations can be used in your scene middles to drive your narrative forward, but they can also be used to end a scene on a note of surprise or intensity, especially in the form of dialogue. The end of a scene is a fantastic place for a sudden and surprising piece of information to come out of the mouth of a character. "I shot her!" the man who is presumed innocent might suddenly proclaim during his trial. Revelation zooms the reader's focus in on the character and builds suspense for the next scene. When the reader meets this man again, she will undoubtedly see the consequences of his actions.

The revelation can be quieter, too, more on an emotional level. "I don't really love you," the new bride might confess to her husband on their honeymoon, changing their fate for the worse on what is supposed to be the happiest night of their lives.

The Cliffhanger Ending

If you really want to be sure that your reader will not stop for breath, and will press forward, you're best off employing the cliffhanger ending. Cliffhangers can happen in a variety of ways and in almost any scene when you want to leave the reader on the edge and uncertain of the outcome: A character is left in grave peril; an action is cut short at the precipice of an outcome; or the tables are turned completely on your character's perception of reality. What all of those scenarios have in common is suspense. They leave the reader wondering every time.

Take this example from Justin Cronin's third novel in The Passage trilogy, *The City of Mirrors*. A remaining village of humans, the last survivors of a "viral" attack that turned humans into vampire-like "virals" and wiped out most of humanity, find themselves on the defensive against a surprise attack:

> Hands reached up through the opening in the floor to help the children, who funneled into the hatch with a slowness painfully out of sync with everything else that was occurring. People were pushing and shoving, women screaming, babies crying. Caleb smelled gasoline. An empty fuel can lay on its side on the floor, a second by the pantry door. Their presence made no sense—it was in the same category of unaccountable details as Sister Peg's rifle. Men were hurling dining chairs through the windows. Others were upending tables to act as barricades. All the things of the world were colliding. Caleb took a position at the closest window, pointed his rifle into the darkness, and began to fire.

The cliffhanger draws the reader so deeply into the action that there is very little chance she will put down the book at that point, and when you have a cliffhanger that involves a danger that throws more than a few beloved characters into a state of peril, as above, the reader will be desperate to find out what happens to them.

Cliffhangers have a tendency to pump adrenaline into the reader's heart, so you want to be careful not to end every scene on such a note without offering an occasional reprieve. Cliffhangers can be an integral part of controlling suspense if they are not overused.

ZOOM-OUT ENDINGS

Zoom-out endings pull away from intimacy or immediacy. The reader often needs a bit of emotional relief from an intense scene, and pulling back provides him an opportunity to catch his breath or reflect on all that has transpired.

Visual Descriptions

There are many reasons why a writer might choose to end a scene with a visual description. Visual passages in general ground the reader concretely in the present moment. A visual description simply shows what is; it doesn't have to be, or suggest, something else. In these instances, you will use more of the senses.

If there has been a lot of action in a scene—running, dancing, or fighting, say—drawing back to let the reader see something in a concrete visual way can be a very effective way to end the scene. If a fight has taken place during the scene, you might end the scene with a visual of the beaten protagonist passed out in the street, leaving the reader to wonder how badly injured he is. Or you might draw back to show the reader something peaceful or hopeful: a cow grazing quietly in the moonlight; a woman brewing tea in her kitchen; a child patting the head of a dog. The key here is to use the senses to leave a physical impression on the reader, an imprint that he will take into the next scene.

Visual endings don't need to give the reader anything to chew on beyond what is right there on the page; they are like palate cleansers that show up in between intense scenes, clearing away some of the feelings elicited in the scene to make way for a new one. One of the most masterful short stories ever written, "The Dead" by James Joyce, employs just such cleansing visuals between the end of one scene and the beginning of another:

> The morning was still dark. A dull yellow light brooded over the houses and the river; and the sky seemed to be descending. It was slushy underfoot; and only streaks and patches of snow lay on the roofs, on the parapets of the quay and on the area railings.

The visual ending above provides a gentle transition between the last scene of the party, full of boisterous activity and motion and dialogue, and a quietly emotional, devastating final scene between Gabriel and his wife, in which he realizes that he does not know her as well as he thinks he does. That simple visual paves the way for a truly powerful next scene.

Philosophical Musings

Since writing is symbolic as well as literal, sometimes an ending can reflect back on the events of a scene (or many scenes) with a philosophical bent that explores the thematic undercurrents of the work. Such is the case in this example from Emma Cline's novel *The Girls*, which imagines a girl caught up in a group inspired by the Manson family gang that wound up enacting terrible murders in the 1960s. The scene where protagonist Evie first spots Suzanne, the girl who will draw her into this sordid cast of characters, ends with this following philosophical musing that tells us something about Evie's character:

> Since I'd met Suzanne, my life had come into sharp, mysterious relief, revealing a world beyond the known world, the hidden passage beyond the bookcase. I'd catch myself eating an apple, and even the wet swallow of apple could incite gratitude in me. The arrangement of oak leaves overhead condensing with a hothouse clarity, clues to a riddle I hadn't known you could try to solve.

Evie's seeking of some extraordinary quality to her otherwise humdrum suburban life will be the very quality that gets her into trouble. Cline ends this scene with a feeling of beautiful, but troublesome, foreshadowing of what is to come, which resonates throughout the scenes that follow.

The best way to work in a philosophical angle is often through the use of a comparison like a simile or metaphor, often a visual comparison, and always in the point of view of whichever character is most important to the scene. For instance, a character who is struggling to decide on whether or not to keep an unexpected pregnancy might, at the end of a scene, see a mother cat nursing her kittens and feel revulsion, which helps her understand her own maternal instincts. You could have her reflect upon this philosophically: "I was frightened by the babies' hunger, their desperate need. I was a woman, and pregnant, but I knew in that moment a mother was so much more than that. More than I could ever be." Let these musings seep out through the character's point of view, not through yours as the author.

Philosophical endings tend to work best when:

- You're writing in the omniscient "all-knowing" point of view, which lends itself to musings outside of intimate character experience.
- Your character is already prone to philosophical musing (it's better not to try for the philosophical ending if your character is literal or not very introspective).

- Your novel or story has a strong theme (redemption, empowerment, loss) that lends itself to philosophical summaries
- Your novel or story is more character driven than plot or action driven; it's hard to get philosophical when a character is about to fall from a cliff or is running from the police

THE CONCLUSIVE ENDING

There comes a time when a scene simply needs to end without anything fancy to get in the way. In these instances, your ending doesn't need to portend any future event or lend thematic resonance; its job is just to conclude something that has happened or to tie up a plot point. This might be the place you kill off a character that you know must die. Death is a momentous act, and placing a death at the end of a scene gives the reader time to decide how she feels and if she is ready to continue reading right away.

There are many other conclusive kinds of endings. You can answer questions that have been posed throughout the scene or the story. Who really *is* Superman, Lois Lane wants to know. At the end of a scene, he can reveal himself as Clark Kent. You can unmask murderers, reveal the results of blood tests, and lay down jail sentences at the end of scenes in as straightforward a fashion as you need to get the job done.

A conclusive ending bears a feeling of finality, which will leave the reader with a very different experience than if you end with things hanging in the balance, dangling at the edge of a cliff. Eventually there will be places in your narrative where one plot avenue or character detail needs to be tied up so that others can be handled.

For instance, in Michelle Richmond's novel *The Year of Fog*, protagonist Abby Mason loses sight of her fiancé's daughter, Emma, for just a brief moment, long enough for the child to disappear. She is not seen again for nearly a year. Even after Emma's father, Jake, gives up searching for his daughter months after her disappearance, Abby keeps up the search on her own. When the child finally is found, that event concludes a major plotline in the novel, but the novel doesn't end there.

She comes out grimacing, holding her fingers to her nose. It's a nothing gesture, universal among children, and yet I'm strangled with emotion just to see her doing this thing, this normal thing. Alive.

Because it strikes such a resounding note of conclusion, this terrific scene ending could easily be the end of the novel. That said, there is, in fact, much more for Jake, Abby, and Emma to cope with due to all they've been through over the course of the story.

Conclusive scene endings are not the ultimate end of the story or novel, just conclusions to plotlines or events that were set in motion by the inciting incident.

In part three, we'll look at ways to end the many different types of scenes that will compose your narrative. Ultimately, though, you will have to choose each scene's ending individually to ensure that it fits the mood, the pace, and the plot.

PART II

CORE ELEMENTS OF THE SCENE

"Do not hoard what seems good for a later place in the book, or for another book; give it, give it all, give it now."

—ANNIE DILLARD

5

SETTING

Imagine entering the chilly, ornate cavern of the Vatican, expecting to be amazed by its historical and artistic beauty, only to find yourself disoriented by all the gilt and marble and the cathedral's sheer size. Imagine you did not know where to look first and soon got a headache. Unfamiliar surroundings can make us feel unsettled and overwhelmed. This is also true of the fictional surroundings you create in scenes. You must act as a tour guide through each scene, expertly guiding the reader to all the important details, pointing out only what is necessary and what will help the reader understand what he sees.

While setting is a core element of every scene, its purpose is almost always to support and contain the action of the scene, and rarely to be the star. Still, setting requires careful consideration, because you want to ground the reader in it and move your character through it purposefully.

Though we'll discuss the implications of setting in specific scene types in part three, it's good to absorb the essential types of setting and props you'll eventually be using.

The first element of building the stage for any scene is describing what can be *seen*. When you create a physical world in each scene, you provide a solid framework to which you can affix all the ineffable details to come, like feelings and thoughts. The more clearly you describe what can be seen, the more likely your reader is to feel right at home.

Humans have a funny tendency to look for verisimilitude—elements of real life—in fiction. Though the fun of fiction is that you can make up the world and the characters to your specifications, even fantasy writers know they must develop a rich and believable culture, history, and physical geography to sell the reality of their fantasy world. Place is one of the first things that make your story real to the reader.

SETTING THE STAGE

Settings are as varied in fiction as they are in the world: a humid Southern bayou; icy Norwegian fjords; a crumbling Victorian mansion; a stable, pungent with the stench of animals. These are just a few of the infinite number of places in which you might set your characters. Though they may seem like merely the backdrop to the action and drama of your narrative, they are more like the rich soil in which you plant your seeds. *Do not* forget to set the scene. Unless you have a good reason to set your novel or story in a vacuum, establishing a physical setting is one of the most important and literal ways to ground the reader and keep them from visualizing your characters as floating heads.

There are so many details to consider when writing fiction that setting can seem like the least important aspect and, therefore, an obligation, something you dread or do only because you have to. Yet you don't need to have the setting perfectly figured out at first. You can begin with a vague idea and flesh it out over further drafts. If you've ever seen or starred in a stage play, you're familiar with the ambiguous visual details that constitute settings and places onstage. Often a vague outline of a city is meant to represent a sprawling metropolis, or a couple of paper trees stand for a forest. If you struggle with setting, there is nothing wrong with sketching it out loosely to begin with and filling it in later, when you have a better feel for it.

You can make notes to yourself in your scene, such as: "Set in some kind of park with lots of loud children and a pond," or "Paris, turn of the century." Research foods and smells later.

Setting may not come to you all at once, because there are many layers to it. Just make sure your "sets" are finished before the final draft. Some of the basic settings you should keep in mind include geographic location, natural environments, and homes and buildings.

Geographic Location and Natural Settings

Do you know where in the world your story is set? Is it a world you've made up, like the planet Rakhat in Mary Doria Russell's novel *The Sparrow*, off in the Alpha Centauri solar system? Or is it Memphis, Tennessee, USA, Earth?

The geographical location is the one thing you need to decide as quickly as possible, as it will have more bearing on your characters than other details of setting. Every location comes with information that is useful to the reader (and to you as a writer), from dialect to politics to climate, and that information bears on the characters who turn up there. A born Southerner, for instance, is likely to feel at home in Alabama, while a character from California might struggle to handle Alabama's hot climate, politics, or racial inequality.

It makes sense for scenes to take place in nature, the most prolific of all natural settings, but remember that cool, snow-piled ski slopes affect characters far differently than scorched deserts. If someone takes a drunken spill into a lush garden full of flowers, the results will be different than if that character had tumbled into a wall of cacti. It is your job to attend to these specifics. The reader cannot be physically transported to the sharp cold of Vail, Colorado, or to the dry heat of the Mojave Desert by reading your book, but you want him to *feel* as though he has been. On the other hand, you don't want to have to give a lengthy geological explanation for the formation of mesas in Arizona if your goal is simply to have a character leap off one of them.

Author Arundhati Roy uses natural settings in her novel *The God of Small Things*, which is set in India. There, the weather and nature—in particular, the constant activity of monsoon rains—have a profound influence on the characters:

> Heaven opened and the water hammered down, reviving the reluctant old well, greenmossing the pigless pigsty, carpet bombing still, tea-colored puddles the way memory bombs still, tea-colored minds. The grass

looked wetgreen and pleased. Happy earthworms frolicked purple in the slush.

In this small paragraph, Roy creates a feeling for what it's like to experience a monsoon rain in India (with wonderful descriptions, no less). Imagine having to set your schedule around these torrential rains, and how this might shape your characters' relationship to natural forces and to each other.

Houses, Buildings, and Rooms

In the course of a novel, characters might live in houses, huts, and yurts; they might enter and exit bathrooms, mad scientists' laboratories, and hospitals; they might gather in restaurants, bars, and bedrooms. Rooms and homes must be real, because these are the most essential of living and gathering spaces, and most people are familiar with them, whether they live in shacks or large estates, eat at gourmet establishments or bring home pizza. These spaces are telling and should reveal details about characters.

You've heard the old adage that seeing is believing? Well, how will the reader know for sure that a bedroom "bears a woman's touch" unless a character in the scene sees perfume and lingerie and lovely flowers on the windowsill? How will he know a home is "homey" unless he can see the fire burning in the hearth and feel the soft rugs beneath his toes?

Houses are often representative of the characters that live in them. By describing the state of a house, you can also speak to the soul of a character. Lonely characters could live in empty, sterile quarters. Passionate characters could have a taste for the flamboyant, the colorful, or the warm. Use your rooms, buildings, and houses to add to your characters and scenes, not just to serve as flat backdrops.

SETTING DETAILS

Every setting type comes with its own unique setting details that are just as important as basic physical details for creating a vivid and believable environment in which to situate your protagonist. From the historical period to cultural references, settings are more than just the way things appear—they comprise values and mores that you can work into your narrative to create a truly vivid, believable world for the reader to become deeply involved in.

Time in History

It's important not to forget *when* your novel takes place, because this also has a major influence on your setting. Medieval England will provide a setting completely different from that of 1920s Congo, Africa.

When you pick a particularly memorable time in recent history, say the Free Love and antigovernment movement of the 1960s in the United States, remember that there are people out there who lived during these times and who will have strong feelings about the accuracy of your portrayal of that time period. Not only will your details need to be especially accurate, but the time period itself, whether you intend it or not, will make a comment on its people and events.

If you choose a historically benign year or decade (if such a thing is possible), or at least one that has seen fewer dramatic events, you may have more room to sketch details broadly. Depending on how important the time period is to your storyline, you might be able to get away with generalities like "the early nineties" or "the middle of the nineteenth century."

Cultural References

Culture defines how people behave and what beliefs have shaped their upbringing; the West Coast of the United States differs in many significant ways from the South, from accent and manner of speech to political values. Cultures come with icons of worship, social and religious traditions—or lack thereof—and language patterns. If your characters are living in a culture that you personally have never lived in, you will be in the position of having to do research to get details right. If it's a culture you know well, then you have the advantage of being able to draw on rich material that will authenticate your scenes.

A good example comes from Michelle Richmond's lyrical novel *Dream of the Blue Room*. In it, protagonist Jenny is on a cruise down the Yangtze River in China in a last-ditch attempt to save her failing marriage, while also saying goodbye to her deceased friend Amanda Ruth, who wanted her ashes sprinkled there. Richmond builds a gorgeous and surreal mood out of these foreign elements with descriptions and images, but she does so in a way that renders the scene accessible and authentic. It is easy to believe you are there on that boat, cruising down this mysterious river in China:

> In the night the river turns silver, the mountains shine down upon it, the air goes cool and wet. This is the China Amanda Ruth wanted, her moonlit landscape, her Land of the Dragon. The villages we pass become magical in darkness, carnival-like and throbbing, though in the day they seem filthy, overcrowded, rubbed raw by industry. Apartment rows crouch like creatures gone dumb with hunger, and in the air there is a stench of coal. The mist mingles with black ash and factory smoke. It takes all of my energy just to breathe.

You do not have to present an entire history or cultural overview of the territory of your novel or story, but you do need to provide enough information, description, and cultural detail to allow the reader to believe she is really there in that country, even if it is on another planet. Try to lean into the senses, rendering the foreign land and its culture visible, audible, and so on. Of course, be aware, too, that if the setting is a real place (as opposed to a fantasy world) and is not your own land, or not one you've visited, you run the risk of creating a hollow or empty landscape that will not resonate with readers. Always, always do your research.

A WHIRLWIND TOUR OF SETTING

For a bird's-eye view of all the elements of setting discussed in this chapter, consider these significant elements pulled from scenes in Patrick Süskind's *Perfume: The Story of a Murderer.*

GEOGRAPHIC LOCATION AND TIME PERIOD

The following details set the stage of eighteenth-century Paris, France. Notice how vividly you are drawn into the smells and sights. The main character is anti-hero Grenouille, a man who was born without a scent of his own and who lusts after scents:

In the period of which we speak, there reigned in the cities a stench barely conceivable to us modern men and women. The streets stank of manure, the courtyards of urine, the stairwells of moldering wood and rat droppings, the kitchens of spoiled cabbage and mutton fat; people stank of sweat and unwashed clothes; from their mouths came the stench of rotting teeth, from their bellies that of onions. …

For eight hundred years the dead had been brought here from the Hotel-Dieu and from the surrounding parish churches, for eight hundred years, day in, day out, corpses by the dozens had been carted here and tossed into long ditches, stacked bone upon bone. …

Here, then, on the most putrid spot in the whole kingdom, Jean-Baptiste Grenouille was born on July 17, 1738.

HOUSES AND BUILDINGS

Here is the neighborhood where young Grenouille lives in his early years. In short passages of description, you get a strong visual image of a claustrophobic little village:

The adjacent neighborhoods of Saint-Jacques-de-la-Boucherie and Saint-Eustache were a wonderland. In the narrow side streets … people lived so densely packed, each house so tightly pressed to the next, five, six stories high that you could not see the sky, and the air at ground level formed damp canals where odors congealed.

Süskind gives glimpses into the physical spaces, namely rooms of the perfumer, through Grenouille's fascinated eyes:

He was touched by the way this worktable looked: everything lay ready, the glass basin for the perfume bath, the glass plate for drying, the mortars for mixing the tincture, pestle and spatula, brush and parer and shears.

NATURAL SETTING

After learning all he needs to know about how to make perfume, and then blowing up his perfume master's shop, Grenouille sets off to divorce himself from other people for long enough to be forgotten. He retreats to the wild:

For the spot had incalculable advantages: at the end of the tunnel it was pitch-black night even during the day, it was deathly quiet and the air he breathed was moist, salty cool. Grenouille could smell at once that no living creature had ever entered the place. ... He was lying a hundred and fifty feet below the earth, inside the loneliest mountain in France. ... Never in his life had he felt so secure. ...

PURPOSEFUL PLACEMENT: EVERY OBJECT COUNTS

Another important aspect of setting is the placement of props, or objects that have significance. Most people who went through public school as children had to construct, at some point, something known as a diorama—a still life representing a book they had read, recreated with tiny props and presented in a shoe box. You could not possibly fit all the details of a famous novel, for instance, into a diorama, so you would have to pare down to the essentials that were most representative of the book. This is a good way to think about the objects that will show up in your scenes: Imagine that each scene is a diorama. You should strive to add only the props that will bring a scene to life—a mechanic will have his tools, a musician his instrument, perhaps—without imbuing these objects with unnecessary power.

If you make the effort to put an object in a scene, the reader will believe that object has significance. This is not to say that every comb, pack of cigarettes, and cup of tea needs to get up and dance the tango, or that you should keep your settings bare, but remember that the more attention you give to descriptions of objects, the more readers will assign import and meaning to those objects. From art on the walls to cigarettes left burning in an ashtray, objects carry emotional weight and may often appear as clues. This is important to consider if your intention is simply to describe a man's possessions to reveal his character; the reader may assume that a cigar is a lot more than just than a cigar, depending on how much description each object gets.

Mood Objects

Some objects are used to symbolize the narrator's feelings and do not play an important role in the plot; thus, they can be considered mood objects.

They add to the tone of a narrative and deepen our understanding of a character's feelings.

For example, in his novel *So Long, See You Tomorrow*, William Maxwell uses a multitude of mood objects in the narrative. The narrator in this novel, now an adult, is writing his memoirs in relation to a murder that took place in his small hometown, and he describes his childhood home just after his mother's death:

> I have never been inside it since that day, when a great many objects that I remember and would like to be reunited with disappeared without a trace: Victorian walnut sofas and chairs that my fingers had absently traced every knob and scroll of, mahogany tables, worn Oriental rugs, gilt mirrors, pictures, big square books full of photographs that I knew by heart.

These objects in and of themselves do not bear any one particular meaning to the narrator; rather, they add up to a feeling of familiarity, of comfort, which he lost when his mother died. The fact that they are very quickly sketched and lumped together in a list, so that no single item stands out as more important than another, tells us that no specific object is particularly important. Though the reader gets a quick picture of the knobs and scrolls of the mahogany table, these details are passed over just as quickly for the "worn Oriental rugs."

The closest this narrator can come to admitting that he misses his mother is to miss the objects he associated with her. While these details certainly add texture to the scene, they are merely representative, placed to call attention to the feelings and memories they elicit in the narrator.

When you describe objects clumped together like this, remember that you're setting mood more than imbuing an object with symbolic power. This is why it's important to be aware of how much description you give to any one object. If you want an object to be innocuous, just background dressing, then be brief about it. If you want an object to mean something inside your narrative, then it needs to stand alone or be given more attention than other objects, as described next.

Significant Objects

Significant objects should call a certain amount of attention to themselves. What makes an object significant? When it directly affects plot or character development. Let's take a careful look at each type to get a better feel for what makes each unique and meaningful.

Plot-Significant Objects

Obvious significant objects, such as evidence sought by police in mystery plots, stolen heirlooms, lost Egyptian tombs, and buried treasure, change your plot once they are introduced or found in a scene.

If your story is about the search for a holy artifact, then it's safe to assume that whenever the object turns up, some sort of drama, danger, or other conflict will be involved. Also, whether the protagonist or the antagonist has the artifact is likely to sway the course of your plot. You may in fact tease the reader with a significant object and have it turn up in every scene, but continue to elude those who want it most.

In J.R.R. Tolkien's Lord of the Rings series, the significant object is merely a tiny ring, but it holds the power to corrupt good people and ultimately destroy anyone who possesses it for too long. Every time that ring turns up in a scene, everyone's attention is focused on it—characters and readers alike—and the balance of power continues to shift as the ring works its diabolical magic on everyone it touches. That's a powerfully significant object, and one that continues to shape the course of the plot from start to finish.

A plot-significant object does not need to be quite as weighty as one that holds the balance between good and evil, but it should have a direct link to your plot. It might be a murder weapon, a stolen piece of jewelry, or an item that incriminates a character for adultery.

Character-Significant Objects

Objects have value to people for sometimes very bizarre and personal reasons. A person cherishes a ratty old jacket because of its sentimental power. People collect items that have meaning only to themselves—figurines, dolls, coins—to satisfy an emotional need in a material form, or for purposes of greed, or to feel safe. People also have talismans—objects that hold religious or spiritual meaning and help them feel loved or lucky.

Character-significant objects do not need to change the course of your plot, but they do need to be described in enough detail that the reader understands their value or importance to the character. If a character always kisses a medallion of St. Christopher before he travels, this will reinforce in the reader's mind that this object means something to him. You might even find it useful to write the scene of when he first obtained this object and how it became significant to him.

While these objects are indeed important, you can introduce them without a great deal of description so long as you effectively demonstrate a character's relationship to the item.

Avoiding Vague Objects

Would your protagonist buy a "vehicle," or a white Toyota Corolla? If someone opened his cabinets, would he find "aspirin," or Advil? Does your character own a "parrot," or a rainbow macaw? The difference is, of course, in the specifics.

It's very important to avoid the vague. If you lead the reader into a "building," she will wonder if it is a bank, an embassy, or a hotel, and this is already too many options for her to have to hold in mind. Remember, it is your job to be the tour guide. If your protagonist carries a gun, the reader deserves to know if it's a tiny derringer or a semiautomatic rifle. What you want the reader to wonder about is what happens next, not where the characters are and what can be seen. If you were a painter and you made some loose charcoal sketches, then displayed your work and told people, "some green paint will go here, and some blue there, and probably a little yellow here," they would have absolutely no idea of the painting you intended to make. So try to avoid making that same mistake in your writing. Be clear and visual.

Your objects are opportunities to reveal information about your characters. Objects are the physical manifestations of characters' personalities and moods. Since you can't spend too much of the text in narrative summary describing a character's personality without losing the reader's attention, these props serve to convey information on the character's behalf.

Tim O'Brien, award-winning author of the linked collection of short stories *The Things They Carried* about soldiers who fought in Vietnam, uses objects as biographies of each person:

> Norman Bowker carried a diary. Rat Kiley carried comic books. Kiowa, a devout Baptist, carried an illustrated New Testament that had been presented to him by his father, who taught Sunday school in Oklahoma City, Oklahoma. As a hedge against bad times, however, Kiowa also carried his grandmother's distrust of the white man, his grandfather's old hunting hatchet.

To use objects properly, you have to get to know your characters, and to do that, you need to ask yourself a series of important questions about who your characters are. What do they love or hate, collect or throw away? What do they like to see around them in their house? Are they art snobs or philistines? These, and many others, are questions that only you can answer.

Remember that great characters and the wild plot actions they undertake need solid ground and meaningful props to support them. Always ask: What needs to be *seen* in this scene?

STRIKING A BALANCE

Setting is where many writers get lost in chunks of narrative summary because it's easy, and even fun, to describe the setting. It's crucial to remember that setting exists mostly to serve as a way of both creating authenticity and grounding the reader in the scene (and story) at hand. If setting takes too much precedence and distracts from your characters or storyline, then it needs to be pruned back.

Here is an example of well-balanced setting description, filtered through the character's perceptions, punctuated by small actions, from Jane Alison's lyrical novel *The Marriage of the Sea*:

> Max landed in New Orleans like a sprinter. His cab barreled over the toxic empty highway into town, the battered streets and battered sidewalks and battered, crooked houses. He'd chosen the most romantic hotel, just beyond the Garden District, lopsided and seedy. Once he'd checked in

he ran up the staircase, noting with delight the stained glass promise in the window: *Let my beloved come into his garden and eat his pleasant fruits!* Then he had barely put down his bag, barely phoned Sea & Air to provide a temporary number (should his fur teacup and cookbooks and secondhand Paul Smiths be lost at sea in their nailed, stamped crates), before he washed his hands, looked at his teeth, tried to order his fly-away ringlets, paced once up and down the room, lifted the receiver and dialed.

While a lot of detail is given to setting in this paragraph, it feels intimately connected to Max's perceptions and makes clear that he is setting the stage for the woman he is in love with.

When you describe setting details, to strike a nice balance and not overdo it, keep the following in mind:

- Setting helps create mood or ambiance that sets a tone for the scene. In the scene above, there's a sense of preparation, of nesting almost, as Max prepares to see his love.
- Your protagonist needs to interact with the setting. I cannot stress this enough. The best use of setting is to show your character engaged with it, not to simply observe it. The reader sees New Orleans through Max's eyes here—words like "romantic" and "battered" reflect his opinion.
- The setting needs to support your plot. Max is in New Orleans because he has come to be with a woman—a woman, it turns out, who will break his heart.
- Small actions help break up setting description. Because Max is moving around, the reader doesn't feel as though he is looking at a static scene. The scene comes alive.

STAYING CONSISTENT

Once you've done the work of establishing the place in your scenes and fleshing out the settings so the reader is clear on where your characters are, it's important to stay consistent. If there are long tendrils of night-blooming jasmine on the porch in one scene, be sure they don't later turn into wisteria.

Don't forget which way the front door faces as your characters enter and exit. If a character sleeps in a room without windows, don't allow in a sudden, unexpected beam of sunlight.

For anyone who has a complicated setting, I often recommend keeping a notebook with all the small details in it as a kind of reference guide in case you get lost. I recommend this for any amount of significant research. If you have trouble organizing, keep your notes ordered into chapters and scenes in a linear fashion.

THE SENSES

Before language, humans were like other animals; we came to know our world through our most primary set of tools for understanding and learning—our senses. The senses are as core a scene element as you can get and are very important in writing fiction: They transform flat words on a page into three-dimensional, realistic scenes and reveal the depths of character experience in a visceral way. However, many writers overlook senses other than sight and sound. In a scene that takes place in a garden, for instance, you might forget to allow readers the opportunity to *smell* the jasmine and lilacs that draw your character out to the garden. Or you might show a character eating an entire tin of cookies without telling the reader what flavor they are. No matter *when* you add in sensual details—upon revision or at the start—remember that they are key tools for bringing your written world alive for readers.

AUTHENTICITY OF DETAIL

The sensual experiences that you describe should be realistic and believable. If a character is baking blackberry pie, but the scent emanating from the oven smells "savory and meaty," you're off base; obviously a blackberry pie would smell sweet and a little tart.

Also, the senses are a part of everyday life, so they should, in fact, be blended into your scenes as an integral part of the stage you set. If your scene's stage is a meadow in County Cork, Ireland, then there ought to be the nutty smell of grass and the sweet perfume of wildflowers, and possibly the musky scent of animals and mud. There might be birds trilling or sheep baaing or the gentle slicing sound of a scythe cutting hay. Characters will feel the wind on their faces and the ropy knots of lavender stems between their fingers. The more seamlessly all these sensual details emerge, so that they become the backdrop to the scene in which a young boy confesses to his angry father that he is leaving Ireland, the more the reader will feel transported to that very spot and time, her own senses activated.

SIGHT

Sight is perhaps the most important element of scene writing, and the most ironic: At no time do you actually draw images or pictures while writing, yet the reader must come away from your wall of text with an experience of *seeing*. He must be able to draw in his mind images of what your characters look like, what the world in which your characters interact looks like, and all the minutiae in between. This means that you must have a pretty good visual idea of the world you're writing about so that you can help provide the appropriate cues that will turn words into pictures in the reader's mind.

All that can be seen in your scenes is the fictional equivalent of evidence provided in a court case. In court, you can't get away with saying, "The bloody knife was about yea long, and imagine a carved wooden handle here, and some speckles of blood here. Trust me, it was a big, nasty-looking knife, and definitely the murder weapon!" The lawyer must provide an *actual* knife that meets those specifications for the jury members to set their eyes upon. So must you provide evidence in your scenes. No matter if the piece of evidence proves that someone's lover was just at the house—a cigarette butt covered in suspicious lipstick still smoldering in the ashtray—or if it's graffiti on the side of a house that gives away a vandal; until the reader can *see* proof, it simply does not exist.

When including details of sight in your story, remember that point of view is not only a vehicle for revealing character; it is also the camera through which the reader sees whatever your characters see. A fictional world takes shape to the reader through the eyes and experiences of your characters implicitly, but many writers fall into the habit of pointing out that a character sees something—"Jimmy saw a huge cloud of dust rise up on the horizon." I call this habit double vision. The point of view establishes that Jimmy is the one seeing; therefore, when you tell the reader that Jimmy saw, you are literally calling attention to the act of sight rather than to the huge cloud of dust on the horizon, which is the important point of action in the scene. You are saying to the reader: "Look, Jimmy is seeing!" rather than, "Look at that huge dust cloud! Wowsers, I wonder what it could be!"

This doesn't only apply to sight. The more you can place readers inside the vision and point of view of your characters and remove the *act* of them sensing, the more directly the reader will interact with the sights, smells, and other senses in the scene.

Blindness

When a character loses sight, or never had it to begin with, the writer is no less obliged to describe the physical world, even though that world no longer exists through the character's eyes. Blindness gives way to all the other senses, which must take over. This is a powerful technique to use, as it not only forces the character to experience the settings in a unique way, it also provides you with unique challenges.

José Saramago's stark novel *Blindness* has the entire world going blind in the course of a few days—except for one woman, a doctor's wife. The novel centers on a quarantined ward of people who are among the first to go blind. Chaos soon erupts as the ward fills to overflowing and is eventually abandoned by the government when they, too, go blind:

> You can count me out, said the first blind man, I'm off to another ward, as far away as possible from this crook. … He picked up his suitcase and, shuffling his feet so as not to trip and groping with his free hand, he went along the aisle separating the two rows of beds. Where are the other wards, he asked, but did not hear the reply if there was one, because suddenly he found himself beneath an onslaught of arms and legs. …

Saramago relies heavily upon the next sense, touch, to delineate the world for the reader.

What the characters see, the reader sees. Remember to extract yourself, the author, from the picture, so that the reader is looking directly through your characters' eyes like he would through a pair of binoculars focused on a far-off stage.

TOUCH

Though philosopher René Descartes would have us believe it is our thoughts that make us who we are ("I think, therefore I am"), touch is one of our first ways of knowing. Young babies do not think about their blocks and stuffed animals; they grab and grope, prod and poke their toys (and their parents) to learn about them. Touch is a bodily experience. Every character in your fiction will have a unique relationship to his body and to touch, and as the writer, you will need to determine these zones of comfort and contact and the meanings that are layered in.

Practical Touch

What are practical forms of touch? Perhaps a character rubs a piece of beach-weathered glass between his fingertips to feel its surface; touches the rough bark of a tree; inspects the edge of a knife for sharpness; runs his fingers over piano keys; or smooths the wrinkles out of a bedspread. These forms of touch aren't necessarily significant to the character or the plot; they are actions taken between dialogue or other actions. However, practical touch is sort of like punctuation—you need a little bit in strategic places because without it the scene would not be fully formed, but it shouldn't call attention to itself.

Practical touch can come in handy when you have a lot of uninterrupted dialogue between characters. A character could stop to touch the smooth surface of a marble countertop before launching an angry salvo, or he might grip a beer bottle tightly in his hand before defending his action. People tend to be tactile. When we're nervous, we fidget, fumble, or unconsciously drum our fingers. In fact, a character won't get more than a couple of minutes into a day before he begins to interact with the world by touching things.

Perhaps your character has a phobia of germs and wears gloves or refuses to touch certain things—like doorknobs or glasses. This example still shows details of touch. Whatever you determine for your characters, remember to let their fingers do the walking at least a little in your scenes, and know what kind of "toucher" each of your characters is.

Personal Touch

Personal touch is a *range* of physical contact that expresses information about your characters and relates to how they physically interact with other people. While personal touch refers to contact between characters (from the platonic to the downright naughty), it also refers to ways that your characters interact with the world—offering readers insight into your characters' personalities. For instance, you might create a character with a form of obsessive-compulsive disorder who cannot refrain from touching strangers' noses, light switches, mailboxes, etc. Another character might have an involuntary habit of gesturing wildly with his hands when he talks, knocking things off shelves because he lives in his head, not his body. The way your characters touch their physical world is important information about who they are.

When characters touch *each other* (or themselves—for instance, your character might be a "cutter" who wounds herself for emotional release from trauma), the reader will also take notice. Touch between people is important because it's a way of communicating with one another. In real life you notice when a stranger puts his hands on your shoulders without permission. Your characters should also pay attention to these forms of touch between each other. A character who was sexually abused may not like to hug or be hugged. Yet another character might come from a culture where close physical proximity is normal and has to learn the hard way that another character does not appreciate this. Remember that when characters touch each other, they are *communicating*, so try to be conscious of this communication and what it means to your scene and your plot.

In chapter seven, we'll talk about body language as a way to develop and build characters without using dialogue.

SMELL

Remember a time when you caught a whiff of the scent of a flower or food, and the smell evoked a childhood memory, making you cry, laugh, or even get embarrassed? It's as if memories are housed inside scents, and once your nose gets a whiff, the memory and associated feelings are unlocked. The sense of smell—our olfactory sense, as scientists call it—has a direct link in the brain to memory and emotion. Since encountering a scent is one of the most common experiences that people have, your characters need to have these experiences, too, and you can use the sense of smell to dramatic effect in scenes.

For a moment, let's classify smells into two basic groups: those that smell good, and those that smell bad. If your scene involves a conflict between a morally good character and morally corrupt character, but you don't want to overtly inform the reader which is which, scent can help you get this distinction across. If Jack, your bad guy, smells of cigar smoke and day-old, greasy Chinese food, while Bill, your good guy, smells like juniper and fresh air, who do you think the reader will see as bad or good?

Now, I can already hear you saying, "What if I hate the smell of juniper?" Point taken. However, in the world of scents, even an unsophisticated reader is likely to believe that juniper smells better than cigar smoke and that there is a reason you've gone to the trouble to make Jack smell worse than Bill. Or you might opt for a smell that is generally considered good, like the scent of roses.

Also, a character might use perfume or cologne for sentimental or vain reasons. A woman might wear Joy perfume because her mother and grandmother wore it; it's a part of her wardrobe, and therefore a part of her character. Another character might choose not to bathe as a way to keep others from getting too close to him. There are ingenious ways to use scent to reveal details about your characters.

Have you ever been to the movies or out to dinner and *smelled* a person entering before you saw her because of her perfume? Scent is a fabulous way to demonstrate that a character has arrived on the scene: "The pungent sting of bourbon in the air told Jeannie that Sam had let himself into the house *and* the liquor cabinet."

Finally, harking back to the link between smell and memory, you can invoke scent as a way to transition into a character flashback. If you need to go back in time to a scene from your character's past and you can use the smell of peaches at a grocery store to drop Becky into the peach orchard where she first met Eduardo, the love of her life, by all means do it. Scent is a subtle way to transition that won't jar the reader.

SOUND

Sounds can describe a physical setting almost as effectively as visual descriptions. With eyes closed, you can probably tell the difference between a train station and an airport. The places your characters show up have sound signatures, which you can use to enrich a setting's other details.

In a restaurant, for instance, your character, with eyes closed, can hear dishes, glasses, and silverware clinking and the sounds of waitstaff calling out orders to cooks and taking orders from customers. There is a certain kind of buzz of conversation that goes on in restaurants that is different from the sound of a real estate office, for instance. The more you pay attention to these small details when building a scene, the more real the scene will become.

Here are a few different examples of the way sound creates or enhances atmosphere and contributes to the tone and theme of a story.

In Irène Némirovsky's novel *Suite Française*, set in German-occupied France, 1942, sound marks the contrast with the silence of people hidden away in fear of air raids:

> The streets were empty. People were closing their shops. The metallic shudder of falling iron shutters was the only sound to break the silence, a sound familiar to anyone who has woken in a city threatened by riot or war.

In Justin Cronin's novel *The City of Mirrors*, the simplest sounds reveal that something terrible has happened:

> Peter, Apgar, and Chase were looking over Michael's passenger manifest when shouts erupted in the hall: "Put it down! Put it down!"
> A crash; a gunshot.

Finally, here is a description of the first time the character Francis Macomber hears the lion that will change his fate, from Ernest Hemingway's story "The Short Happy Life of Francis Macomber":

> It had started the night before when he had wakened and heard the lion roaring somewhere up along the river. It was a deep sound and at the end there were sort of coughing grunts that made him seem just outside the tent, and when Francis Macomber woke in the night to hear it he was afraid.

Sounds enhance mood, set tone, and create atmosphere, and should not be forgotten when setting the scene.

TASTE

One of my pet peeves about writing is that you don't very often see characters eating. Food is an important part of life and, I believe, an important part of a good story, too, when it can be factored in organically. While many of your scenes may have no need to invoke the sense of taste, you might ask yourself if there are places in your story where you could add in the act of tasting something. Taste provides great moments of potential conflict and intimacy. For example:

- A mother asks her a son to taste her soup, which provides an opportunity for him to be honest with her about her terrible cooking, leading to either conflict or unexpected closeness.
- A character who has just learned of a terrible loss might bite into a piece of his favorite cake only to discover that, in his grief, he cannot taste a thing.
- A character hoping to impress his gourmet lover with a home-cooked meal might see her true colors when, in rejecting his cooking, she also rejects his love.

Taste provides a fabulous opportunity for feelings and interactions between your characters to arise. Through the simple act of lifting a fork to mouth, your characters can come to epiphanies, exalt in simple pleasures, and enact conflicts that enliven your scenes.

. . .

Though the senses appear separately in this chapter to help you look at them individually, you will probably find that a majority of these sensory details will emerge naturally in combination when you begin writing scenes. Your own observations will deliver themselves as you write. But when you go back through to do a revision, ask yourself if you have underwritten one of the senses and been too heavy-handed with another, and take opportunities to add or subtract some for sensory balance.

CHARACTER DEVELOPMENT AND MOTIVATION

When you put down a book, what do you remember most? Just think about it for minute. Is it the lovely descriptions of city streets? Or the moody, powerful, potent characters who populate them? I'm sure it comes as no surprise that most of us identify most closely with the characters. Though passages of pretty scenery or buildings collapsing capture the reader's attention for a moment, maybe two, characters bring scenes to life and are the natural focal point of a strong scene. After all, scenes are the primary vehicles for developing your protagonist (and co-protagonists, when you have more than one).

ACTION, EMOTION, AND THEME

In every scene, just as in every plot, there are three key layers, known as Action, Emotion, and Theme. Martha Alderson and I elaborate on these layers in our book, *Writing Deep Scenes*, but it boils down to this: In each scene, you have to create opportunities for your characters to reveal and enrich themselves (Emotion) and to drive their stories forward in connection with your plot (Action) in a way that allows them to transform and make meaning (Theme).

If your characters are the same at the end of your narrative as they were at the beginning, you most likely didn't balance your layers of action, emotion, and theme.

Here we'll discuss the basics of character development and motivation as a core element of the scene.

CHARACTER DEVELOPMENT

In chapter eight, we'll talk more about character development over the course of your plot, but for now I want you to think on the micro level. The moment your characters are born in your imagination, you should ask, how do they behave in public? With family? Under pressure? Sometimes people act out when they're with family members; a normally compassionate character might have a prejudice that leads him to behave in a cruel or sadistic fashion around people of certain ethnicities; or your character might always be on his best behavior *only* around his priest or his girlfriend. Your characters won't behave the same way in every social situation, and for the purpose of drama you should try to build in moments where they misbehave or respond to unusual or unexpected events in ways that surprise others.

How does your protagonist develop over the course of your narrative? Since you can't invite the reader into his entire history at the beginning of the narrative, you only have the elements of the scene to work with. The scene is sort of like improvisational theater. Look at the following formula.

1. Every plot ultimately begins with an incident or situation, after which every scene will involve a consequence or result of that seed event and the events that follow. However, each scene should provide your character with the following things:

   • **AT LEAST ONE PLOT EVENT OR NEW PIECE OF INFORMATION TO REACT OR RESPOND TO.** (Of course, you can have more than one, if needed.) Whatever you choose, it must unravel from the scenes that came before and drive the story forward by giving your character something to react to (see chapter eight for types of plot information).

- **A CATALYST OR ANTAGONIST WHO PROVIDES OPPOSITION AND CONFLICT TO YOUR PROTAGONIST.** Other characters are catalysts—they facilitate change and reaction in your protagonist; or they are antagonists—they thwart, oppose, and even sometimes outright sabotage the intentions of your protagonist. Through the interactions your protagonist has with these other characters comes the necessary leverage to develop them into complex people with a compelling story goal. When there is no other character in the scene, your protagonist will interact only with himself or with forces of nature or the world around him, in which case you get contemplative scenes (see chapter fifteen).

2. In every scene, your protagonist should be motivated by two things:

- **THE PROTAGONIST'S INTENTION FOR THE SCENE.** A scene intention is ultimately a goal or decision your protagonist makes that drives the direction of the scene. A scene without an intention feels anecdotal and disconnected from the plot. Whatever intention you give your protagonist in a scene will fuel his motivation and action. A scene intention (discussed at length in chapter eleven) must be related to the inciting incident of your narrative, but your protagonist may have different intentions in each scene. In fact, one intention might even lead to another or more within the same scene. For example, in one scene the protagonist's intention might be to contact the agency that facilitated his adoption to try to track down his biological mother, and in another scene it might be to confront the adoptive mother who withheld that information all his life. We'll discuss how to make sure that a character's intentions stay strong throughout your storyline in chapter twenty-three.
- **THE PROTAGONIST'S PERSONAL HISTORY.** One other factor will motivate your character in every scene: his backstory. And while you can certainly show insight into your protagonist's nature or history through reflective flashback scenes or summary dialogue, characters are always demonstrating backstory in words and deeds, and it's best to integrate that backstory rather than reveal it through

lengthy narrative summaries. It is our histories, for the most part, that dictate how we think, feel, and behave (with room for genetic underpinnings, of course). You can also use a character's history to inform how she will behave next. Mostly you want to be sure that she behaves in line with her history and doesn't make dramatic leaps of character before plot events have had a chance to transform her.

3. Each situation or interaction should make your plot and its consequences for the protagonist either more or less complicated:

- **MORE COMPLICATED.** When the consequences become more complicated, as described in chapter three, you build dramatic tension, create character conflict, and heighten the energy of the scene. Lean toward building more complications in every scene in the first two thirds of your narrative.
- **OR LESS COMPLICATED.** There are a few good cases for making situations less complicated for your protagonist: In the final stretch of your narrative, when you want to resolve plot threads and head toward resolution; when you want to pull back on the intensity of a scene; and when you want to lull the reader into a false sense of complacency to spring a plot surprise on him.

4. Through these complications, your protagonist should change. He can change beliefs, behaviors, attitudes, allegiances or loyalties, appearances, and motivations.

By narrative's end, your protagonist—thanks to the many opportunities you gave him to develop and change in scenes—will not be in exactly the same place emotionally, or even spiritually, as when you began. He will have changed (see chapter twenty-three).

Now, using the formula from above, let's walk through a scene example from M.R. Carey's *The Girl with All The Gifts*, a postapocalyptic novel set after a strange, viral-like fungus has wiped out a significant part of the population. The novel opens in a military stronghold and is told in alternating points of view between Melanie, a ten-year-old girl who spends most of her day, like the other children in her "class," strapped into a special chair she can't get out of or in her locked cell; a somewhat sympathetic Sergeant; a coldhearted doctor working on a cure; and Melanie's teacher, Miss Justineau, who continues to get in trouble with her superiors for treating her charges with too much concern.

In this scene, Justineau breaks orders and enters Melanie's cell alone during off hours. She feels bad for these children who don't know what they are and with whom she's forged a bond, against protocol.

Someone unlocks Melanie's door and pushes it open.

Miss Justineau stands in the doorway. "It's okay," she says. "I'm here, Melanie. I'm here for you." [*Miss Justineau has a clear intention to rescue Melanie. Though the scene is told in Melanie's POV and she doesn't yet know that, the reader does.*]

Miss Justineau steps forward. She wrestles with the chair like Hercules wrestling with a lion or a snake. The arm strap is partway undone, and it opens up really easily. Then Miss J goes down on her knees and she's working the leg straps. [*Already we have added complication to the scene. She shouldn't be doing this at all, much less alone.*] Right. Then left. She mutters and curses as she works. "He's frigging insane! Why? Why would anyone do this?" [*This reveals aspects of Justineau's backstory: She doesn't fully understand the danger before her, still believing Melanie to be a normal child. This causes immense tension in the scene because the reader understands these children wouldn't be locked up for no reason.*] Melanie feels the constriction lessen, and sensation returns to her legs in a tingling rush.

She surges to her feet, her heart almost bursting with happiness and relief. Miss Justineau has saved her! She raises her arms in an instinct too strong to resist. She wants Miss Justineau to lift her up. She wants to hold her and be held by her and be touching her not just with her hair but with her hands and her face and her whole body. [*This reveals important information about how Melanie feels for Miss Justineau, which will define their relationship later on.*]

Then she freezes like a statue. Her jaw muscles stiffen and a moan comes out of her mouth. [*The scene suddenly becomes more complicated when what started out as a salvation turns bad.*]

MAKE A SCENE REVISED AND EXPANDED

Miss Justineau is alarmed. "Melanie?" She stands, and her hand reaches out.

"Don't!" Melanie screams. "Don't touch me!"

Miss Justineau stops moving, but she's so close! So close! Melanie whimpers. Her whole mind is exploding. She staggers back, but her stiff legs don't work properly and she falls full length on the floor. The smell, the wonderful, terrible smell, fills the room and her mind and her thoughts, and all she wants to do is … [*This is the first time it has occurred to Melanie that there might be a reason she's always strapped to a chair. It's the beginning of a painful awareness.*]

"Go away!" she moans. "Go away go away go away!"

"Go away, or I'll fu**king dismantle you!" Melanie wails. She's desperate. Her mouth is filled with thick saliva like mud from a mudslide. Her jaws start to churn of their own accord. Her head feels light, and the room sort of goes away and then comes back again without moving.

Melanie is dangling on the end of the thinnest, thinnest piece of string.

"Oh God!" Miss Justineau sobs. She gets it at last. She takes a step back. "I'm sorry, Melanie. I didn't even think!"

About the showers. Among the sounds that Melanie heard, one big absence: no hiss of chemical spray falling from the ceiling to settle on Miss Justineau and layer on its own smell to hide the Miss Justineau smell underneath. [*New plot information. Earlier in the story we see all the characters undergo these chemical baths but don't know why. Now, we have an inkling.*]

The scene, though very short, adds great complexity to the plot and to both characters. What was simply a relationship of mutual admiration before is now one that cannot be, meaning that Justineau can't rescue Melanie from the inevitability of Dr. Caldwell's lab (or so we think). Justineau has been our hope for Melanie's salvation, so this scene presents a major complication when even she can't rescue Melanie. Moreover, it's the first awakening Melanie has to her own condition, which plants a growing fear and confusion in her.

SCENE STEALER

Sheila Kohler, author of the novel *Becoming Jane Eyre* and many others, finds that there is nothing more memorable than what she calls "first glimpse scenes," in which main characters see each other for the first time, setting the stage for their relationships to unfold.

. . .

There are so many great ones. Almost every great book has a great first-glimpse scene when the hero and heroine meet or the hero or heroine meets an adversary (when Pip first meets Miss Havisham in *Great Expectations*, for example). Others include the following:

- The first time Charles Bovary sees Emma in Gustave Flaubert's *Madame Bovary*. Charles, a doctor, arrives on his fearful horse. He is then taken by Emma to her father's bedside, where she sews pads for her father's broken leg and pricks her fingers and sucks them (with all the connotations of such an act). Charles is surprised by the whiteness of her nails in a wonderful moment that will cause him, ultimately, great sorrow.
- The first time protagonist Aschenbach sees Tadzio, the young man who captures his mind, in Thomas Mann's novella *Death in Venice*. In this wonderful scene, Tadzio's sisters arrive dressed "with almost disfiguring severity," in sharp contrast with the appearance of Tadzio, strolling in late with all his golden curls, his English sailor suit, and his spoilt, exquisite air.
- When Anton Chekhov's "lady with the dog" is sighted by the eponymous short story's protagonist. "Sitting in Verney's pavilion, he saw, walking on the seafront, a fair-haired lady of medium height, wearing a beret, a white Pomeranian dog was running behind her." It is a brief first description without the many details that are gradually introduced throughout the story, but wonderful in its superficial simplicity.

CHARACTER AND PLOT

Hopefully the illustration above made it clear that plot and character are married to one another. Your protagonist ought to be indelibly caught up in the plot situation and information of every scene, and should bear or participate in the consequences that follow. Similarly, your plot should not be able to advance or get more complicated without the active participation of your protagonist.

With that in mind, when developing your characters you should always be thinking about how the plot situation of a given scene will affect the character and what it will cause him to do, think, or feel.

When reviewing your scenes, you should ask: What is plot relevant? What is character relevant? How are the two related? Your plot should be unable to carry on without your protagonist.

A Note on Character Behavior

If you've ever turned up in the aftermath of an exciting incident like a fight or a police chase, you will probably agree that hearing a bystander's account is never as dramatic as witnessing it for yourself. The same is true of character behavior in scenes; inevitably you'll take shortcuts, hoping the reader will take your word for it that "Charles didn't want to live any longer," or "Frederika had a magnetic personality." Well, okay, both details might be true, but unless the reader gets to witness the plot situation of Charles standing at the edge of the bridge ready to leap off or, through character interactions, sees multiple characters fall in love with Frederika, the reader has no proof of what you have tried to quickly summarize.

. . .

If you follow the formula set forth in this chapter for developing characters, your characters will have no choice but to become complex, plot-relevant people who feel vivid and real to the reader.

PLOT AND YOUR CHARACTER'S EMOTIONAL JOURNEY

Without the human mind to give significance to what happens to us, life is just a series of random events unfolding over time. This randomness is one of the reasons that many people turn to literature. Inside the pages of a book, you trust that you will be led on a meaningful journey revealing insights and giving your spirits and emotions a jolt. In fiction, this is called a plot.

Some people confuse plot for story and think it is enough to have a sequence of events lined up, one after the other. A story is just a string of information about a cast of characters in a given time and place. Boy meets girl. Stranger comes to town. The doctor is found dead.

A plot is the method by which that story takes on tension, energy, and momentum and urges a reader to keep turning pages. Plot transforms "boy meets girl" into *Romeo and Juliet*—with secret love, wild fighting, and tragic conflicts along the way.

In short, plot is the related string of consequences that follow after the inciting incident in your narrative, consequences that must be addressed, become complicated, and be resolved through engaging, well-crafted scenes. Some people refer to this relationship of events as causality, but that's a sterile-sounding word. Here we'll just call them consequences.

In chapter two, we discussed how any narrative is a series of scenes strung together like beads on a wire. This chapter will look at the two elements inside each scene that are essential to plot: new information and character transformation.

Plot is constructed out of crucial bits of information—the consequences of, and explanations for, the inciting incident and the characters who must deal with it. Plot is best delivered teasingly to the reader in small bites to keep them hungry for more. In a well-written plot, the reader gets just a little bit smarter, a little bit more clued in to the puzzle, as he reads each scene.

PLOT INFORMATION BASICS

Most writers are as fond of a beautiful sentence as they are a good plot element. It's fun to write lyrical passages, to wax philosophical, and to create images of beauty. Surely there's no harm if a scene digresses from the plot to meander and muse, right?

Nope!

Sorry to be the plot police, but here's the cold truth: Every scene in your narrative must pertain to your plot. Every single one. Even if a character muses or meanders, that activity must be plot related. A character under suspicion of murder may drift off into thought, but those thoughts had better be about why he's been wrongfully accused, how he's going to prove his innocence, or who the true murderer is, not random memories of whale watching or hiking.

Scenes exist to make the events in your fictional world real to the reader. You want the reader to be knee-deep in your action and emotional drama, to feel for your characters, to hope and dream and want for them.

Each scene, then, must deliver, at minimum, one piece of new information that speaks to one of the following questions: Who? What? Where? When? Why? How?

Every scene.

The way to do that is simple—don't end a scene and begin another one until new information has been provided. Providing information is one of the most important functions of a scene and is the foundation of a plot.

New information has three main responsibilities:

1. It must fill in another piece of the puzzle, so that both the character and the reader get a little bit smarter.
2. It must deepen or change the course of your main character's thoughts, feelings, or actions.
3. It must lead to new consequences, actions, or behaviors that carry your plot forward.

Here we'll look at the different types of plot information more closely.

Who

Much scene time is devoted to characters, since they are typically the most important element of any fictional narrative. You'll want to include a bit of general character information in your narrative—what kind of work your protagonist does, his religion or lack of one, his habits. Does he, for instance, go to AA meetings twice a week or sing in a gospel choir? These details tell us who your character is in general, not necessarily who he is in relationship to your plot. Character-related plot information, on the other hand, tends to come up over the course of a narrative, often having to do with identity or hidden origins being revealed, someone's past catching up with him, a dark secret being brought to light, or a surprising change of heart. Here's an example of plot-related character information from Ann Patchett's novel *The Magician's Assistant*, in which a lawyer tells the protagonist, Sabine, that her recently deceased husband (and business partner) was not who she thought he was.

> "Parsifal's name wasn't Petrie. It was Guy Fetters. Guy Fetters has a mother and two sisters in Nebraska. As far as I can tell the father is out of the picture—either dead or gone. ..."
> "That isn't possible," she said.
> "I'm afraid it is."

When it comes to characters and plot, think about how your characters can surprise each other, and the readers, by revealing new information about themselves (not necessarily after death), about things they have hidden or covered up, or about something that is being denied or protected.

Most important, when you reveal this character information, you should do it directly—through dialogue and action, if possible, or if the person has died, either in the form of correspondence he left behind or through the mouth of another person. Try to rely as little as possible on the thought bubble, in which a character *thinks* a revelation.

What

What is perhaps the widest possible category of all plot information. It is, in essence, what is often described as your hook—the storyline or angle that makes your narrative unique, and from which all other plot events will flow.

In *The Magician's Assistant*, for instance, Parsifal's death is the novel's inciting incident—the first big piece of *what* information—that launches the book. The necessity of sharing the information about Parsifal's death with his family sets the next plot events in motion and leads to great insight and change in Sabine and the other characters. These two main pieces of information drive the entire plot, and both have their own string of consequences that each scene deals with in one way or another.

In every scene you should ask yourself, literally: What is next? What piece of important information do I need my characters to learn and my readers to become aware of? Remember that every scene needs a new piece of information, or else there's no point to including it.

Where

Where is one of those bits of information that does light duty in terms of plot, most of the time. Undoubtedly setting is crucial to your plot, especially if one must trace the steps of a murderer or revisit a place to learn something new, or if your narrative is specific to a geographical location. However, most of the time, place serves as a backdrop for the other bits of information and should be limited. In Sabine's case, she has to travel from Los Angeles to Nebraska, two vastly different worlds. Sabine meets with cultural challenges due to the differences between Nebraskan and Californian lifestyles, but the plot does not depend upon much information being imparted about place in every scene.

Other than the space your characters directly interact with, setting often serves more as a spoken reference—the maid was found dead in the drawing room; Jacques had last been seen in Cancun before he disappeared; my father had a second family in a small town in Florida.

If place does turn out to be crucial to your plot, remember these points:

- **NEW DETAILS MUST BE REVEALED IN EVERY SCENE TO MAKE IT PLAY INTO YOUR PLOT.** For instance, a mansion might turn out to be haunted, or a beautiful countryside might also be a Native-American burial ground.
- **THE NEW INFORMATION ABOUT THE PLACE MUST HAVE AN EFFECT ON YOUR CHARACTER.** His thoughts, feelings, or actions in the scene should all reflect the information given. For instance, say Jack and Jill planned to honeymoon in the mansion; once Jack learns the mansion is haunted, he refuses to stay, causing a fight with Jill.
- **THE ACTIONS GENERATED BY THE NEW INFORMATION MUST LEAD TO OTHER PLOT-RELATED CONSEQUENCES.** For instance, Jill decides she will stay in the mansion by herself and that Jack can stay in a motel, causing conflict and building tension.

When

When, in relation to your plot, is the time at which some important action in your narrative takes place: either time in history or time of day. *When* tends to be important in mystery plots for determining when a murder or a crime was committed, employing alibis, and figuring out how long a victim has been dead. Time as a form of information often comes into play in reference to when a crucial plot action takes place. For instance, a soldier may learn that his wife got pregnant when he was stationed abroad, and therefore the baby can't be his. Or a mother may learn that her missing child was actually held hostage in the neighborhood in the days after she thought he was gone. Or a character's innocence may be called into question when it turns out he does not have an alibi.

Since, generally, *when* is not in and of itself a compelling detail, new *when* information will best serve your plot when it brings to light startling, contradictory, or unexpected results. When can also be effective when you use it as a ticking clock technique, to create tension by employing a time countdown for your protagonist.

Why

Ah, motive—that tricky devil. *Why* is very much at the crux of plot, and what the second half of this chapter will focus on. Betrayal, murder, deception, unusual kindness, obsessive love, and many more facets of human behavior will fill the pages of many a plot. *Why* is often the very thing the reader and the protagonist are seeking to understand. Small explanations will be necessary along the way if the reader is to keep up with your plot, but *why* is the driving force of any novel.

It can be easy to toss this type of information into narrative explanations and pace-dragging passages of backstory because it may seem easier just to tell the reader *why* than to let actions, dialogue, and even flashback scenes tell the truth for you. However, don't fall into the habit of *explaining* why in narrative summary. If your scene needs to reveal why a character behaved a certain way, committed an action, or kept a great secret, return to the chapters on character development and scene intentions in order to get *why* across—primarily, rely upon demonstration to reveal *why*. That is, let your characters discover, uncover, act, speak and actively participate in revealing *why*. To aid you in this, you will also need to establish backstory and scene intentions for characters other than your protagonist (even if only in your mind). After all, your antagonist is attempting to thwart your protagonist's intentions because those intentions clash with her own, not just because your protagonist needs some conflict along his journey.

How

How—the method by which things are done—plays a great role in plot. It's usually the piece of information that ties up the investigation, reveals the missing clues to tragedies, and explains how the impossible really was possible. Law and science often play a role in revealing how something was done. Was the heiress murdered with a gun or a poisoned cup of tea? Was the fire started by arson or by a cigarette butt tossed carelessly aside?

How is often linked directly to *why*. If a character is plotting revenge, for instance, the method of his crime will probably be specific to the injury he believes he suffered—a spurned boyfriend might try to publicly shame the woman who dumped him by scrawling inflammatory words on her house. An insulted bigot might attack a person's race.

How really can't be an afterthought. You need to know how things were done by the time you get to the scene in which it is revealed, and then the information should be imparted in as direct a way as possible, most often through dialogue: the reading of police reports, evidence in court, a deathbed confession, and so on. But you may also choose to use a device like a letter, a message played back from a machine, or an e-mail found on a computer—something that a character stumbles across that contains the answer to how.

WHEN TO DOLE IT OUT

How you reveal information is just as important as what that information is. The most tempting way to pass on plot information is to narrate in a rushed, matter-of-fact way. But information is best served like food at a fancy French restaurant—in small, elegantly presented courses that neither stuffs the reader nor leaves him overly hungry. You want the reader to have room for dessert—which is, of course, the end of your book or story.

Some scenes will involve revealing multiple kinds of information, while others may be all for the purpose of revealing one very important kind of information. There's no way to know what to advise without seeing a specific manuscript, but as long as you know that you must have at least one piece of new information in every scene, you're on the right track.

You must always be thinking about the span of your narrative. The length of your narrative, whether it's a ten-page story or a five-hundred-page novel, will affect how soon information is revealed to the reader. A short story has less time to get things across and often has to drive the narrative to a brisk emotional impact with a less complex plotline.

Character Transformation

Plot comprises not only the events that happen in your story, but also the emotional and spiritual changes that occur to the characters affected by those events. In fact, you can think of the plot as the series of compelling and complicated events that cause your character to undergo a transformation or discovery, or to come to a greater understanding of something important. While all people undergo some change in life, characters in fiction have a dramatic imperative to change in significant and noticeable ways in order to give meaning to the narrative they star in. These transformations, however, can't happen all at once, or too easily. The reader tends to be suspicious when a character starts out mean and becomes kind too quickly, for example. So how can you change your characters in ways that feel authentic in the course of your narrative? Gradually, and scene by scene.

PLOT STRUCTURE AND THE ENERGETIC MARKERS

All plots must have a beginning, middle, and end, so it makes sense to divide your plot structure in this same way (though there are books written with more than just three acts). Martha Alderson, author of *The Plot Whisperer*, and my co-author on *Writing Deep Scenes*, coined the term "Energetic Markers" to discuss the places in a story where the character pivots in a new direction, often under pressure by the antagonist or through an act of discovery. These markers are like pillars that hold up the entire framework of the plot, and they are very important because they also reflect emotional and spiritual shifts in the inner landscape of your characters.

Beginning Scenes

- Introduce protagonist and her "ordinary" world—this means the world she knows, with all its problems, perks, and characters. Introduce only enough information to ground your reader. Avoid entering any sort of lengthy backstory explanations or summaries here. Keep the reader guessing.
- Create a sense of mystery or suspense by withholding information, whether backstory or revelations.
- Thrust the character out of her ordinary world into the action of the inciting incident, setting the story engine of the plot in motion. This is known as the **FIRST ENERGETIC MARKER: POINT OF NO RETURN**.

The beginning of your narrative is all about establishing the nuts and bolts of characters with their basic conflicts and plot problems, and setting in motion all the seeds for conflict and challenges to come. In these opening scenes, the reader is meeting your characters just as if they were new guests over for dinner. Their words, actions, and reactions to other people will all serve as introductions, and these first impressions will be remembered and set the stage for their later behavior. We'll now look at the ways you can establish information and set up your characters for change in the first third of your narrative.

Establishing Character-Related Plot Threads

While establishing your smack-talking hooligan protagonist with seductive eyes and a mop of brown curls or your lonely librarian who reads mystery novels and winds up investigating an actual crime in this first section of your narrative, you also need to establish:

- **INVOLVEMENT.** What is your protagonist's relationship to the events of the inciting incident? Is the event his fault, centered on him in some way? Did he accidentally stumble into it, or is he integral to it?
- **THE STAKES.** What does he stand to lose or gain as a result of the above-mentioned events? How will this create necessary tension and drama?
- **DESIRES.** What does he desire, from material goods to deep and abiding love, and how will that inform the stakes and his intentions?
- **FEARS.** What does he fear? From bodily harm to not obtaining his desire, how will these fears also inform the stakes?
- **MOTIVATION.** What reasons does he have to act upon the events of the inciting incident? What drives him onward?
- **CHALLENGES.** How does the inciting incident challenge his life, views, status, his status quo, needs, etc.?

The Middle Scenes: Emerging and Deeper

The middle is really the bulk of your book, encompassing the majority of the scenes. Thus, Martha and I divided it into two parts: the Emerging Middle and the Deeper Middle. In both, you should drive the plot forward by providing more information than you did in the first part, without giving away secrets or crucial plot information that belong in the end scenes.

Emerging Middle Scenes

- Protagonist enters a "new world" or new situation and can't easily turn back.
- Protagonist is tested, stretched, pushed in new directions—some pleasurable, and many painful or fraught with danger. Here he makes new allies and enemies.
- All key characters should have been introduced or hinted at by the Emerging Middle.
- New plot information should lead to conflict and danger that forces your characters to change or redirect. Life should never be too easy for your protagonist.
- Throw in red herrings, or false leads, that let the reader think you're filling in missing information or, in the mystery genre, that you're solving the mystery.
- This leads to the **SECOND ENERGETIC MARKER: THE REDEDICATION**. Once a character has left behind her known world or reality, things should become more complicated, tense, and even dangerous. Eventually, these may begin to feel overwhelming or unmanageable to your protagonist. She may experience fear, fatigue, doubt, insecurity, and a desire to stop or turn back. For the sake of plot, however, she has to move ahead. "Rededication" is an important pivot point where your character rallies inner emotional resources, the support of an ally, or the determination to keep going.

Deeper Middle Scenes

After the rededication point, every scene should take your protagonist closer to his goal, but also into deeper waters and more dangerous territory, whether literally or emotionally. Writers who get stuck in this section should ask the following questions:

- How can things get more complicated for my protagonist?
- What secrets or flaws can come back to trip him up?
- Are any allies actually enemies?
- What more can my protagonist lose?

- The deeper middle is a process of stripping things away—support, hope, illusion—that leads up to the **THIRD ENERGETIC MARKER: DARK NIGHT**.

This is the lowest point of your protagonist's entire journey. It's where the antagonist appears victorious and your protagonist defeated. Here there might be a literal death, a betrayal, or the loss of the hope that your character held up to this point. Though this is the darkest period for your protagonist, it's also the last dark period. From here on out, your protagonist, now matured and transformed, rises from the ashes with greater strength and clarity. She will gain strength on the remaining journey to the Triumph, the high point of the story.

By the time you've made it to the deeper middle section of your narrative, the reader should be riddled with anxiety and worry for your characters, tense and upset as he wonders what will happen next. Inflicting discomfort upon your reader in this way sounds like a mean thing to do, but uncomfortable is exactly what you want him to be. Your protagonist should be in a similar state. After all, you've dangled his desires just out of reach and pushed him toward, or into the midst of, his fears. And you've added a series of challenges along the way so that he can't get out of conflict too easily. The middle part of your narrative—both in the emerging middle and the deeper middle—is where he'll do the most work. He will be tested and stretched here because you will provide your protagonist with the following character-building opportunities:

- **OPPORTUNITIES FOR CRISIS AND CONFLICT.** Now that you've destabilized him and given him problems to contend with, you want to mount the challenges. Complicate his problems. Give him new ones. Add other stressors.
- **OPPORTUNITIES FOR DRAMATIC AND SURPRISING CHANGES.** Under all this pressure, your protagonist is going to start to change. She might act out in bursts of rage or find that she is far more capable than she ever imagined. Either way, the complications you provide in the middle should cause her to act *differently* than she has before, for better or worse.

- **OPPORTUNITIES FOR PLOT COMPLICATIONS.** You may feel that your protagonist's inciting incident was bad enough, but if you leave him with no new complications, you also stop the storyline. In this middle section, more difficulties will need to happen. Each new scene should provide a new complication or add complexity to the existing problems.
- **OPPORTUNITIES TO TEST-DRIVE NEW BEHAVIORS.** Even logical people react emotionally to situations—react being the key word. Therefore, under all that pressure and stress you've put on her, your protagonist can now legitimately get away with doing something that was previously out of character. That's the nature of conflict—it changes a person. So if you've complicated things enough, then your previously timid protagonist can now pick up the gun and threaten to kill someone, for example.
- **OPPORTUNITIES FOR DRAMATIC TENSION.** As author Steve Almond said, "You have to love your characters enough to put them in danger." This danger, emotional or physical, will create an aura of tension that will drive the reader deep into your narrative.

If all your characters' desires and intentions were met in the middle of your narrative, your story would be done already. Middle scenes are not about resolutions. Middle scenes are the place for characters to experience the classic "dark night of the soul," desperation, uncertainty, and a host of other trials. This element of uncertainty and crisis will bring out a wide range of emotional responses in your characters that will change them, reshape them, cause them to undergo epiphanies and behavior shifts as you move toward the climax of your narrative.

End Scenes

The most dramatic scene in your entire plot essentially kicks off the end of your narrative. After your character has recovered from the Dark Night, all forces move toward a final clash or collision of some kind. This is the **Fourth Energetic Marker: The Triumph.** Here, at last, all the work your protagonist has done, all the pain she's suffered and the hard-earned wisdom she's gained, will come to bear in a final clash of forces resulting in the protagonist's victory; this is also where the antagonist is finally quashed (or driven off licking his wounds, at least). After the Triumph, your story ebbs into final answers and the tying up of loose threads.

The end scenes of your narrative might seem the most difficult, because here you must tie up all threads you started earlier in the story. The ease or difficulty with which you can tie up these threads at this juncture will reveal to you how well constructed your plot is and whether you still have much work to do. The reader should not have very many, if any, questions by the time they reach the truly final scene (unless you're writing a sequel). End scenes should do all of the following:

- Answer questions and reveal truths.
- Conclude drama. Don't introduce new information, but you may introduce surprising endings to plot avenues.
- Let characters settle into their changes.
- Lead the reader toward a sense of conclusion by turning down the emotional and dramatic tone of information revealed.

The end scenes are where many writers discover the holes in their plot, simply because they can't tie up all the threads. If that happens to you, you may need to revisit your plot goals, ask what information is missing, and fill in those holes.

Resolution

After the Triumph, where the greatest amount of stress or tension has already been exerted on your protagonist, you want to show who he is in the aftermath. You can do this by determining (and demonstrating) the following:

- What are the consequences of having any desires met?
- What are the consequences of having any fears realized?
- Did your protagonist's desires change? How so?
- Did your protagonist's fears change or lessen? How so?
- How does your protagonist feel now about the inciting incident?

Demonstrate Character Changes

Depending on the answers to the questions above, you want to show, through some form of behavior, action, or speech, that your protagonist really has changed. Perhaps he turns himself in for the crime that his best friend is in jail for. Maybe she finally is able to visit the grave of her dead husband. Maybe he moves to a new town after being hung up on the past. Or the change might be as simple as a statement: "I'll never go back," a soldier might say, deciding he's ready for peace.

You're going to have to tie up all the consequences that stemmed from the inciting incident. Whatever questions you raised must be answered or concluded. Murders must be solved. Stolen property must be returned or found. And the thread of action and events in which your protagonist has been involved must taper to its final end.

In literary fiction, this will probably come as more of an internal resolution or transformation for your protagonist. In a romance novel, your protagonist will finally be ready for the right man and will find him or consummate the romance that has already begun. In a mystery novel, your protagonist will not only solve the case, or be exonerated from wrongdoing; he will see himself and the world differently. In a science fiction novel, your protagonist may get in touch with his humanity or understand the power of the cosmos. There are many ways to tie up plot events in the final part of your narrative—and they all share these elements in common:

- The protagonist has learned something.
- The protagonist's behavior or attitude has changed.
- The protagonist has embarked on a new direction or path.

The key to successful character transformation is to let your character changes unfold dramatically, but also realistically. Let the reader see your characters change through how they act and speak, and by the choices they make within the framework of scenes, not through narrative summaries.

Putting the Plot Pieces Together

Of all the core elements, plot can seem like the most complex because it weaves its way through every scene. A strong plot allows for the reader to experience a sense of mystery, as scenes withhold just the right amount of information for just long enough. The reader should see only one bread crumb at a time in the dimly lit forest of your narrative. Of course, the mystery must be solved eventually, and the plot information must add up to a satisfying whole.

Following are examples from Toni Morrison's acclaimed novel *Beloved*, in which plot information is doled out carefully and builds on itself. A scene in the first part of the book opens with a woman called Beloved walking out of a pond fully dressed. She is soon discovered by Denver, one of the main characters, and taken home to Denver's mother, Sethe—a woman with a past full of dark secrets. Through dialogue, the reader learns that Beloved is not like other people. She has hazy origins and behaves unusually. This information is delivered bit by bit over multiple scenes.

> "Something funny 'bout that gal," Paul D said, mostly to himself.
> "Funny how?"
> "Acts sick, sounds sick, but she don't look sick. Good skin, bright eyes and strong as a bull."
> "She's not strong. She can hardly walk without holding on to something."
> "That's what I mean. Can't walk, but I seen her pick up a rocker with one hand."

That scene achieves the three responsibilities of new information. One, the reader and the characters get smarter: Under the category of *who*, they learn that Beloved is not like other people—she behaves quite oddly. Two, Beloved's strange behavior and the impact she has on other characters lead the reader to start questioning her state of mind and intentions. Three, motivation comes into play—*why*. Because the characters now see Beloved differently, they begin to act differently with one another in response to her, and their changed behaviors affect the plot consequences.

In the middle of her narrative, Morrison drops even more plot information about who the mysterious Beloved is, though she does not come out and say it; she lets the readers piece it together:

> Beloved closed her eyes. "In the dark my name is Beloved."

Denver scooted in a little closer. "What's it like over there, where you were before? Can you tell me?"

"Dark," said Beloved. "I'm small in that place. I'm like this here." She raised her head off the bed, lay down on her side and curled up.

Denver covered her lips with her fingers. "Were you cold?"

Beloved curled tighter and shook her head. "Hot. Nothing to breathe down there and no room to move in."

What does Beloved's description sound like? A mother's womb. The reader slowly learns of Beloved's origins, which is a crucial piece of plot information, within the context of scenes that build upon the plot and reveal character. This slow build gives Morrison time to create a character that is strange and vivid, who represents the sacrifice that her mother had to make in her journey to freedom. If she gave Beloved's identity away immediately, there would be very little dramatic tension or character building.

As the book moves toward its close, the plot begins to move into its final stage. No longer do the characters wonder who Beloved is; now they've started to fear her. Beloved has become pregnant and begins to take up all the joy, eat all the food, and consume everything that Sethe and Denver need in the household (which is a fabulous metaphor, incidentally, for how grief works). She absorbs Sethe's attention and time, inspiring jealousy and rage in Denver. As the plot comes to a close, the reader begins to root for a terrible end for Beloved, despite that she seemed so needy and frail earlier in the narrative. She has become a parasite. Either Beloved will have to go, or something terrible will happen.

Without giving away the ending, I can say that Morrison brings her plot to a close that makes perfect sense—with all threads tied up.

SCENE STEALER

Gayle Brandeis, author of *My Life with the Lincolns*, *Delta Girls*, and many others, discusses plot in Amanda Eyre Ward's *Sleep Toward Heaven*.

. . .

Years later I still get goose bumps whenever I think about the ending of Amanda Eyre Ward's novel *Sleep Toward Heaven*. The beautifully written plot braids together the stories of three characters—Celia, whose husband Henry was murdered; Karen, the murderer, who is awaiting her execution on death row; and Franny, the doctor who has been treating Karen for cancer.

Celia is reeling throughout the book, trying to find her place in the world after the senseless death of her husband. In the final scene, she recounts how, during a meeting in a bar with Franny, Henry's ghost came to her and told her to find Franny's notebook in her purse and write down the code for Karen's morphine machine while Franny was in the restroom. Celia memorizes the code, not knowing why until she visits Karen in the prison. The book ends with Celia saying, "The numbers to the machine lined up in my head. I opened my mouth." Giving the woman who murdered her husband the means to end her own suffering without having to endure the spectacle of an execution is such a profound act of forgiveness and compassion. It infuses the entire book with a sense of grace, weaving all the threads of the book into a perfect, deeply moving whole.

SHORING UP YOUR PLOT

If a plot is built out of strong, vivid scenes, then the most logical place to start when writing a new scene is to refer to the previous scene first. You create your own blueprints scene by scene. So before you go on to write the next scene, in which you move your plot forward just a little bit more, you must see how far, and from what direction, you've come. Which of the Energetic Markers has your character passed? In between each of the markers, your character is in a process of change. In a different, dramatic way at each marker, your character should gain awareness, strength, resources, and more on the journey toward a transformation at the Triumph of the novel.

You would be amazed at how often writers repeat information, forgetting that they already revealed it or that their character already had that realization in the last scene. Reviewing sometimes as many as two or three scenes back can be crucial to moving your plot forward.

Once you've reviewed the last scene, or scenes, you will come to a decision point. What happens next? Harking back to earlier chapters of this book, you know that you must up the ante on your characters and keep the action moving forward, making sure it continues to grow more complicated until the novel's resolution.

If you're unsure whether your idea for the next scene will work, you can run it through this criteria test. The next bite of plot information should do the following:

- Involve your main character(s)
- Be related to the inciting incident or one of its consequences
- Give the readers more knowledge or clues, or the impression that they're smarter because some new information is revealed
- Add complications or resolve an earlier complication

SUBTEXT

No matter the grades you got in school, you're probably someone who's willing to give writing your best try; after all, you're reading a book on scene writing. At the very least, you can follow the recipe in chapter one and combine all your ingredients to create a rudimentary scene. So don't get discouraged now when you learn that a competently written scene can still fall flat.

Scenes often need depth, or subtext, a texture that fleshes out your scenes and links them to the themes and larger plot of your narrative. A theme is the underlying message, idea, or moral of the narrative. Building in this subtext may take a second draft or more because, as I often say when teaching, your first draft is where you tell yourself the story and get to know your characters; later drafts are where you pull in the nuance and depth.

Scenes that lack subtext read as if they've been dictated by a court reporter: "Bailiff had to escort the defendant, in pearls and red sweater, out of the room. Sunlight filtered in. Courtroom was quiet."

There is nothing wrong with the details above, but a scene full of sentences like that is guaranteed to lack dramatic tension and emotional complexity. A good scene should ideally have a surface—the visible and palpable, from setting to physical descriptions of characters to spoken dialogue—and an underbelly, a subtext, where your characters' emotional baggage, agendas, painful secrets, and unconscious motivations lurk.

TECHNIQUES FOR CREATING SUBTEXT

Think about the deeper layers of your scenes. The subtext is the layer that contains unconscious information, clues to behavior, and even elements of backstory. You can use several different techniques to draw out your story's subtext.

Thematic Imagery or Symbols

To work with thematic imagery, naturally you need to know the theme of your book or story (although, for many writers, theme is determined after the first draft is done). Think of the theme as the overall message or idea of the narrative, as opposed to the plot, which includes the specific events and new pieces of information that take place or are dropped into the narrative.

Thematic imagery refers to the images that metaphorically and symbolically conjure your theme. Some thematic imagery will find its way into your narrative through the magic of the unconscious without you realizing it, but most of it will require conscious application upon revision.

Emma Cline's novel *The Girls* introduces its naïve young protagonist, Evie, a teenager in the summer of 1969, to the world-weary, "feral" characters of several itinerant girls, whom she sees digging through a dumpster in a local park and eventually joins up with. Cline uses many images interspersed throughout the book to add subtext to her scenes, like this one:

> I looked to Suzanne—even our brief history seemed to ratify my presence among them—but she was sitting off to the side, absorbed by the box of tomatoes. Applying pressure to the skins, sifting out the rot. Waving away the bees.

Images of decay and rot recur in the story, nicely reflecting the derelict "ranch" where Suzanne and these other girls live communally under the charismatic leadership of a man named Russell. Russell, too, has a dark and decayed center of morality, and it is at his urging that things will eventually take a very dark turn.

This decayed morality is suggested the first time Evie meets Russell:

> Russell's buckskin shirt, smelling of flesh and rot and as soft as velvet.

Images can also be simple, just tiny highlights in your larger scene: A tree in the night could suddenly look like a face, portending danger; a character who longs to be pregnant could see the faces of babies in her mashed potatoes; and so on.

Of course, you can always opt to work with the more abstract world of symbols. The great mythologist Joseph Campbell said, "The function of symbols is to give you a sense of 'Aha! Yes. I know what it is. It's myself.'"

Symbols elicit meaning without having to be explained; they add a subtle touch of texture to your narrative.

The Argentinean writer Jorge Luis Borges was very fond of using symbols—like labyrinths, hexagrams, and even books—to represent the complexities of human thought and spiritual mystery.

If your theme is about finding peace, you might plant a dove in the eaves outside a scene, or use an olive branch or a white flag somewhere along the way. The key is to plant your symbols subtly so that the reader doesn't feel as though this subtext is being waved in his face in an obvious manner. You don't need your character to say, "Look, a dove, that makes me think of peace!" A symbol could just turn up as a design on a character's shirt or on the cover of a book on a desk in someone's office.

In Tana French's mystery novel *The Trespasser*, she never lets the reader feel too at ease. In an early scene in the novel, as Stephen Moran and Antoinette Conway, the two detectives working a case, take a break in a local park to eat a bite and go over new information, French plants an image guaranteed to elicit discomfort and tension:

> The dinosaur kid has fallen off his scooter and is sitting on the path trying to work up a convincing wail. We dodge around him and we're heading for the gate, me dialing the floaters to tell them to bring Fallon in, when I catch the plastic bag in the corner of my eye and realize what's sticking out of it: a dead cat, fur plastered sleek against its skull, lips pulled back to show spiky teeth open wide in a frozen howl of fury.

It's even more potent because Conway is one of the very few women in the Murder department, and she has been on the receiving end of greater and greater harassment from her fellow detectives. But she can't show her outrage because that will only give them more fuel. The cat not only plants a sense of general unease about the plot, it reflects her own inner "howl of fury" that nobody can see.

Innuendo

It is inevitable that characters in your fiction, as in life, will come across truths that they don't want to admit to themselves or to others. Sometimes this information is obvious to those around them first.

It's important when developing each scene that you plant seeds of things to come later on. Innuendo is a great way to deal with plot developments that haven't come to pass yet. It also helps round out your characters, since innuendo can come in the form of teasing or accusation and usually elicits high emotion.

For instance, say the princess of a medieval kingdom cannot let on that she is in love with a peasant boy because their match can never be. There's nothing more wickedly juicy than a scene in which this piece of information, which she can't accept, is pointed out to her by someone she'd rather not hear it from—perhaps one of her ladies-in-waiting, who is supposed to keep her opinions in check, or the princess's sister, who will inherit the crown if the princess abdicates it.

"Nice tights," the sister might say to the princess when the peasant boy stops in to deliver a herd of sheep.

The princess, of course, will be shocked and outraged. "As if I'd noticed!" she might say with a rosy hue of indignation on her cheeks.

Innuendo can go further than teasing. You can use it to suggest that someone is responsible for murder or robbery, or to suggest that a character wants another character dead or gone. Innuendo is a way to subtly point fingers so that the reader's attention begins to move just slightly ahead of the scene at hand, layering complication into your scene.

Unconscious or Uncontrollable Behavior

Characters will do all kinds of things intentionally in your scenes, from tenderly caressing an injured animal to jumping out of flame-engulfed buildings. But there is a whole world of behavior that you can employ in scenes that adds subtext not only to the present scene, but to the reader's understanding of the characters and your plot.

A character with a secret history of having been locked in closets for punishment as a child might break into a sweat each time he is in a confined space. Perhaps you don't reveal this detail about the character's past until near the very end of your book, but you can plant seeds in the reader's mind through subtext. If your character sweats each time he's in a car, an elevator, or even a small New York apartment, this registers in the reader's unconscious without having to be plainly stated, thus creating a question that the reader is curious about (why is he sweating?) but does not yet have an answer for.

In Sheila Kohler's psychologically tense novel *Crossways*, protagonist Kate has been forced to leave her life in Paris and return to her childhood home in South Africa due to a tragedy: A car accident has killed her sister, Marion, and left her brother-in-law, Louis, injured and in the hospital.

Louis, a surgeon, is used to being in control of everything in his life—including his wife and their three children. Now that he is injured and his sister-in-law, Kate, is around to question him, he has a difficult time controlling the rage he used to be able to suppress.

> The nurse leans over his bed. She pats the back of his hand. He has a sudden, strong urge to smack her across her pretty face with it. It is the same urge he had when his wife would ask him what he was doing.

The reader begins to question what it is in Louis's past that causes him to behave so badly toward people less powerful than himself and, of course, the answer is eventually provided and brings with it the final piece of the plot that explains Marion's death.

SCENE STEALER

Elizabeth Cox, author of *The Slow Moon*, discusses the use of images in Cormac McCarthy's *Suttree*.

. . .

My favorite section provides imagery (a spoon, a cup of coffee, or spilled cream with "flies lapping like cats") to deepen tension and to expose the profound sadness felt by Suttree when he learns that his boy is dead.

As he was going up Gay Street J-Bone stepped from a door and took his arm. Hey Bud, he said.

How you doin'?

I was just started down to see you. Come in and have a cup of coffee.

They sat at the counter at Helm's. J-Bone kept tapping his spoon. When the coffee was set before them he turned to Suttree. Your old man called me, he said. He wanted you to call home.

People in hell want ice water.

Hell Bud, it might be something important.

Suttree tested the cup rim against his lower lip and blew. Like what, he said.

Well. Something in the family. You know, I think you ought to call.

He put the cup down. All right, he said. What is it?

Why don't you call him?

Why don't you tell me?

Will you not call?

No.

J-Bone was looking at the spoon in his hand. He blew on it and shook his head, the distorted image of him upside down in the spoon's bowl misting and returning. Well, he said.

Who's dead, Jim?

He didn't look up. Your little boy, he said.

Suttree set his cup down and looked out the window. There was a small pool of spilled cream on the marble countertop at his elbow and flies were crouched about it lapping like cats. He got up and went out.

It was dark when the train left the station. He tried to sleep, his head rolling about on the musty headrest. There was no longer a club car or dining car. No service anymore.

Students, when writing dialogue, focus on patterns of speech and verisimilitude, but often they do not know that dialogue needs to move the action forward, giving information and creating a tension within a particular moment. I tell them to imagine one person saying, "Please, please" and the other saying, "No, no" no matter what is being said. This example offers fast-paced dialogue (even though the moment seems to move in slow motion). The dialogue carries the action forward as it reveals some new information to a character, and McCarthy produces a true pattern of speech used by the country people that populate the book. The understated quality of McCarthy's dialogue and imagery add clarity and power to the moment described, and give to that moment a dramatic tension of human life happening before our eyes.

Foreground and Background

Scenes can have backgrounds the same way that paintings do, and *backgrounds* refers to more than just setting. While you draw the reader's attention to what is happening most noticeably in the foreground, you can plant subtle messages and emotional layers in the background through actions. For example, if a couple is about ready to make love in the scene at hand—the foreground—while another couple is fighting in the next room—the background—not only is this a great setup for comedy or drama, but it plants the idea that perhaps the loving couple is moving toward the fate of the fighting couple. You can add suspenseful texture to your scenes without having to resort to narrative summary or intruding into the narrative with statements about how this couple might be destined for failure.

Jane Hamilton's novel *A Map of the World* opens when protagonist Alice, a school nurse, agrees to babysit her neighbor's two little girls. When Lizzy and Audrey arrive, however, Alice's own daughters, Emma and Claire, are giving her such grief that she takes a moment of respite to collect herself, barely a couple of minutes. It is enough time for young Lizzy, a toddler, to make her way down into the pond and nearly drown.

In the next scene, Alice is at the hospital waiting for Lizzy's family to arrive and for the doctors to disclose the child's prognosis. She has no idea if Lizzy will live, and if any of their lives will be the same from here on out. Hamilton sets us up for the direction of Alice's (and Lizzy's) fate by throwing this into the scene subtext:

> I remember glancing across the room and noticing Robbie Mackessy's mother. Robbie was a kindergartner at Blackwell Elementary. ... He was frequently sick, because of his mother, I thought, because of her negligence. She was leafing through a magazine looking, not at the print, but at me. She was squinting, as if she couldn't stand to have her eyes wide

open, to see all of me at once. … It was her ugly mouth, her sneer that made me feel like crying.

The talk of negligence, the details about not being able to "see all of me at once" are all subconscious suggestions of a dark and tragic turn for the worse for both characters.

. . .

Each scene is a multidimensional creation. Don't forget the many ways you can deepen and add complexity to it by enriching subtext, a subject that will be addressed in each of the scene types discussed in part three.

DRAMATIC TENSION

Imagine you're watching a game of tug-of-war between two strong men. Separating them, a length of rope stretches over a pit full of angry, poisonous vipers. One man pulls the rope his way, and the other man teeters on the brink of falling in. Then the teetering man pulls back, and soon it's the first man whose life is at risk. This is a visual analogy for the effect of one of the most crucial core scene elements of all: dramatic tension.

Dramatic tension is the *potential* for conflict in a scene. When trouble is brewing, or resolution balances on a pinhead, the reader will be psychologically, and even physically, tense; this tension, believe it or not, keeps a reader reading. It's very hard to walk away from that tug-of-war match without knowing what's going to happen to both men!

Dramatic tension relies on the reader's knowledge that something is about to go down—she just doesn't know exactly how or when. Tension keeps the reader waiting with breath held and fists clenched, hoping that the protagonist makes it out of the scene alive, in love, or with his goal achieved (and no viper bites).

As a core element, dramatic tension must be present in every scene. It may take the shape of the prickly feeling of unease your protagonist has when he enters the dark building where the killer was last seen, an unsettling exchange of dialogue as he wonders if he has just picked an argument with a dangerous man, or a potent image that evokes dread.

Scenes need tension to avoid being mundane. A fiction narrative is a heightened experience of reality in which life is more intense, unusual, and dramatic than real life; otherwise, why bother writing about it? Therefore, you want to employ techniques that keep the world inside your narrative from resembling too closely the quotidian life that most people actually lead. By building a sense of trouble—or the potential for it—into every scene, you will hook the reader.

We'll be looking at several techniques for building tension in different scene types in part three, but it's useful to have an overview of how tension works first.

Dramatic tension has the power to turn a domestic scene into a nightmare. To create it, you must do the following:

- Thwart your protagonist's goals—delay satisfaction
- Include unexpected changes without immediate explanation
- Shift power back and forth
- Pull the rug out—throw in a piece of plot information that changes or alters your protagonist in some way
- Create a tense atmosphere through setting and senses
- Utilize the poetic, rhythmic power of language to create sentence-level tension

EXPOSITION AND TENSION

The language that runs between all the other major scene elements is often referred to as exposition or narrative summary. Just like tendons connect muscle to bone, narrative summary links your scene elements so they don't merely float, leaving your scene disjointed or weak-kneed. Too much exposition, however, quickly bores the reader and kills the possibility of dramatic tension. These passages of *telling* prose should be used strategically to build tension or to act as theater ushers, directing the reader's attention to the important moments in the scene.

Condensing Time

No matter how fascinating your story and how interesting your characters, you can't show every moment of their lives in a single narrative. To select the moments to dramatize, you also must select which moments in time to condense or to summarize. Below is an example from Richard Gwyn's novel *The Color of a Dog Running Away*. Lucas, a translator living in Barcelona, has just begun a love affair with the beautiful and enigmatic Nuria, whom he met following a mysterious invitation to an art gallery. The author has already dramatized the initial throes of attraction and the activities in which the blissful new couple have engaged over the past few weeks. Now he needs to speed the plot forward, which he does with narrative summary:

> In the two weeks that followed, Nuria and I spent every free moment with each other. We ate together, slept together, phoned each other when she was at work, and lived for the evenings and the nights.

Gwyn skillfully collapses two whole weeks into quick summary and then gets back to the action:

> One lunchtime I was already on the bench, having spent some time there reading over proofs in the morning sun with a bottle of cold beer. Nuria arrived, exuberant, flushed.

By condensing small passages of irrelevant events in short windows of time, you cut the flab from your prose and keep tension alive.

Condensing Information

Your characters will be doctors and architects and tradespeople of all kinds. They will weave intricate designs out of silk, build plans for large skyscrapers, and study the flora and fauna of their worlds. What they do as a vocation, a hobby, or for pure survival may be of great interest to you, and may even play a crucial role in your narrative, so it's possible you'll want to describe the breathtaking minutia of a heart surgery or the drafting of a blueprint. Too much description, however—whether in dialogue or through narrative passages—reads like a technical manual and provides no possibility for tension. You want to first digest this information and then filter it through the point of view of your character, offering a condensed version of the facts that gives the reader a taste, a flash, or an insight into your character.

In Anne Patchett's novel *State of Wonder*, Marina Singh, a doctor who works for a pharmaceutical company in the Midwest, has agreed to head to the Amazon to see what she can learn of a missing colleague and attempt to make contact with the long-silent project lead, Dr. Swenson. Through much trial and error, she eventually finds Dr. Swenson and calls her boss to report the details:

> She did not wait for him to ask her because he had asked her every time they spoke, as if finding Dr. Swenson was something that might have happened and then slipped her mind. She told him about the opera house, about Easter, and the dinner. She told him what had been said about Anders and, in trying to re-create the conversation, she realized how little of a conversation it had actually been. She could report that the project was moving forward.

The reader needs to know that Marina has told her boss what she found, but does not need a rehashing of all the events. Condensing does the job well enough.

The same is true of information that comes as a result of crime scene investigations or any mystery that can be solved—from the ancient origins of a sacred relic to a murder to how an entire civilization disappeared. Any line of investigation and inquiry will naturally come with lots of clues and information that you need to convey to drive the plot forward and explain things.

Your job is to condense it in a way that adds to the tension and drama of your narrative. For example, in Joanne Harris's novel *Sleep, Pale Sister*, Henry Chester is a painter fascinated by one model in particular—Effie, a young girl upon whom he projects innocence. He becomes obsessed with her and paints her many times, but rather than showing a bunch of dull sittings, Harris gives the reader an overview of all the sittings in quick, expert lines of exposition that, rather than being boring, add up in their condensed description to an eerie feeling of tension and concern:

> I must have drawn or painted Effie a hundred times: she was Cinderella, she was Mary, she was the young novice in *The Passion Flower*; she was Beatrice in Heaven, Juliet in the tomb, draped with Lilies and trailing convolvulus for Ophelia, in rags for "The Little Beggar Girl." My final

portrait of her at that time was The Sleeping Beauty, so like My Sister's Sleep in composition, showing Effie all in white again, like a bride or a novice, lying on the same little girl's bed, her hair, much longer than it had been when she was ten—I had always urged her never to cut it—trailing on to the floor, where a century's worth of dust lingers.

When you condense information like this, try to do so in a way that creates a feeling of brewing trouble. Add up elements that give the reader concern for your protagonist, or suggest a behavior that is a little off-center, or obsessive, or potentially volatile. If the devil is in the details, then use these details strategically to build tension when you tell the reader about the vocation and activities your protagonist (or antagonist) engages in.

OTHER TENSION-BUILDING TRICKS

A writer can create dramatic tension in so many different ways that there's really no reason not to use it. Keep the following set of techniques in your writer's kit and pull them out whenever you want to infuse tension into individual scenes.

Including Foreboding

Foreboding is a feeling that something bad or unpleasant is coming for your protagonist. Unlike foreshadowing, which hints at actual plot events, foreboding is purely about setting a mood. It heightens the feeling of tension in a scene but doesn't indicate that something bad actually will happen.

Here's an example from Don DeLillo's novel *White Noise*. In this scene, the young son of Professor Jack Gladney and his wife, Babette, wakes up one day crying and doesn't cease for seven hours straight. Though they can find nothing physically wrong with him, the crying is so abnormal that they take him to the doctor—where they get no answers. His crying instills terror in the family, and it presages a more dramatic situation that is to come later in the book—that of an airborne toxic cloud that descends over their town inexplicably. Notice how something simple like a crying child creates tension and foreboding in the following passage:

> As I started the car I realized his crying had changed in pitch and quality. The rhythmic urgency had given way to a sustained inarticulate and mournful sound. He was keening now. These were expressions of Mideastern lament, of an anguish so accessible that it rushes to overwhelm what immediately caused it. There was something permanent and soulstruck in this crying. It was a sound of inbred desolation.

Since the child is preverbal, one gets the feeling that he feels on some level what is to come, and DeLillo conveys this tense, uneasy feeling without dropping any direct plot information. The scene is eerie, tragic, and unnerving, full of dramatic tension as the reader wonders what on earth is going on.

When you create foreboding, remember to think about atmosphere and mood. Invoke the senses. Think about how you can use sound—like the plaintive cawing of seagulls or a crying child—or smell—think of what kind of effect a foul odor will have on a character. Foreboding happens in the moment; you don't have to make good on it the way you do if you use foreshadowing. You're painting an atmosphere to establish a feeling of unease and worry in the reader.

Thwarting Expectation

When a character has an expectation or desire in a scene (as they always should!), you have a great opportunity to create tension by making the reader (and the character) worry that the expectation will not be met. This can be a large expectation, like the bride waiting at the altar, or something seemingly small, like in this example from Diane Setterfield's novel *The Thirteenth Tale.*

Protagonist Margaret Lea is an amateur biographer and book lover who has been asked to write the biography of the enigmatic and famous writer Vida Winter. In preparation, she begins to read Winter's famous work, concluding with a book of stories called *Thirteen Tales.* Notice how the simple act of expectation—of reading the thirteenth tale—takes on tension as Margaret's expectations are thwarted:

> It was while I was reading "The Mermaid's Tale"—the twelfth tale—that I began to feel stirrings of an anxiety that was unconnected to the story

itself. I was distracted: my thumb and right index finger were sending me a message: Not many pages left. The knowledge nagged more insistently until I tilted the book to check. It was true. The thirteenth tale must be a very short one.

I continued my reading, finished tale twelve and turned the page.
Blank.
I flicked back, forward again. Nothing.
There was no thirteenth tale.
There was a sudden rush in my head, I felt the sick dizziness of the deep-sea diver come too fast to the surface.

This sets up a mood for the rest of the novel. Things are not as they seem. Pieces of the story are missing. It's a brilliant stroke of dramatic tension.

To carry this out, you must put something at stake for your protagonist regarding whatever it is he expects, something emotionally meaningful or consequential. A man waiting to learn the contents of his mother's will, for instance, has a great deal invested in the results. If the lawyer continues over a long period to read out assets that are granted to cousins and relatives less directly tied to his mother, the scene will take on tension. What, if anything, has his mother left your character?

Thwarting expectations is a technique I recommend you use frequently. For if your protagonist gets what she wants or expects in too many scenes, there will be little tension to keep the reader hooked.

Making Changes Without Explanation

People like to know why things happen, especially when it comes to change. Therefore, if you want to create tension in a scene, you can change something in your protagonist's life without giving him an immediate explanation. The change can be life altering, or it can be something more befuddling, like in this example from a scene in another of Joanne Harris's novels, *Gentlemen and Players*:

As the door closed I saw a pile of flat-packed cardboard boxes propped up against the wall.

"Busy day today?" I asked him, indicating the boxes. "What is it? Invading Poland?"

> Gerry twitched. "No, ah——just moving a few things around. Ah——to the new departmental office."
>
> I regarded him closely. There was an ominous ring to the phrase. "What new departmental office?"
>
> "Ah——sorry. Must get along. Headmaster's briefing. Can't be late."
>
> That's a joke. Gerry's late to everything. "What new office? Has someone died?"
>
> "Ah—sorry, Roy. Catch you later."

All that has really transpired in this bit of a scene is that Professor Roy Straitley has learned about the creation of a new department at the school where he teaches. Yet it feels tense because Roy is a longtime professor at St. Oswald's School for Boys, and it is very atypical for him to be uninformed about a major decision. The reader instantly wants to know why Roy hasn't been informed, and the way that Gerry hems and haws makes it clear that the answer to come will not be pleasing to Roy. Harris could easily have made that a boring scene, or just cut to the chase of Roy finding out, but she creates dramatic tension over the simplest interactions because it sets a tone of intrigue, which she follows through on later.

You can do the same thing in your own work by throwing change at your characters, the kind of change they don't have an explanation for.

It's not useful, however, to create a change just for the sake of it or out of the blue. Change without explanation must have a basis in your plot. It must motivate your protagonist to learn more and to take his fate into his hands.

TENSION KILLER: ON MELODRAMA

There's nothing that kills tension more quickly than melodrama. Author Charles Baxter writes in his book of essays, *Burning Down the House*, that melodramatic writing enacts a kind of "emotional violence against the reader." He goes on to say, "One often feels bullied in its presence, pushed around."

The reason for this bullied feeling is that melodrama contains over-the-top or excessive emotional intensity, or it shifts too quickly to be plausible. You'll recognize melodrama when the emotional content of a scene is so hot it is almost embarrassing, or when it's so hollowly sentimental that the reader feels his intelligence has been insulted. Melodrama lacks nuance. It slams a feeling or a weak character or a theme into the reader's face without doing any deep, foundational work. In essence, melodrama *tells* loudly, with explosions and screaming ladies. It does not show.

Less Is More: The Art of Subtlety

Have you ever seen a real gross-out, gory horror movie like *A Nightmare on Elm Street* or one of the *Saw* slasher films that seemed to come out every year for a while there? The drama is all very in-your-face, with pretty young victims screaming bloody murder as they're sawed in half (for no apparent reason), and the mangled villain jumping out of the shadows with tools of violence (with no apparent motive). There is nothing subtle about that kind of horror. Subtlety—or cool emotions—goes a long way toward building drama.

In Vendela Vida's novel *Let the Northern Lights Erase Your Name*, protagonist Clarissa has undertaken a search for her mother, Olivia, who left her fourteen years before. In a powerful moment, shown in the scene below, Clarissa finally makes contact with her mother. There's plenty of opportunity for melodrama—an abandoned daughter has a lot to be angry about. But with so much at stake for the protagonist, Vida takes the quieter path:

> "I have something to tell you," I said.
>
> "Yes I know," she said. "You're my daughter."
>
> I nodded.
>
> "I knew the second you walked in the door," she said. The corners of her mouth turned upward. I believed she might hug me.
>
> "I knew this might happen one day. ... I thought it was Richard who would track me down. ..."
>
> She traced a flower, transforming the line into a stem. "I don't have anything to say to him, and I don't have anything to say to you. If I had, I could have written you a letter."

The characters don't cry and fight and yell at each other. There is a delicate pause after the sentence "I believed she might hug me" in which no hug follows, and the reader suddenly knows what's going to come. Olivia is not about to stand up and become a loving mother. Clarissa is devastated, and the reader feels this devastation for her without any need for Clarissa to get emotionally loud. Her pain is evident in the silence, in the lack of tenderness from her mother. The reader can feel her grief in the previous paragraph, and in her actions that follow, without any need for melodrama.

With subtlety, you let the reader figure out certain things for himself. You let the impact of information hit in its own time, without ramming it down the reader's throat. You deliver hints and images, rather than swooning ladies and strutting saviors.

The Traits of Melodrama

Believe it or not, you can still have wild situations with large and exciting actions without sliding off into melodrama if you know what to avoid. The most common traits of melodrama follow:

- **SENTIMENTALITY.** Think of the kinds of sentiments written in greeting cards for lovers. Think of cliché, trite, or corny dialogue. "'You are my everything,' he said passionately to her." "'The Earth wouldn't turn if I couldn't be with you,' she said to him."
- **HYSTERICS.** Think crying, screaming, arguing that gets too loud, too emotional, or too angry. Allowing hysterics to go on for too long is a surefire way to lose your readers.
- **GRAND OR UNREALISTIC GESTURES.** These are often found at the end of sappy romance movies, in which the changed man arranges for something utterly implausible, like hiring a famous football team to serenade his love. Big gestures may work for Hollywood, but they rarely fly in writing.
- **AFFECTED SPEECH.** Be careful that your characters don't sound like divas and English barons (unless they are), dropping phrases that real people wouldn't likely utter. Often what seems melodramatic in a character is just a bad affectation or poorly crafted dialogue.

- **KNEE-JERK REACTIONS.** When a character changes his mind or behavior too suddenly, flip-flopping from meek to brave, from kind to villainous, the scene can read as melodrama.
- **DESCRIPTOR OVERLOAD.** On the technical level, remember that an overuse of adverbs or adjectives can lead to a feeling of melodrama. Often just cutting them away will solve the problem.

How to Cut Melodrama

The kindest thing you can do for your writing—and the reader—is to cut the heart right out of your melodramatic passages using these techniques:

- **CHECK THE EMOTIONAL INTENSITY.** Your first order of business is to go through your scenes looking specifically at the emotional content. Are people fistfighting and launching soap-opera-style accusations at each other? Are lovers a little too profuse in their expressions? Are your characters saying too much about their feelings rather than demonstrating them? Try to take the temperature of the emotional content of a scene. If it feels too hot, bring it down.
- **RETOOL DIALOGUE.** Go over your dialogue with the finest-tooth comb around. Read it aloud—heck, read it to someone else—until it sounds like things people might actually say to each other (dialogue can still be stylized, but it should not make the reader want to gag or feel insulted).
- **SMOOTH OUT CHARACTER BEHAVIOR.** Take the diva or the preening prince out of your characters. Get to know who they really are so that their behavior stems from true motivations, not affectation or empty behavior.
- **GROUND GESTURES IN REALITY.** Your characters can be bold and passionate, but think twice about having them do things that are too implausible or over the top if you want them to be believed.
- **EQUALIZE CHARACTERS.** Try not to make one character so much larger than life that he seems out of proportion to the others. Villains often get very colorful in first drafts, since villainy is so much fun to write. But if your bad guy outshines your good guy in his speech and behav-

ior, the scene will feel off-kilter, and the reader will become confused about which character to pledge allegiance to.

Tension comes from the stakes you set for your characters. If there is little or nothing at stake, there will be little tension. The more you practice creating authentic tension, the less likely you'll be to dip into melodrama.

No matter what genre of story you're writing, tension techniques will ensure your readers' undying attention.

SCENE INTENTIONS

An important way to keep your protagonist from wandering aimlessly about your narrative (and in the meantime build a strong plot) is to give him an intention in every scene—a job that he wants to carry out and that will give purpose to the scene. The intention doesn't come from nowhere—it stems directly from the inciting incident of your plot and from your protagonist's personal history. To clarify, an *intention* is a character's plan to take an action, whereas a *motivation* is a series of reasons, from your protagonist's personal history to his mood, which accounts for some rationale of *why* he plans to take an action. In every scene, these intentions will drive the action and consequences; they will help you make the scene relevant to your plot and character development. Intentions are also an important way to build drama and conflict into your narrative because, as your protagonist pursues an intention, you will oppose it, thwart it, intensify his desire for it, and only at the end of your narrative, grant him the satisfaction of achieving it and more.

Every time you begin a scene, you want to ask yourself these questions:

1. **WHAT ARE THE MOST IMMEDIATE DESIRES OF THE CHARACTER?** An intention is a character's desire or plan to do something, whether it's to rob a bank, propose to a woman, go to the store for cigarettes, or tell off a misbehaving family member.
2. **WHEN WILL YOUR CHARACTERS ACHIEVE THEIR INTENTIONS OR MEET WITH OPPOSITION?** An intention should meet with complications to

build drama and suspense. Therefore, try not to allow your characters to achieve their intentions right away or too easily. Know when and where you will complicate or resolve things. Some intentions will have to be achieved or else your plot will stop cold.

3. **HOW DOES THIS INTENTION RELATE TO PRIOR SCENES AND TO THE PLOT?** Intentions are not arbitrary; they stem from the actions and consequences of prior scenes. They should be organically derived from the story that is already fully in motion. Be careful not to take tangents and side paths that, while fun to write, don't contribute to the main drama; every intention should be related to the inciting incident and its consequences.

4. **WHO WILL HELP YOUR CHARACTERS ACHIEVE THEIR GOALS? WHO WILL OPPOSE THEM?** Decide what other characters or conditions will support or thwart your protagonist's intentions, and keep constant tension in the scene so that intentions are not achieved too soon, nor delayed beyond what feels realistic (except, of course, when you intentionally leave the reader hanging to build suspense).

These basic questions will help direct you when you begin thinking about the actions your characters need to take in a new scene. Now we'll look at the two kinds of intentions you'll want to focus on: those that are plot based and those that are scene specific.

PLOT-BASED INTENTIONS

The first imperative any character has in any scene must always be tied to the inciting incident of your plot or else your scenes will seem to be free-floating, like vignettes. An intention, at its most basic, is a course of action your protagonist plans to take (and sometimes *needs* to take) in the scene that arises first out of the inciting incident and then from the consequences that ensue.

For example, Tess Gerritsen's thriller *Vanish* launches its inciting incident when medical examiner Maura Isles prepares to do an autopsy on a Jane Doe—an unidentified female corpse—and the dead woman opens her eyes. No, this isn't a zombie story—the woman is alive, though barely. Maura's overarching plot-based intention, no matter the scene she stars in, is to figure out who this woman is and what has happened to her—how did she end up in a body bag in the morgue when she wasn't dead? The consequences of the inciting incident get underway very quickly, creating new intentions for Maura: For example, the press gets wind of what happened and begins to harass Maura and misquote the medical examiner's office. The nearly dead Jane Doe, once she's in the hospital, turns out to be livid with rage and violent in defense of her own life. These are the consequences that spin out from the inciting incident, and they drive scene-specific intentions (discussed in the next section).

So, here's an example of Maura Isles engaged in a plot-based intention. Maura is visiting the hospital after Jane Doe has been admitted:

> "I'm here to visit a patient," said Maura. "She was admitted last night, through the ER. I understand she was transferred out of ICU this morning."
>
> "The patient's name?"
>
> Maura hesitated. "I believe she's still registered as Jane Doe. Dr. Cutler told me she's in room four-thirty-one."
>
> The ward clerk's gaze narrowed. "I'm sorry. We've had calls from reporters all day. We can't answer any more questions about that patient."
>
> "I'm not a reporter. I'm Dr. Isles, from the medical examiner's office. I told Dr. Cutler I'd be coming by to check on the patient."
>
> "May I see some identification?"
>
> Maura dug into her purse and placed her ID on the countertop. *This is what I get for showing up without my lab coat*, she thought. She could see the interns cruising down the hall, unimpeded, like a flock of strutting white geese.

So, referring to the points mentioned earlier, we will want to ask these questions:

1. **WHAT IS MAURA ISLES'S MOST IMMEDIATE PLOT-RELATED INTENTION?** To interview Jane Doe and determine her identity, and discover what, if anything, she remembers of how she came to be left for dead.

2. **WILL SHE ACHIEVE THIS INTENTION OR BE THWARTED?** The reader doesn't know when in the scene (or if) Maura will achieve her intention, but Gerritsen does—and in a moment, I'll show you how she complicates

this intention unexpectedly, creating drama and action. Though the exchange with the clerk may seem inconsequential, it's quite crucial to building tension. If Maura walked unobstructed into the hospital, which is thronged by press clamoring to get in, and went straight to her patient's room, the lack of barriers to her intention would kill any element of dramatic tension. Here, the reader wonders if she's even going to get in to see the woman; since the reader wants to know what happened to Jane Doe (and who she really is) as much as Maura does, thwarting Maura's intention keeps the reader on his toes. On a larger scale, other law enforcement officials will aid Maura, and members of the press and Jane Doe herself will thwart her.

3. **DOES THE INTENTION MAKE SENSE TO THE PLOT?** Yes, absolutely—naturally Maura will want to speak to the woman who seemingly survived death. For the plot to move forward, something new will have to be revealed about Jane Doe.

4. **AND FINALLY, WHO HELPS MAURA ACHIEVE HER INTENTION?** In this scene, after questioning her and scouring her ID, the clerk lets Maura through, helping her achieve one part of her intention—she gets into the hospital. But will she get to interview Jane Doe? Who will help her? In the rest of this scene, as it turns out, no one.

Gerritsen ups the ante on the plot when Jane Doe, who is more than awake—in fact, she's volatile and has to be restrained—gets ahold of the guard's gun and shoots him, then takes Maura as her hostage. Afraid of the woman, no hospital personnel want to get involved. Maura ends up relying on her own wits and skills to keep from getting shot.

Complicating intentions is a crucial part of building suspense and tension. Remember that if you allow your characters to achieve their intentions too early in the scene or in the narrative, you dissipate any tension or suspense you might have created. Always imagine your plot, no matter its actual genre, as a kind of mystery, or puzzle, in which every scene fills in one or two more of the missing pieces, but never the entire thing, until the end.

Plot-related intentions can be demonstrated by the protagonist's direct responses to the inciting incident through:

- Interior monologue that shows his thoughts and feelings
- Actions he takes to try to change or influence the outcome of the inciting incident
- Dialogue in which he expresses his feelings or thoughts about the plot

SCENE-SPECIFIC INTENTIONS

Now, while your protagonist has an umbrella set of plot-related intentions that drive him no matter what is happening in the scene, he will also have more immediate, scene-based intentions, like finding shelter after his car has been bombed or contacting a friend he can trust before the cops find him. These immediate intentions still must relate to the plot, but they are more likely to be related to *consequences*—the many smaller actions and events that stem from the inciting incident. Scene-specific intentions keep your characters from being aimless.

Let's look at an example from William Trevor's novel *Felicia's Journey*, the story of a lower-class Irish girl named Felicia on a trip to England. Her plot situation is that she's pregnant and on a journey to meet up with "a friend" (as she tells customs) who is actually Johnny, the father of her child, with whom she hasn't had any contact since their whirlwind dalliance. She doesn't have his address and he doesn't know she's coming, but Felicia, who is desperate to get out of her small-town life, chooses to believe he is going to marry her when he hears the news.

Now, in an early scene, she has arrived in England. Her plot intention is to get Johnny to marry her and be a father for her baby. Her scene-specific intention—her most immediate need or desire—is to find the lawn-mower factory where Johnny works:

> A man in a Volkswagen showroom is patient with her but doesn't know of a lawn-mower factory in the vicinity. Then an afterthought strikes him as she's leaving and he mentions the name of a town that he says is twenty-five or -six miles off. When it occurs to him that she's bewildered by what he's saying he writes the name down on the edge of a brochure. 'Not the full shilling,' is an expression her father uses and 'Nineteen and six in the pound': she wonders if the man is thinking that.

So her intention in the excerpt was to find the lawn-mower factory where Johnny works, but since she doesn't know the town or have an address, she goes to a place that is as close to a lawn-mower factory as she can think of: a car dealership. Driven by her overarching plot intention to be with Johnny, her scene-specific intentions are directed by whatever information she obtains that will help her find him. In this case, she receives for her trouble the name of the town the factory may be in.

Her scene-specific intention then quickly becomes complicated, as the town she needs to go to is twenty-six miles away and she has very little money and no form of transportation. Her next scene intention, therefore, is to find transportation to this city (which, of course, leads to more trouble).

Scene intentions lead to complications, which lead to new scene intentions, and so on, until you begin to resolve your plot toward the end of your narrative.

Intentions give your protagonist a purpose on a large scale (plot) and on a present-moment scale (scene) so that you get to the action at hand and don't leave the reader wondering what is going to happen next. They help you structure your plot and direct your characters. Then, by complicating the intentions through opposition or some other kind of twist, you build tension, drama, and energy and create new intentions.

INTENTION OPPOSITION

So now, hopefully, it's clear that intentions are the most immediate actions your characters plan to take to fulfill their larger plot goals. Once your character's intention is established and in motion in a scene, you want to build tension and keep a sense of urgency alive for the reader by thwarting the intentions in various ways. Here are some ways you can do it:

- **PREVENTING THE COMPLETION OF THE INTENTION.** Another character intervenes, a rainstorm pours down, a car accident occurs, etc.
- **THROWING IN A TWIST.** The protagonist learns that what he intends to do is impossible, illegal, or wrong (and he decides to do it anyway, or he gives up completely).

- **COMPLICATING THE INTENTIONS.** Allow your protagonist to set out with one intention in mind, only to have circumstances beyond his control or awareness intervene and change his course of action.
- **CREATING A NEW INTENTION.** Upon having his original intention thwarted, complicated, or twisted, your protagonist may need to change course altogether and come up with a new intention.

The longer you delay fulfilling your protagonist's intention, the more tension and drama you build. It's useful to delay and oppose intentions for most of a scene so that the reader is compelled to keep reading to find out when, and how, the intention will finally be achieved—if at all.

INTENTION SUPPORT

Eventually, you will want to provide your protagonist with *some* support of his intentions along the way. You can't delay a desire forever or your narrative will end unresolved. At certain junctures along the way, then, you need to give your protagonist allies and assistance in achieving his intentions. Whether these come in the form of friends in high places—like headmaster Albus Dumbledore, who always seems to help Harry Potter out of tight fixes—or simply a kind stranger offering shelter to a weary protagonist running from a pursuer, these little acts of assistance will keep your character from getting stuck.

If you only thwart intentions, after all, eventually your protagonist will become completely stymied, and the plot will come to a halt.

Keep in mind that no character should be superhuman in his ability to get through difficult trials. In the Lord of the Rings trilogy, Frodo needs his group of companions to get him to Mordor, where he can get rid of the malicious ring for good. Protagonists need friends and supporters, small acts of kindness, insight, and clues that lead them on in their journeys.

· · ·

Ultimately, some plot-specific intentions will carry over from one scene to another, particularly if you are good at thwarting them. These intentions will also likely change slightly over the course of a narrative, once some aspects of the plot are revealed or wrapped up, but they should arise and continue organically, spinning off from the inciting incident that launches your book. Scene-specific intentions, on the other hand, while also distantly related to consequences that unravel from the inciting incident, can vary and shift from scene to scene as needed to drive your plot forward and create various effects—including tension and drama—in your characters' lives.

PART III

SCENE TYPES

" Every novel is an equal collaboration betwen the writer and the reader and it is the only place in the world where two strangers can meet on terms of absolute intimacy. "

—PAUL AUSTER

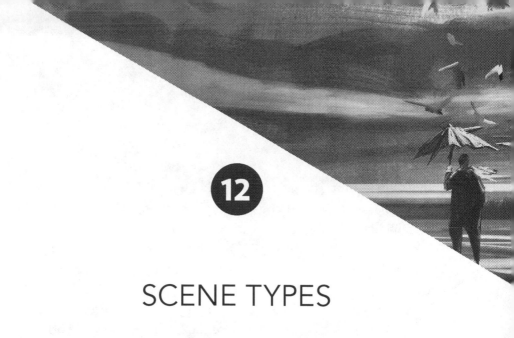

SCENE TYPES

The first two parts of this book have been about introducing you to the core elements of scenes so that you know how to construct them, how they build character, and how they add up to equal plots. In part three, we'll take a deeper look at the types of scenes you have in your tool kit. If you never before considered that there might be different types of scenes, you may find this section elucidating as your scene palette expands.

If you think of plot structure as the backbone of your novel or story, and scenes as the flesh that turns it from skeleton to fully realized creation, then scene types are what add color, texture, and shape along the way.

In my book *Writing Deep Scenes*, co-authored with Martha Alderson, we have identified a number of significant scene types that you might use in a story:

1. Climax Scenes
2. Contemplative (or Sequel) Scenes
3. Crisis Scenes
4. Dialogue Scenes
5. Epiphany Scenes
6. Escape Scenes
7. Final Scenes
8. First Scenes
9. Lay of the Land Scenes
10. Love Scenes

11. Recommitment Scenes
12. Resolution Scenes
13. Transition Scenes
14. Suspense Scenes
15. Twister Scenes

These are not necessarily all the scene types in existence, but the list is a good sampling. These scene types are explained in detail in *Writing Deep Scenes*, so I won't go into them all here, but in this next part I'll give you an in-depth look at the most key scene types you'll need to know to write a strong story. Think of them as your primary colors, from which all other scenes can be mixed.

At the end of each chapter in this section, I have provided a short list of "Muse Points," a shortcut to the key points to remember about that particular scene type. If you can use them to master these scene types, you'll have the essential structure you need to write a strong plot.

PROLOGUES

WHAT IS A PROLOGUE?

Many writers don't understand the distinction between a prologue and a first chapter, so this chapter aims to make that clear. A prologue is a short scene that you find at the very beginning of a narrative—the very first scene that will be read, even before the "official" first scene or chapter. But here's where it can get confusing: A prologue has the liberty to take place at any time—the future, a few minutes ago, even the distant past—and may not fit into the linear chronology of the narrative. Its purpose is to provide information that the narrative can't or won't just yet, but that is necessary for understanding some key component of plot or character. Some writers use a prologue as a hook to tempt readers with information that the plot will not deliver for many more hundreds of pages, if ever.

Consider using a prologue in the following circumstances:

- The reader needs to know key information that falls outside the linear time line of the story. This will help you avoid dense backstory or exposition.
- In lieu of flashback scenes that would reveal the same info but might also slow the pace and jar the reader's focus.
- To offer the POV of a character who is not the protagonist but whose story is in some way crucial to the protagonist's story.

- To hook the reader. Since a prologue can start at any point in time, you can choose one that is high on action and drama, especially if your first scene starts a little slower.
- To create foreshadowing. By giving a hint of what's to come, or what's gone before, you can entice a reader into a story.

Let's take a look at some prologues and their different functions.

Using a Prologue to Reveal Key Character Information

Here's one from Tana French's mystery novel *The Trespasser*. The protagonist, Dublin Murder detective Antoinette Conway, the only woman on her squad, is hazed and teased by her squad members in ways she doesn't see them treat each other, and thus is paranoid that they have it out for her. The prologue is almost completely exposition, in Antoinette's first-person POV:

> My ma used to tell me stories about my da. The first one I remember, he was an Egyptian prince who wanted to marry her and stay in Ireland forever, only his family made him go home to marry an Arabian princess. She told a good story, my ma. Amethyst rings on his long fingers, the two of them dancing under turning lights, his smell like spices and pine. … The story held my chin high for years, till I was eight and told it to my best friend, Lisa, who broke her shite laughing.
>
> A couple of months later, once the sting faded, I marched into the kitchen one afternoon, stuck my fists on my hips and demanded the truth. My ma didn't miss a beat: squirted Fairy liquid and told me he was a medical student, over from Saudi Arabia. … By the time she found out I was on the way, he was gone, back to Saudi, without leaving an address. She dropped out of nursing college and had me. … That lasted till I was twelve and got detention for something, and got an earful from my ma about how she wasn't having me end up like her, with no Leaving Cert and no hope of anything but minimum-wage cleaning jobs for the rest of her life. I'd heard it all a thousand times before, but that day it occurred to me that you need a Leaving Cert to study nursing. …
>
> My birth cert says *Unknown*, but there are ways.

I'll be honest, even as a seasoned reader and writing teacher, I wasn't entirely sure of the purpose of this prologue at first, though it certainly establishes important character details about Antoinette and makes me care about her more. It wasn't until later in the novel that it hit me why French had included it. Antoinette is bothered from the beginning of the case because she recognizes the deceased woman, Aislinn Murray, but can't recall why. In the middle of the case, as they've hit a dead end with their one suspect, Conway finally remembers how she knew the girl. Back when she worked in Missing Persons, Aislinn had come around wanting help finding her missing dad. Notice how Conway responded:

> I had zero intention of busting my arse trying to help her find Daddy.
>
> Which is what I told her, in a slightly more tactful way, wondering how hard I would have to blank her before she would fu*k off out of my face. ...
>
> And of course then she whipped out the tears. *Please couldn't you just look up the file, you can't imagine what it's like growing up without* yada yada yada, and some Hollywood-style puke about needing to know the truth so it couldn't control her life any more—I can't swear she actually used the words "closure" and "empowered," because I'd stopped listening, but they would have fit right in. By that stage my happy buzz was well and truly wrecked. All I wanted was to shut the bitch up and kick her out the door.

Thanks to the prologue, we have no trouble understanding why Conway, who grew up not knowing who her dad really was and harboring a secret anger about it, has no sympathy for the girl. We don't need any clunky flashback scene or heavy-handed dialogue to reveal this key detail of Conway's life; the prologue set it up, and the reveal of Aislinn's backstory recalls the detail. The prologue also helps explain why Conway is so wary of her male squad members, especially the older ones, and why she steels herself against trusting people. Moreover, it sets up for a tenser situation when a character turns up claiming to actually be her father.

Using a prologue to reveal nonlinear information to hook the reader

In my first published novel, *Forged in Grace*, protagonist Grace Jensen hasn't seen her childhood best friend, Marly Kennet, for thirteen years. The last time Grace saw Marly was the night of the terrible accident that left Grace horrifically burned, forever changing her life. Grace does not have full memory of that night and has always wondered why Marly abandoned her. I didn't want the reader to get antsy or bored wondering if these two were going to find a way to reconnect, address the past, and resurrect their friendship. I also wanted the reader to understand that Marly was a loose cannon, and therefore to both root for the two friends' reunion and be nervous for Grace. The prologue is actually a snippet of a scene from much later in the novel, when things get intense:

> I feel swimmy, high, adrenaline on full tilt, though I haven't consumed a drop of alcohol. "We need to subdue him first," I hear myself say. "Can't just slap a hand on his face and hope it knocks him out."
>
> Marly nods, though she is too encumbered to move quickly, and me—there's no guarantee of what I can do.
>
> "I have pepper spray." She fidgets with her purse as though she's about to withdraw the cannister. "And it's not like we have to break in, Grace. He'll let us in, when he sees it's me. Think I'm coming to talk."
>
> "Okay, then," I say, before I lose my nerve. And we get in her car and drive.
>
> We park and walk four residential blocks. The streets are lit by yellow halogen lamps, but there's also a nearly full moon. Its bold light makes me feel bolstered, sanctioned. Marly points to his condo, one square box among many in a beige world of homogenous residences.
>
> "This could have been my life," Marly whispers, her face a portrait of disgust. "I should be in that kitchen right now making dinner, then go spread my legs for him. I can't *believe* he thought he could get away with what he did to me."
>
> The guilt surges through me again. If only I hadn't healed away the evidence. But we didn't know. Nobody could have known.
>
> "Let's do it soon, before I chicken out." My palms have begun to ache with heat.

"Damn straight," she agrees, and the toss of her hair is so familiar it's like we're fifteen again.

Simultaneously, we take a deep breath.

Marly repeats her lines, "I'll say we're here to talk—that I brought you as my friend and witness. That will put him on his best behavior. And you?"

I choke a little on my own saliva, cough, and answer, "I'll ask for a glass of water, say I got too much sun today. He'll take one look at me and have a hard time refusing, right?"

Marly pats her purse. "Let's go."

She's always one step ahead of me.

It plants foreshadowing for the reader—maybe hooking up with Marly again is not such a great idea for Grace, after all. On the other hand, it hints to the reader that Grace will be capable of leaving the small, safe life she's established for herself in the aftermath of her accident. And it creates a sense of intrigue, as the reader wonders exactly what the two of them are up to.

Anytime you have information to deliver from a time period outside of the linear narrative, a prologue can be incredibly effective, especially if it lends itself to a tense, compelling scene.

Using prologues to reveal information the POV character or reader could not otherwise know

Whether your plot is based upon an old family secret or an event that has taken place before the story starts, you can drop just enough of that history into a prologue to get readers up to speed.

Myfanwy Collins's novel *The Book of Laney* takes place in the aftermath of a terrible massacre by two boys on a school bus. The protagonist, Laney, is the sister of West, one of the killers, and her life has gone belly-up in her small community in the aftermath of the tragedy. The story begins with a prologue, ostensibly in Laney's first-person POV, but very quickly it slips into something else, a vision, inside West's POV, back at the time of the massacre:

My story starts months ago and hundreds of miles south of where I am now. My story starts in the place I used to call home. My story starts with violence and heartbreak.

My story starts with a vision.

Mark is up ahead of me, pushing to the back of the bus. The light smearing through the windows is a dull toothache of yellow. I rub a hand over my eyes to clear them. It's my hand. It's not my hand. I feel what it feels and when I look at it, I recognize it, but I don't know it to really be mine. But I'm here. I'm still here. There is nowhere else I could be and this is real. One kid starts screaming and Mark points his machete at the kid and tells him that if he doesn't shut his face, he's next. It could be a scene from a movie or a game but it's real. It's real. I keep saying, "This is real. This is real," to remind myself that I'm in this place with Mark. …

But here we are now and her eyes meet mine and I lift the hand with my knife in it, raise my arm right up over my head. I know she's frightened but she won't let her eyes show it. I want her to show her fear. It would be easier for me to kill her then.

"Aren't you scared to die?" I ask her. I will stab her. I will hurt her. I might even kill her. She doesn't deserve to live. The pain.

"Please don't hurt me, West," she says.

She knows my name. She said my name. West.

This vision-as-prologue brings the reader up to speed on the horrible event of the recent past, which Laney did not experience firsthand (except in news story sound bites), since she was not there. However, it also serves to establish a key plot device: that Laney has visions. It's a compelling use of both devices that is more effective than Laney simply recounting the horrible details of her brother's terrible act after the fact. By being inside West's head at the moment of the massacre, the real horror is driven home, which helps us to connect more deeply to all the characters.

When a Prologue Is Not Right

Sometimes you try your hand at a prologue only to find that really you're just starting the story too soon or too late. In either case, you'll probably receive feedback that the prologue is confusing, or people will ask why it's there—it may have the not-quite-complete quality of a vignette. If the prologue doesn't establish something key to the story or hook the reader, you can skip it and just write a first scene. If, after you've written a first draft, you see an obvious prologue begging to be written, then go ahead and do it.

PROLOGUE SCENE MUSE POINTS

Use prologue scenes to do the following:

- Offer key plot or character information that comes before or after the front story
- Reveal the POV of a character who is not part of the current story, or no longer alive, but crucial to the story
- Hook the reader
- Create foreshadowing
- Deepen our understanding of a character

14

THE FIRST SCENE

Your first scene is like a window thrown open at the sound of a scream. Novels, like life, are driven by curiosity: The reader must be curious about what the window of your first scene opens onto—say, lovers quarrelling, a murderer fleeing from a body, a strange and beautiful dance—to compel him to keep reading, or not. In many novels, the inciting incident takes place in the first scene. (A prologue, remember, is not your true first scene—it's a scene that hints at actions to come.) In other novels, the first scene is an introduction to all the key players and their problems just before the inciting incident shatters them apart.

The first scene in your narrative bears the greatest burden because it *must* do all of the following:

- Launch your inciting incident or set the reader up for its imminent arrival
- Introduce your protagonist and a brief glance into his inner or outer struggles in his ordinary world
- Establish a distinct setting through a subtle evocation of the senses
- Set up dramatic tension that hints at future complications and conflict

A first scene should accomplish the above, yet still avoid the items on this list:

- Revealing the entirety of your protagonist's backstory
- Listing descriptions and histories of the setting and time period

- Introducing every character in your protagonist's life
- Explaining the situation when action can unfurl naturally

First scenes are most successful when they begin with an air of mystery, a question or situation that requires an answer, or a crisis from which the protagonist needs to be extricated. The first scene should include enough action and plot information that the reader does not need any backstory or expository summary to keep from getting confused.

In relationship to the larger narrative, the first scene should set the tone and resonate in the reader's mind like a haunting tune throughout.

INTRODUCING THE INCITING INCIDENT AND YOUR PROTAGONIST

Burn these words into your consciousness, now and forevermore: *Plot and character cannot be separated.* Your inciting incident is something bad, difficult, mysterious, or tragic that happens to your protagonist. This monumental event is what sets your story in motion and compels your character to take action; the problem belongs, first and foremost, to your protagonist. Through other plot twists and complications, the inciting incident may lead to trouble for a whole host of other characters, but not on page one. The opening scene belongs to your main character and should occur in real-time action, as if happening at the moment of reading. Don't begin with narration in exposition or a flashback scene: The action is happening *now!*

If yours is a novel in which the inciting incident takes place in the first scene, then get to it within the first couple of paragraphs. If you force your readers to wait too long for the first main event, you stand to lose them before ever getting to it.

For example, in Jennifer McMahon's novel *The Night Sister,* the first scene opens right in the thick of unexplained action:

> Amy's heart hammers, and her skin is slick with sweat.
>
> *Focus,* she tells herself.
>
> *Don't think about the thing in the tower.*
>
> Amy knows that if she thinks too hard about it she won't be able to do what needs to be done.

She looks down at the photo, the old black-and-white print she's kept all these years, hidden away in the drawer of her bedside table. It's been handled so much that it's cracked and faded, one of the corners torn.

In it, her mother, Rose, and her aunt Sylvie are young girls, wearing crisp summer dresses as they stand in front of a sign that says World Famous London Chicken Circus. Each girl clutches a worried-looking hen, but that's where the similarities end. Amy's mother is wearing a scowl beneath tired eyes, her hair dark and unkempt; Sylvie is radiant, the one who was going to grow up and go to Hollywood. Her blond hair is movie-star perfect; her eyes are shining.

Someone had scrawled a date on the back: June 1955. If only Amy could travel back in time, talk to those two girls, warn them what was coming. Warn them that one day it would all lead to this moment: Amy alone and out of options, on the verge of doing something terrible.

She bites her lip and wonders what people will say about her once she's gone.

The reader is instantly hooked. Amy, whom we know nothing about, is clearly in a difficult situation, possibly danger. In the first few lines, we learn that she has to do "what needs to be done"—an ominous sounding statement—about "the thing in the tower." Creepy, spooky, full of tension, you bet the reader will turn the page to find out what happens next, especially after that last line in which Amy thinks ahead to "once she's gone."

When you kick off your inciting incident, be sure that it directly involves—or at least directly sets up consequences for—your protagonist (or protagonists; see chapter twenty-three for more on multiple protagonists). In either case, remember that your incident should challenge your protagonist's sense of normal and knock her off-kilter somehow. Plot and character are bound together, and one without the other will cause your first scene to flop.

In your first scene, you aren't going to focus too much on character development, though; rather, your goal is to introduce your protagonist as quickly and with as much intrigue as possible, getting your story started and hooking your reader. So, what does your first scene need to be successful? The following, for starters:

- **AN INCITING INCIDENT, OR THE HINT OF ONE TO COME, THAT CHALLENGES YOUR PROTAGONIST'S STATUS QUO.** Amy is clearly about to do something dangerous, possibly fatal.
- **A CATALYST WITH WHICH THE PROTAGONIST CAN INTERACT.** That thing in the tower is likely the catalyst or antagonist with which Amy must contend.
- **A QUICK INTRODUCTION TO YOUR PROTAGONIST'S IMMEDIATE INTENTIONS.** She's decided to go out to the tower and deal with whatever is out there.
- **A GLIMPSE OF YOUR PROTAGONIST'S PERSONAL HISTORY AND PERSONALITY, WHICH SHOULD SHED FURTHER LIGHT ON HER MOTIVATION.** Here we get details about her family history, which, we learn later, plays a large part in the plot.
- **A COURSE OF ACTION OR A DECISION ON THE PART OF THE PROTAGONIST THAT LEADS IMMEDIATELY TO MORE COMPLICATIONS.** As the scene progresses, Amy heads out into the hallway, "willing herself not to run, to stay calm and not wake her family."

Some first scenes don't include the inciting incident. In Gina Frangello's contemporary literary novel *Every Kind of Wanting*, a cast of characters, some of them already related by blood or marriage, are all driven forward by the desire of a gay couple to have a baby. The scene that starts the novel, after the prologue, is not the inciting incident of the entire book; it's our introduction to the pivotal character, Gretchen, who agrees to donate her egg:

> Something is wrong with Gretchen's son Gray when he sits down in the breakfast nook. He looks different, alien, but Gretchen can't place it. She keeps staring at him and it's like she's taken someone else's black coat accidentally in the pile of coats at a party, when she's a little bit drunk and the coat looks like hers and maybe is even the same designer but something is implacably wrong. She watches Gray as though feeling inside the pockets of this wrong coat, hoping for some evidence of its wrongness, or better yet, clues to whom it actually belongs.
>
> Troy saunters into the room for coffee, looking sexy and angular and hateful like someone who would be cast to play a Nazi in a miniseries, and takes one look at Gray and says, "Where the hell are his eyebrows?"

"Huh?" Gretchen says.

"Why doesn't our kid have eyebrows?" Troy snaps, and they both turn back to Gray, who is shoveling cereal into his mouth. For an instant, their eyes meet above his head in a rare moment of collusion: Is it possible that Gray has never had eyebrows? Has he been eyebrowless from the get-go, and somehow Gretchen and Troy forgot to … *notice* until now?

This quirky bit about Gretchen's son Gray has very little to do with the plot that develops. Yet it does set the stage, introducing us to Gretchen and her husband and reflecting Gretchen's feeling of unbalance in her own life. In an opening scene that doesn't launch the inciting incident, you still have to grasp the reader's attention, but there are different demands to meet:

- **INTRODUCE THE CHARACTER IN A COMPELLING WAY.** Here Frangello sets the stage of Gretchen's "ordinary life"—that is, the life she leads before the inciting incident—and reveals her character: Gretchen is in the midst of a midlife crisis, which positions her to agree to donate her eggs when the time comes, a decision she may go on to regret (at least for part of the novel).
- **ESTABLISH SOME SORT OF PROBLEM.** As the scene unfolds, we quickly learn of several problems: Gretchen's son may be on the autism spectrum and isn't receiving the support he needs, she's found incriminating evidence of adultery on her husband's computer, and she is considering divorce.
- **PREPARE TO TAKE THE CHARACTER TO THE POINT OF NO RETURN.** Remember the First Energetic Marker. It is a powerfully charged threshold that, once crossed, can't be reversed. In books like Frangello's, where the inciting incident doesn't happen in the first scene, the early scenes will establish the pressure cooker of your protagonist's life, setting her up for an inciting incident to take place at the Point of No Return.

BALANCING SCENE ELEMENTS IN THE FIRST SCENE

Now let's look at how other scene elements—setting, subtext, dramatic tension, pacing, and scene endings—come into play. Getting the balance right is crucial because too much or too little of any one element can throw off the symmetry of the entire scene. For instance, too much setting description can slow your pace to a crawl, bore your reader, and stall your story before it even begins. Too little, on the other hand, can make it hard for the reader to picture the lay of the land and your character's location within it.

Setting

It's tempting to paint a dramatic canvas of setting in the first scene, but be careful not to let setting stand in the limelight. You don't always need to make it clear what room, building, city, or even planet a character occupies to ground the characters in physical space successfully. Consider Megan Abbott's novel, *You Will Know Me*. The first scene opens with a sentence of crisp setting details that provide a visual without going overboard:

> The vinyl banners rippled from the air vent, the restaurant roiling with parents, the bobbing of gymnast heads, music gushing from the weighty speakers keeled on the window ledges.

And just a page later, another brief set of details:

> Everything was glowing: the disco ball spinning above, and the Sterno lights flickering under the kebabs and lomi-lomi atop long tables skirted with raffia, candles in coconut shells and pineapples that Katie had helped hollow out with ice cream scoopers.

In your first scene, setting should be sketched lightly unless the setting itself is part of your inciting incident in some dramatic way (if your protagonist is lost in a wild jungle or scaling a mountain, for example).

Let's look at how another author infuses her first scene with setting to further the development of her inciting incident. In the novel *The Handmaid's Tale* by Margaret Atwood, the inciting incident is a radical shift in government that takes away women's freedom overnight. One day protagonist Offred has a normal life with her husband and daughter, the next it has been stripped away. In this first scene, she is nothing more than a slave kept by the new ruling class for the sake of reproduction. Atwood uses setting to create tension and unease from the very first sentence. She describes a familiar setting—that of a high school gymnasium—but there's something wrong with the picture. Why are the protagonist and these others sleeping there? Who are these "Aunts" that patrol the room with "cattle prods slung on thongs from leather belts?"

Even in Atwood's matter-of-fact style of writing, the use of a normal setting in an abnormal way creates an aura of fear and uncertainty that drives the plot forward.

> We slept in what had once been the gymnasium. The floor was of varnished wood, with stripes and circles painted on it, for the games that were formerly played there; the hoops for the basketball nets were still in place, though the nets were gone. A balcony ran around the room, for the spectators, and I thought I could smell, faintly like an afterimage, the pungent scent of sweat, shot through with the sweet taint of chewing gum and perfume from the watching girls, felt-skirted as I knew from pictures, later in miniskirts, then pants, then in one earring, spiky green-streaked hair. ...
>
> We had flannelette sheets, like children's, and army-issue blankets, old ones that still said U.S. We folded our clothes neatly and laid them on the stools at the ends of the beds. The lights were turned down but not out. Aunt Sara and Aunt Elizabeth patrolled; they had electric cattle prods slung on thongs from their leather belts.

Notice how the first line makes you feel nervous and curious, and how the careful descriptions of a gymnasium and their few belongings—"flannelette sheets, like children's and army-issue blankets"—add to a feeling that something bad has happened and that worse things are to come (complications!). The protagonist also describes the setting with a keen note of nostalgia, suggesting that this familiar place is no longer used for familiar activities. Atwood unbalances our sense of what is normal.

You, too, can unbalance the reader's sense of normalcy by having your inciting incident take place in a familiar setting in an unexpected way. For instance, after establishing the domestic scene of a cozy little cottage, a murder could occur; or against the backdrop of a dingy back alley where homeless people sleep, a man could propose marriage.

Unbalancing normalcy with setting is a great way to start your scene off with a visual and emotional pitch.

Subtext

Once you have your physical world in place, you can begin to think about your subtext. Subtext, as discussed in chapter nine, foreshadows aspects of your plot through the strategic placement of thematic imagery, subtle character behavior, or parallel actions in the background of the scene. Not all genres need much subtext. Action-driven narratives such as thrillers and mysteries, for example, often bypass the subtle for action, while literary fiction—a genre characterized by lyrical language, slow pacing, and rich character development—tends to rely more heavily upon subtext.

Harking back to the excerpt from *The Night Sisters*, the subtle subtext about Amy's mother, Rose, and her aunt Sylvie in the first scene foreshadows the later focus of the plot. In the photo that Amy looks at, Amy's mother is "dark and unkempt" and her aunt Sylvie is "radiant" and "movie-star perfect." This subtext of inequality (and competition) between the sisters will play a key role in the main plot of the story.

With the subtext of your first scene, you want to develop a mood, foreshadow your protagonist's plot direction, and plant thematic images in the reader's mind.

Dramatic Tension

Whether or not your first scene employs subtext, it definitely needs to have dramatic tension. Dramatic tension creates the expectation that something will go wrong for your protagonist, whether it's due to forces working against her or due to her own ill-advised or unwise choices. You want to be sure that your inciting incident gives your reader cause to worry about your protagonist.

Once your inciting incident is underway, you'll want to be sure that you keep the tension alive throughout the scene. Without dramatic tension, the pace of your scene will become sluggish, your character's dilemmas may seem to lack stakes, and you stand to lose your reader's attention.

Pacing

First scenes need to get things moving —start big or dramatic, ratchet up the suspense or lay on the fear, throw us off balance, make the reader deliriously curious—since this is your one chance to hook them.

In Philip Pullman's young adult fantasy novel *The Golden Compass*, the first scene opens with an air of nervous anticipation, and the quick pace mirrors that feeling. Protagonist Lyra, a ten-year-old girl, and her animal "daemon" Pantalaimon live at Jordan College in Oxford, England. In the first scene, Lyra is snooping in the chamber of the Master of the college, despite Pantalaimon's fretting that she will get in trouble. The action is quick, and the exposition and reflection are kept to a minimum.

> "What d'you think they talk about?" Lyra said, or began to say, because before she'd finished the question she heard voices outside the door.
>
> "Behind the chair—quick!" whispered Pantalaimon, and in a flash Lyra was out of the armchair and crouching behind it. It wasn't the very best one for hiding behind: she'd chosen one in the very center of the room, and unless she kept very quiet …
>
> The door opened, and the light changed in the room; one of the incomers was carrying a lamp, which he put down on the sideboard. Lyra could see his legs, in their dark green trousers and shiny black shoes. It was a servant.
>
> Then a deep voice said, "Has Lord Asriel arrived yet?"
>
> It was the Master.

Within a few paragraphs of quickly paced action and brief description, Lyra finds herself in the midst of her inciting incident: As a result of being where she isn't supposed to, she sees someone slipping poison into the brandy of their visiting guest, Lord Asriel, and overhears a private conversation that sets the plot in motion. To save Lord Asriel's life, she'll have to let on that she was in a forbidden room, thus facing punishment—putting her in quite the dilemma, a great way to thrust the reader into a first scene!

Your first scene is like a cold pool—the reader needs to dive in and get moving fast or he'll be too cold to stay in. In other scene types to come, you'll have more leeway with pacing. In the first scene, however, a quick pace—more action, less reflection and exposition—will be an easier sell.

To keep the pace quick, think in terms of action. What actions can your protagonist take that stem directly from the inciting incident? You might want your protagonist to take a risk or be surprised in some way. First scenes are great for reactions—that is, characters being taken off guard in one way or another and having to think quickly about what they'll do next.

Ending the First Scene

Eventually your first scene will have to taper off to its close. No matter what kind of plot you choose—quiet and character driven or action based—if you end your first scene with a feeling that the trouble, conflict, crisis, or dilemma has only just begun, you will almost certainly guarantee your reader goes on to the next scene. Be sure to do the following:

- Leave the consequences of the inciting incident unresolved, with a promise of more to come. For example, if your protagonist has just been caught at the scene of a murder, don't let him be arrested or proven innocent before the first scene's end—leave the reader guessing.
- End the scene before the character makes a major decision or just after she makes a bad one, as with Amy in *The Night Sister*.
- Allow your protagonist to have a disturbing realization that will change everything about his life—he must flee the country; her husband is a double agent; his evil nemesis has found where he is hiding.
- Let your protagonist have a knee-jerk reaction to the inciting incident that makes things more complicated for her.

Take a look at how McMahon wraps up the opening scene of *The Night Sister*:

> Amy takes each step slowly, willing herself not to run, to stay calm and not wake her family. What would Mark think if he woke up and found his wife creeping up the steps with a gun? Poor, sweet, clueless Mark—perhaps she should have told him the motel's secrets? But no. It was better to protect him from it all as best she could.
>
> The scarred wood beneath her feet creaks, and she thinks of the rhyme her grandmother taught her:
>
> *When death comes knocking on your door,*
> *you'll think you've seen his face before.*
> *When he comes creeping up your stairs,*
> *you'll know him from your dark nightmares.*
> *If you hold up a mirror, you shall see*
> *that he is you and you are he.*

While you want to taper the action of the first scene to a close, you don't want it to feel too conclusive. Here the reader still doesn't know what Amy's going to do, and the eerie poem just adds a layer of foreboding.

Finally, leave your protagonist in a little bit of trouble, so the reader feels anxious enough to keep reading. Choose whichever path will create the most potential for conflict and change in the character. A shy, fearful character, for instance, might be faced with a big, brave decision at the end of your first scene—hopefully one that is a consequence of his inciting incident. Whatever path you take, leave your protagonist's fate up in the air.

FIRST SCENE MUSE POINTS

- The inciting incident must happen to your protagonist.
- Match your pace to the emotional content of the scene.
- Use thematic images to foreshadow an outcome. If your protagonist's life is in danger, set an eerie mood, use setting objects that conjure images of death or darkness—a knife, a raven, even a shift in light from bright to dark.
- Unbalance the reader's expectations through setting by employing the unexpected, such as featuring a monastery as the site of a violent crime or a prison as the setting of a surprising revelation of innocence.
- Keep the pace tight. Notice if your exposition or description drags the pace, and watch for lengthy passages of dialogue or action without break that push the pace too quickly.
- End with your protagonist in trouble or with an uncertain fate, setting up the next scene.

CONTEMPLATIVE SCENES

Contemplation—the act of careful consideration or examination of thoughts, feelings, and small details—is the antithesis of action. When a character contemplates, time slows, or even disappears, and the scene zooms in tightly and intimately to the character's perceptions. Contemplative scenes tend to be used sparingly. However, as you'll see throughout this chapter, for some genres and styles, especially traditional literary fiction, contemplative scenes play a crucial role.

A well-crafted contemplative scene typically does the following:

- Has more interior monologue (thought) than action or dialogue
- Moves at a slower pace, allowing the reader a deeper, more intimate look into the protagonist's inner life
- Shows the protagonist interacting with himself and the setting more than with other characters
- Allows the protagonist time to digest actions, events, and earlier epiphanies and to decide how to act next
- Gives pause before or after an intense scene so that the character can reflect and the reader can catch her breath

Contemplative scenes rarely appear as a first scene or even among the earlier scenes in a narrative, as they work best following plot events and dramatic interactions that are worthy of being digested or reflected upon.

Too many of these scenes in a row make the pace drag, so scenes involving some action should be interspersed among contemplative scenes.

INTERIOR MONOLOGUE

The defining characteristic of a contemplative scene is that your character spends more time thinking than he does in action or speech. These passages of thought are called interior monologue (since they happen inside the character's mind) and are meant to be overheard by, and somehow revealing to, the reader; therefore, even if nothing concrete happens in the scene at hand, they have bearing on plot and character development.

While the old convention was to set off thoughts by putting them in italics, I'm more of a fan of embedding thoughts within the narrative voice as simple, elegant exposition.

For example, in Lidia Yuknavitch's novel *The Small Backs of Children*, the narrator, named only The Writer, describes the stillbirth of her daughter in interior monologue:

> The day birth came at last, the labor had lasted two days. I nearly gave in. I kept thinking, To what end? It seemed true that at any point I could simply surrender to the pain of an ordinary body and … leave.

Interior monologue falls outside of time—it free floats, which is why it tends to feel slow. The Writer is not actually in scene, in the labor. There's no action involved. Notice how her thoughts feel ethereal. You don't get a sense of when or where, just the feelings and memory of that time. Still, it evokes emotions, sets a tone, and helps the readers better understand the protagonist.

Here's a passage of interior monologue from José Saramago's novel *Blindness*, in which it's a little more obvious what the point-of-view character, the doctor's wife—the only character in the narrative who has not gone blind—is thinking:

> Now, with her eyes fixed on the scissors hanging on the wall, the doctor's wife was asking herself, What use is my eyesight? It had exposed her to

greater horror than she could ever have imagined. It had convinced her that she would rather be blind, nothing else.

Notice how her thought "What use is my eyesight?" is in first person, so the reader knows these are her thoughts. But the exposition that follows is still coming from her point of view and can also be considered her thoughts, integrated into the narrative voice.

Interior monologue is very intimate and allows readers to temporarily step inside the mind of a character. Characters really only have a few ways of reflecting that invite the reader in to experience it: Your protagonist can speak his thoughts to another character; he can write his thoughts down; or, through interior monologue, he can think and reflect on what's happened. Dialogue fails as a contemplative technique because most of us don't reflect aloud—we quietly ruminate in thought, or occasionally in writing.

Since interior monologue naturally slows the pace of your prose, use it sparingly in noncontemplative scenes. In a scene wholly devoted to contemplation, however, you have an opportunity to step back from the action and delve into the world of thoughts, which is why these scenes need to be placed strategically in your narrative. Use a contemplative scene purposely when you want to slow things down and shed insight on your character that dialogue and action simply can't convey.

OPENING CONTEMPLATIVE SCENES

In the aftermath of an action, suspense, or dramatic scene in which big plot events and emotional extremes were central, you want to get to the contemplation early and signal to the reader that a slowdown is taking place from the very beginning of the scene. If you open a contemplative scene with a lot of action, for instance, the reader may feel unfairly detoured by the contemplation that follows. Some of the most common ways to open a contemplative scene include using interior monologue, setting description, or transitional action.

Opening with Interior Monologue

The main requirement for opening your contemplative scene with interior monologue is that the character's thoughts be related to the scene that came before. Don't force the readers to guess what your protagonist is reflecting on—make it clear.

In Charles Dickens's novel *Great Expectations*, protagonist Pip—a young boy who lives with his older sister and her husband—is accosted one morning by an escaped convict who demands that Pip bring him food and drink. Out of terror, Pip does so, at great risk to himself. The next scene, which also happens to be the first scene of a new chapter, opens with Pip reflecting on the fact that he has not been arrested or punished for what he's done:

> I fully expected to find a Constable in the kitchen, waiting to take me up. But not only was there no Constable there, but no discovery had yet been made of the robbery.

The opening lines let the reader know that this is going to be a scene in which Pip is reflecting on his actions. A couple of lines is enough to let the reader know there will be thinking going on, but the interior monologue can continue for much longer. Back to our *Great Expectations* example: Though the scene includes some small actions, for much of the remaining scene, Pip can barely pay attention to what is happening around him because he's so focused on his inner experience, worrying about the trouble he's sure to get in:

> Joe and I going to church, therefore, must have been a moving spectacle for compassionate minds. Yet, what I suffered outside was nothing to what I underwent within. The terrors that had assailed me whenever Mrs. Joe had gone near the pantry, or out of the room, were only to be equaled by the remorse with which my mind dwelt on what my hands had done.

When you open with interior monologue, you get straight to the point and signal to the reader that the character has something on his mind. It's a simple, fluid way to transition into a contemplative scene.

The key thing to remember here is that thoughts are slow and timeless, so pages and pages of them will drag your pace down to a crawl. You want to make sure that the emphasis of a contemplative scene is on thoughts, but that they are not the sole content of the scene—just as Pip's thoughts overlay the regular events of the day.

Opening with Setting Description

Setting description is a nice way to open a scene because it grounds the reader in physical reality first without containing any action—the reader can see where the protagonist is before she delves into his inner turmoil. But this technique works especially well when you can use the setting as a kind of reflective surface off of which the character can bounce or form his thoughts, like in the example below from Jill McCorkle's novel *Carolina Moon*. Mack's wife, Sarah, has been in a coma for years, though he still feels the need to be faithful to her. Yet he's falling for another woman, June, and in the very bedroom where Sarah's sleeping body lies, he and June embraced. In the next scene, he's deeply reflective and concerned.

McCorkle opens the scene with a description of the setting that evokes images of family—which Mack no longer has—and uses it as a segue into Mack's internal world:

> Mack sits on the porch and watches the lights go out in the houses around him. The house to his left has long been dark, the children who run screaming all afternoon tucked into their beds and sleeping peacefully. He imagines the tired mama with her feet propped up, belly swollen, dim lamp swaying overhead. Even the college kids have turned in for the night, the only window lit being the stark white bathroom that glares in full view. Sarah used to wonder why they didn't get a shade, a curtain; instead, there was an all-day parade of young men with their backs turned to the world outside.

Notice how Mack's thoughts are stirred up in relationship to the environment he shared with his wife—a very natural and realistic way for a character to begin reflecting on events. As he looks around their neighborhood, there's no way to avoid thinking about her, and thus his guilt over falling for June, so the setting is effectively used as a way to get his thoughts on the subject of his wife. The scene could have opened something like this: "Mack felt guilty about kissing June in front of Sarah," but that's a narrative technique with no emotional weight. The way McCorkle does it, the reader sees the world that Mack shared with Sarah and understands his complex thoughts and feelings on the subject better, giving the scene greater dramatic impact.

When you use setting details to elicit a character's thoughts and feelings, your character's emotional responses will feel more integrated and the details will give the illusion of action, which contemplative scenes are scarce on; as Mack's thoughts interact with his environment, readers get a sense of action, even though there really isn't any. It's important to keep the energy from falling completely flat in a contemplative scene, and a great way to keep it alive is by having the character's thoughts interact with the setting.

Opening with Transitional Action

Sometimes a contemplative scene is, in essence, a continuation of the scene that came before, so you may begin by concluding the action of the prior scene. For example, at the end of a cliffhanger scene, a woman may have just watched her home erupt in flames. In the next scene, she may be standing by, watching the firemen put out the flames and reflecting on how her life will change.

Ending a scene before an action is resolved—a suspenseful or cliffhanger ending—is actually a strong technique because it keeps the reader worried about the character. If you're coming off of a scene with a cliffhanger ending, you have many opportunities to open a contemplative scene by concluding the actions of the previous scene.

When you do this, don't worry about keeping that same cliffhanger energy alive; when you move into contemplative scenes, it's okay to bring the tension and the energy down—in fact, that's the point. Use a minimal amount of small actions and let them quickly lead to contemplation.

For example, in Steven Sherrill's wonderful allegorical novel *The Minotaur Takes a Cigarette Break*, the protagonist M, an immortal Minotaur (half man, half bull), works as a line cook in a Southern restaurant.

He's lonely and awkward and has trouble making friends, but a waitress, Kelly, has steadily been making overtures to him for months. In one scene they wind up making love, but midway through, Kelly has an epileptic seizure. Afraid and unsure of how to deal with human afflictions, M flees the scene, and neither M nor the reader knows if Kelly is okay or not; M may have consigned her to death. The next scene concludes his flight as M is driving away from the scene:

> Pulling to a stop at the traffic light where Independence Boulevard goes from four narrow lanes to six narrow lanes, the Vega stalls and the Minotaur has to pump the throttle to restart it. He hates this stretch of road. David, a font of useless knowledge, says it's the busiest and most dangerous five miles of asphalt in the entire state.

Notice Sherrill's careful choice of actions here—M is fleeing the scene of Kelly's seizure. The actions at the opening of the next scene serve mainly to let the reader know where M is in relationship to the last scene (and also to offer a metaphor for where he is in his life: stalled, and possibly in danger, if Kelly is dead). Despite the fact that Kelly might be in mortal jeopardy, M is not a human man who knows to call 911, and the reader is wondering what he's going to do next and how he could just leave her like that. Notice how Sherrill shifts gears and moves quickly into the realm of thoughts.

Make sure in a contemplative scene that opens with transitional action that the action relates to or concludes the action from the prior scene, offers some thematic or metaphoric subtext, and then moves quickly into the realm of your characters' thoughts.

CHARACTER AND PLOT

Now that you have an idea of how to open a contemplative scene, it's important to keep in mind its fundamental purpose: to get as intimate as possible with your protagonist as he experiences the consequences of the inciting incident introduced in your beginning scenes. You want to use these reflective scenes to move into his most inner thoughts and reflections. When you focus on your protagonist's thoughts for a prolonged period of time, the reader gets a very intimate experience of his feelings and perceptions. Because of their inherent slowed quality, these scenes should be used sparingly, as noted earlier, after your character has undergone something intense, dramatic, or painful. You want to create a realistic pause for him—and the reader—to process what he's experienced.

To keep the contemplation relevant to your plot, you want to be sure that your protagonist does the following:

- Has realistic and appropriate responses to a plot event; i.e., this is not a time for random memories of childhood, etc.
- Grapples with something that has recently happened in the narrative (the prior scene is ideal), or that is about to happen
- Uses the contemplation scene to make a plan of action, weigh his options, or make some sort of decision related to plot events

Contemplative scenes are not a time for high drama; they provide an opportunity for the protagonist to make sense of the tragedy, wild success, or unexpected turn that has just taken place in her life.

Let's look at these three points in a scene from Walker Percy's novel *The Moviegoer*. In it, playboy Binx Bolling keeps dating the wrong women—those who don't love him, and those he doesn't truly love. When he unwittingly falls for Kate Cutrer, a suicidal beauty (and also his cousin), nobody is pleased about it, especially not Kate's mother, his aunt. Yet their relationship offers the two unlikely lovers a kind of redemption, and after spending a weekend together at Carnivale in New Orleans, Binx is deeply reflective and worried … and truly in love with Kate. Here is a moment midscene where he begins to think about what has happened:

> Nothing remains but desire, and desire comes howling down Elysian Fields like a mistral. My search has been abandoned; it is no match for my aunt, her rightness and her despair, her despairing of me and her despairing of herself. Whenever I take leave of my aunt after one of her serious talks, I have to find a girl.
>
> Fifty minutes of waiting for Kate on the ocean wave and I am beside myself. What has happened to her? She has spoken to my aunt and kicked me out. There is nothing to do but call Sharon at the office. The little pagoda of aluminum and glass, standing in the neutral ground of

Elysian Fields at the very heart of the uproar of a public zone, is trim and pretty on the outside but evil-smelling within. Turning slowly around, I take note of the rhymes in pencil and the sad cartoons of solitary lovers; the wire thrills and stops and thrills and in the interval there comes into my ear my own breath as if my very self stood beside me and would not speak. The phone does not answer. Has she quit?

Notice how this scene achieves the points laid out above. First, Binx grapples with his difficult feelings: He's torn between his desire for Kate, his aunt's disapproval, and his own tendency to use women as a distraction from his feelings. Second, he comes to a decision here, too, to call Sharon—he trusts her opinion and wants to run his feelings by someone who will not shame or scold him. Finally, his reactions, while they are emotional, are appropriate: Here he finally has fallen in love with someone—with a history of suicidal tendencies, no less—and she hasn't shown up to meet him as she said she would. His fear and anxiety are getting the best of him.

When you slow things down to reveal thoughts and feelings in this way, you want to be sure that your protagonist works out issues specific to plot events and comes to a point of change or choice as a result. While people contemplate all kinds of things in real life, from the good to the downright dull, musings in fiction about how great life is tend to get boring fast. Save contemplation for those topics which are most revealing—the ones that are difficult.

DRAMATIC TENSION

In chapter seven, we talked about giving your protagonist at least one new plot situation or piece of information, as well as a catalyst or antagonist to interact with, in each scene. However, a contemplative scene is the one scene type where you're not obligated to do either of those things. What you *must* do, however, is find a way to keep dramatic tension alive without much action and with limited character interaction. How do you do this?

- **INCLUDE INTERNAL CONFLICT.** The reason for a contemplative scene is to allow the characters and the reader to digest and make sense of complex decisions and actions. So, whether your character is forced to have time to himself—through jail, kidnapping, or just waking up alone one morning—or feels the need to take that time to understand what has happened to him, the main criteria of the scene is that he actively struggles to come to terms with something, like Binx Bolling did. You want to show that there is an emotional struggle in your protagonist's heart. She should be thinking about her options and wondering what will happen. She should be struggling to make sense of more than one feeling. She should not know until the scene's end what she wants or needs to do next.

- **INCLUDE UNSPECIFIED DANGER.** An absence of action or other characters does not necessarily mean that a scene will feel relaxed. People contemplate in dangerous situations too, so you can keep the tension alive by creating a sense of danger on the horizon or anxiety in the moment. Maybe your protagonist has been kidnapped, but the captors have left him alone for a few hours. Maybe a man's beloved wife has gone missing and you show him walking through his house, handling her possessions, wondering what has happened to her.
- **CREATE AN EERIE OR TENSE ATMOSPHERE.** Use the setting to your advantage by considering how weather, physical geography, and objects can serve to create an uncomfortable and tense environment for your character to contemplate in. (We'll discuss this more in the next section.) For example, if you want to create a tense contemplative scene and you are considering whether to set it in the protagonist's sunny, cheerful backyard or on the side of a road after his car has broken down, consider that the lonely road in the broken-down car has far more potential for tension—that is, creating a sense of potential conflict or crisis for the protagonist.

In Camille DeAngelis's novel *Mary Modern*, a blend of the literary and the fantastic, Lucy Morrigan, the infertile daughter of a genetic scientist, is preparing to clone a child through the use of her grandmother's DNA and her own womb. As she searches for a clipping of her grandmother's hair, she ventures into the attic, where she finds the scrap of cloth that bears drops of her grandmother's blood. Through careful description, DeAngelis sets an eerie mood for the act that Lucy is contemplating:

> Most attics are unpleasant places: cobwebs swaying in the breath of stale wind stirred up by the opening of the door, or perhaps a draft through a hole in the roof or a broken windowpane: the smells of mildew and dust and mothballs; the fear that any given thing you touch will fall to pieces in your hands. Even the natural oil on a clean fingertip leaves a stain on old wood. Why come here, why putter through all these material reminders of lives long since lived?

These careful details evoke a sense of decay and decrepitude. As Lucy contemplates the illegal act of cloning her own kin, with the intention of creating life, these setting and object details create a feeling of tension and foreboding that causes the reader to worry about the consequences of Lucy's actions.

In a contemplative scene, your setting details should reflect the emotional content of your character's contemplation. A despairing person might best contemplate suicide in a lonely setting—a deserted room, an empty hotel. A person contemplating a rash and violent act, in contrast, could be mirrored by a loud, overwhelming setting, such as a carnival, or by objects that speak to a feeling of anger—a lit match or a nest of disturbed hornets.

SETTING

Contemplation scenes rely heavily upon mood and ambiance. In some cases, setting might even be the reason your protagonist has so much time to think. For instance, a protagonist in prison, trapped in a cave, or making a long, slow journey will obviously have time to contemplate the state of his life. As your scene progresses, you have an opportunity to focus on the small details that often get passed over in dramatic or action-driven scenes. If your narrative is about a family tragedy, a contemplative scene should, through the specific setting details you choose, convey a sense of melancholy and sorrow through dark colors, low light, and any significant objects that can help to convey this mood.

More important, though, you can give your protagonist something physical to bounce his thoughts and feelings off of. Since there is very little action in a contemplative scene, weave in setting details intermittently with interior monologue so that your protagonist isn't just sitting in a vacuum.

In this excerpt of a scene from Neil Gaiman's fantasy novel *The Ocean at the End of the Lane*, the protagonist is returning after many years to the scene of his childhood, where he has some very dark memories. The closer he gets to home in this contemplative scene, the more the setting reflects his growing anxiety:

> The slick black road became narrower, windier, became the single-lane track I remembered from my childhood, became packed earth and knobbly, bone-like flints.
>
> Soon I was driving, slowly, bumpily, down a narrow lane with brambles and briar roses on each side, wherever the edge was not a stand of hazels or a wild hedgerow. It felt like I had driven back in time. That lane was how I remembered it, when nothing else was.

The use of the details "slick, black," and especially "bone-like" create an eerie atmosphere. This setting that gets rougher and wilder the deeper down he goes is also a metaphor for the way the protagonist feels about his childhood, and it provides a dark edge to his contemplation. By the time he reaches the old neighbor's house, he's deep in contemplation:

> I had been here, hadn't I, a long time ago? I was sure I had. Childhood memories are sometimes covered and obscured beneath the things that come later, like childhood toys forgotten at the bottom of a crammed adult closet, but they are never lost for good.

Focusing on specific setting details throughout a contemplative scene—and not just at the beginning, as we saw earlier in this chapter—not only creates a vivid atmosphere and mood, but also keeps the pace from slowing to an absolute drag. Here you can give the reader a chance to literally stop and smell the roses or recoil at the stench of a battle scene, letting impressions sink in and atmosphere build toward decisions that your protagonist will need to make.

ENDING A CONTEMPLATIVE SCENE

Since the pace of a contemplative scene is more like that of a gentle stream than of rushing rapids, when it comes time to end it you will want to change the energy just slightly in preparation for the next scene.

After contemplation, action returns. Once a character has had time to think and reflect, he will need to take some kind of action to get the plot moving forward again.

So, depending on the type of scene you intend to come next, here are some ideas for ending a contemplative scene on an up-tempo beat, building back toward action:

- **END WITH AN ACTION CLIFFHANGER.** After all that myopic thinking or careful attention to surroundings, your protagonist may suddenly find himself backed into a corner, a gun at his neck, or a cliff at his back. Contemplative scenes often allow other characters to catch up to your protagonist—after all, he's been preoccupied. A cliffhanger ending is great preparation for an action scene to follow.

- **END WITH A MOMENT OF DECISION.** If your character has been grappling with a dilemma, the ending is a great place to show the reader that she has made a decision. You don't necessarily need to give away what the decision is, but you could, for instance, end a scene in which the protagonist has been debating whether to tell her husband she's been cheating on him with her picking up the phone; or a man might grab his gun, get in his car, or take a purposeful action that lets the reader know something has been decided. The decision should, of course, relate to whatever issue the protagonist has been grappling with in that scene.

- **END WITH A SURPRISE.** Because contemplative scenes are so quiet and slow, the reader is not focused on the characters or events that are ostensibly taking place outside of the scene. This leaves room for all manner of surprises. While the character is sitting and thinking, something outside of his control could happen, and the very end of a contemplative scene is a great place to drop in such a surprise.

- **END WITH FORESHADOWING.** Since most contemplative scenes don't naturally lend themselves to action in the scene at hand, you can end the scene with a bit of foreshadowing that tells the reader there will be action, or dialogue, or some kind of pace quickening, in the next scene.

At the end of the scene above in Gaiman's novel, the protagonist finds himself before a pond near the neighbor's house. This pond will go on to play a very significant part in the story that unfolds—or rather, in the story that unfolded in his childhood, which he is now about to relive, as well as the forward plot. This contemplative scene sets the reader up to drop into the past, which holds some very terrible memories that the protagonist has blocked out for good reasons:

> The pond was smaller than I remembered. There was a little wooden shed on the far side, and, by the path, an ancient, heavy, wood-and-metal bench. The peeling wooden slats had been painted green a few years ago. I sat on the bench, and stared at the reflection of the sky in the water, at the scum duckweed at the edges, and the half-dozen lily pads. Every now and again, I tossed a hazelnut into the middle of the pond, the pond that Lettie Hempstock had called …
>
> It wasn't the sea, was it?
>
> She would be older than I am now, Lettie Hempstock. … I wondered if we had ever fallen in the water. Had I pushed her into the duck pond, that strange girl who lived in the farm at the very bottom of the lane? I remembered her being in the water. Perhaps she had pushed me in too.
>
> Where did she go? America? No, *Australia*. That was it. Somewhere a long way away.
>
> And it wasn't the sea. It was the ocean.
>
> Lettie Hempstock's ocean.
>
> I remembered that, and, remembering that, I remembered everything.

No matter how you choose to end your contemplative scene, you want to keep in mind that you are setting up the next scene, and action follows contemplation very nicely because it provides the energy necessary to balance the equation of your narrative. You may choose to use your contemplative scene to lead your character toward change, toward action, toward drama or suspense to suit the demands of your plot. Rarely should you place two contemplative scenes back to back, however, as this may slow your pace too much.

CONTEMPLATIVE SCENE MUSE POINTS

- Use contemplative scenes to slow down action in the narrative.
- Signal that the contemplative scene has begun as quickly as possible.
- Focus on the protagonist's inner life.
- Allow the protagonist to grapple with a conflict, dilemma, or decision.
- Select the setting details that will create dramatic tension and set a mood.
- Use the end of the scene to shift the energy toward action.

16

SUSPENSE SCENES

Suspense, at its most primal, is a state of uncertainty that produces anxiety. In fiction, no matter whether the condition creating the suspense is positive or negative (Will she say yes to the handsome rogue's proposal? Will he be flung off the cliff?), the effect on the reader tends to be the same: The heart races, nerves are tight, and an aura of apprehension hangs over the scene. This is a good thing. The way to get the reader to white knuckle her way through a suspense scene is by delaying the inevitable outcome of the trouble your characters are in.

Suspense scenes can be found in almost every genre of fiction, though mysteries and thrillers capitalize on these scenes more so than romance or literary novels do. For a scene to qualify as suspenseful it must display certain qualities:

- The protagonist must find himself in jeopardy or quickly get caught in the middle of trouble or danger.
- The emotional, physical, or spiritual stakes for the character must become more complicated as the scene progresses.
- The emotional intensity must increase for the protagonist, not letting up until the end.
- The events of the scene or the other characters must exert pressure on the protagonist to change or act.
- The outcome of the situation must remain uncertain for more time than it is resolved.

Use suspense scenes to add emotional voltage to your narrative, to up the emotional ante for your protagonist, and to add complications to your plot that will require new solutions. (Half the fun of reading is following a protagonist as he gets into and out of and then back into trouble again.) There's almost no bad place for a suspense scene other than those scenes whose purpose is to conclude and reveal information. They're especially good for raising the tension after a contemplative scene or a dialogue-driven scene whose main purpose is to provide plot information; in those instances, a suspense scene will get the reader excited again and provide your protagonist with new challenges. A reader in the midst of a suspense scene experiences a need to press forward urgently, to relieve the sweet agony of waiting and wondering, so consider using such scenes before an epiphany scene to help drive your characters toward big conclusions and realizations. You can also use them heavily in the middle of your story, where plots often sag.

Pacing, the speed at which action plays out and information is revealed, plays a large role in the success or failure of a suspense scene. When building to painful realizations or inevitable outcomes, it's good to slow the pace by focusing on small details or by using a few well-placed lines of exposition or interior monologue. The key element that creates suspense is the agony of not knowing what is going to happen next. Of course, a fast-paced scene can often add that much-needed surge of adrenaline that propels the reader forward. Generally, though, suspense is built upon slow and carefully measured action that builds and holds tension.

Suspense can be lost if you try to rush into it. Think of how nerve-racking it is to watch a horror movie in which a character walks slowly down a darkened hall toward a room where he has heard a frightening noise. If he runs down that hall, there's no time for suspense. But by walking, slowly and fearfully, he allows the viewers to feel his anxiety. The same technique works to build suspense in your narrative—the more time the reader has to feel nervous, the more effective the scene will be.

OPENING A SUSPENSE SCENE

Suspense scenes should open in a way that gives the reader immediate concern for the protagonist. While your protagonist doesn't need to be dangling from scaffolding just yet, he might be starting the climb. Or you can create a more subtle uneasiness—the protagonist can simply feel that something is not quite right about the unusual silence or overly bright lights of a building. In a suspense scene, you want to give the reader an *uh-oh* feeling, a sense of trouble, which should begin to mount and reach a crescendo of pressure toward the end of the scene.

Let's look at a suspense scene from Paul Auster's novel *The Book of Illusions*. Though a literary novel, he works in suspense masterfully. David Zimmer, a translator recovering from the loss of his wife and two sons in a plane crash more than a year before, has just arrived home after a harrowing drive and a minor accident in the rain. The inciting incident of the plot was a letter he received, inviting him to meet Hector Mann, the elusive silent-screen comedian, thought to be dead, about whom David wrote a book. David is not convinced of the veracity of the letter and has written back demanding proof that Mann is actually alive. His proof shows up in the form of a mysterious woman, Alma Grund, sent to fetch him back to New Mexico. Notice how the scene begins fairly benignly but causes a prickle of anxiety:

> We found the keys with her flashlight and when I opened the door and stepped into the house, I flicked on the lights in the living room. Alma Grund came in after me—a short woman in her mid- to late thirties, dressed in a blue silk blouse and tailored gray pants.

The fact that the strange woman comes in after him is cause for concern. The scene takes on more suspense when, within a couple of paragraphs, David begins to act irrationally even though Alma has done nothing threatening.

> Just give me five minutes, she said. I can explain everything.
>
> I don't like it when people trespass on my property, I said, And I don't like it when people jump out at me in the middle of the night. You don't want me to have to throw you out of here, do you?
>
> She looked up at me then, surprised by my vehemence, frightened by the undertow of rage in my voice. I thought you wanted to see Hector, she said and as she spoke those words she took a few more steps into the

MAKE A SCENE REVISED AND EXPANDED

house, removing herself from the vicinity of the door in case I was planning to carry out my threat.

Here's the brilliant moment of this scene: The protagonist, David, starts out as the aggressor—the reader isn't afraid *for* him, but that he's going to harm this poor woman. But subtly, with a slight shift, Auster turns the tables when Alma "took a few more steps into the house." Those few steps are full of suspense. What does she want? Why isn't she afraid of him? Suddenly, Alma has taken the power. And the suspense has only just begun. David still isn't afraid, but the reader is, and rightfully so, for when David comes back downstairs from his bath and finds that Alma is still in his house, after trying unsuccessfully to convince him with words, she takes desperate action:

> The gun was in her hand. It was a small silver-plated revolver with a pearl handle, no more than half the size of the cap guns I had played with as a boy. As she turned in my direction and lifted her arm, I could see that the hand at the end of her arm was shaking.
>
> This isn't me, she said. I don't do things like this. Ask me to put it away, and I will. But we have to go now.

To build suspense, you don't need to throw in a gun or a physical altercation, though those will work. Suspense can be created by shifting the power back and forth between characters, letting the reader wonder if your protagonist is going to grab the ancient treasure out of the enemy's hands or if he's going to fall into that burning pit of magma.

David later wrests the gun out of Alma's hands and shocks them both by putting it to his own head, jacking up the emotional intensity—the stakes—more and more until David finally pulls the trigger.

To create suspense at the beginning of a scene, you can do the following:

- **INTRODUCE A CATALYST OR ANTAGONIST WHOSE INTENTIONS SEEM SUSPECT TO THE PROTAGONIST.** David, and consequently the reader, does not trust Alma from the very start because of the manner of her arrival—suddenly, without notice, and in the middle of the night.
- **ALLOW YOUR PROTAGONIST TO FEEL THREATENED OR PRESSURED BY ANOTHER CHARACTER OR EVENT AND TO RESIST THE ENSUING DE-**

MAND OR REQUEST. David is tired, wet, upset, and just wants a bath. Alma's presence and her demand that he fly to New Mexico with her puts pressure on him—his family died in a plane crash, remember, and he's emotionally unstable.

- **ALLOW YOUR PROTAGONIST, UNDER PRESSURE, TO REACT OR ACT OUT IN A WAY THAT CAUSES UNEXPECTED CONFLICT.** David becomes emotionally volatile with Alma. If he had just let her talk in the first place, it's likely she would not have used the gun.

Remember that suspense is about *delay*. The longer the anxiety-producing event goes on, and the more pressure you can put on your character in the scene, the more suspense you'll build.

MOOD, SETTING, AND SENSORY DETAILS

The mood you create also has a large impact on suspense. Mood is conveyed through the physical conditions, such as setting and weather, that your protagonist finds herself in. In Auster's suspense scene, he zooms the focus down onto the landscape of the characters' bodies—to the exclusion of the physical world around them—which keeps the reader's attention uncomfortably planted where the action is, in the distance between David and Alma.

Other authors very purposefully use the senses to create a suspenseful mood, as in this example from Tana French's detective novel *The Trespasser*. Detective Antoinette Conway keeps thinking she sees someone casing her house. Added to the fact that she is already paranoid about members of her own squad, the reader doesn't know what to think. In this scene, her paranoia becomes a reality:

> I'm working on my reply when something moves, in the corner of my eye. I whip around, not fast enough. A big dark shape skims away from my window before I can get a decent look.
>
> I grab my keys and dive for the door. By the time I get it open, the road is empty. …
>
> I'm pulling open the car door when the light twitches. There's someone under the street lamp at the top of the road: a tall guy, hovering. I

slam the car door and take one step in that direction and he vanishes, into the dark around the corner, going at a fair old clip.

Notice how just a few well-placed images add up to a mood of suspenseful anxiety: "a big dark shape," and "a tall guy, hovering"—especially since it's nighttime, and Conway is home alone.

Sensory details are tailor-made for suspense because they lend themselves to metaphor and mood well, and through them you can affect the reader's senses, bringing authenticity to the scene. A terrible odor, or the creepy slickness of a dank cellar, can turn an otherwise normal scene into a suspenseful one.

Some great suspense-building setting and sensory techniques include the following:

- **WEATHER.** Using dramatic weather, such as storms, blizzards, or a harsh beating sun, is a great way to create suspense if it imperils your characters, keeps them from their goals, or adds complications. Be mindful that the weather relates to your plot.

- **DECAY.** In the physical world, a house or boat or car in a state of decay will inevitably create suspense. Rotting wood, a half-submerged car in a lake, or a trail of faded old clothing will cause the reader to feel concerned that the protagonist could meet the same fate as those things.

- **COLOR AND LIGHT.** Dark colors lend themselves to dark emotions; dark fabrics or art pieces can add a note of suspense. Intensely bright lights can cause feelings of pressure, as when a character is being interrogated or is caught in a spotlight, trying to escape.

- **TOUCH.** There are many subtle ways to use the sense of touch to create suspense, particularly when a character fears he is in danger. Think of the eerie nature of touch: the feeling of a hand on the back of a neck; the slippery quality of blood on skin; the light pressure of breath in a person's ear.

The beauty of setting and sensory details is that you can add them in minimally—it doesn't take more than a handful of small, well-placed details to evoke a feeling of suspense.

The difference between a suspense scene and other scene types is that you infuse uncertainty and anxiety into a suspense scene in every way possible, not just through setting details. So don't forget that you must introduce new plot information in a suspenseful way, too.

RAISING THE STAKES

Suspense scenes are fantastic when you are about to take your plot in a new direction by changing your character's fate or adding complications to his story. They dramatize these twists, rather than narrate them in exposition.

In Sarah Waters's novel *Tipping the Velvet*, protagonist Nan King, a waitress in her family's oyster bar, comes alive the day she meets Kitty Butler, a vaudeville actress. She is drawn into Kitty's world, joins her on tour, and quickly becomes a part of the act, performing in nineteenth-century London. They also begin a love affair they can carry on only in secret. Nan takes a long overdue leave of absence to visit her home, and when she returns, full of eagerness to see Kitty, Waters builds suspense by hinting at Nan's fate before Nan realizes it herself.

> Our house, when I gazed up at it from the street, was, as I had hoped, quite dark and shuttered. I walked on tip-toe up the steps, and eased my key into the lock. The passageway was quiet: even our landlady and her husband seemed still abed. I laid down my bags, and took off my coat. There was a cloak already hanging from the hat-stand, and I squinted at it: it was Walter's. How queer, I thought, he must have come here yesterday, and forgotten it!—and soon, creeping up the darkened staircase, I forgot it myself.
>
> I reached Kitty's door, and put my ear to it. I had expected silence, but there was a sound from beyond it—a kind of lapping sound, as of a kitten at a saucer of milk.

Waters strategically slows the pace down to a near crawl, so that the reader's focus is delivered very carefully to the most important clue: Walter's cloak on the hook. She also cleverly calls the door "Kitty's door." It has previously been Nan and Kitty's door, but after this scene, Nan will never live there again. While Nan is curious at the "kind of lapping sound" coming from behind the door, she still doesn't realize that her fate is about to change. By keeping Nan ignorant while cluing in the reader, the author keeps the reader in suspense, waiting for the moment when Nan's heart will be broken and her life (and plot) changed forever.

The longer you can delay the moment of conflict through suspense, the more intense the conflict will be for the reader. When you can also keep your own character ignorant of the oncoming conflict, you have far more possibility for a dramatic change, which is the purpose of good suspense.

PLAYING UP THE UNEXPECTED

Strange or surprising actions that challenge a protagonist's sense of normalcy, creating confusion that adds pressure to the anxiety, can drive suspense to a crescendo. Here's a fast-paced moment of suspense in Justine Musk's horror novel *BloodAngel*. Musk is a deft and careful writer who doesn't go for big, melodramatic horror. Instead, she puts her character Lucas Maddox in a very unusual situation and does not give him, or the reader, time to understand what's happening. The effect is disturbingly suspenseful:

> He had been waiting for maybe fifteen, twenty minutes when he caught movement from the corner of his eye.
>
> He turned.
>
> Saw an animal in the yellow grass.
>
> He blinked twice, looked again.
>
> Skittering crab-like on all fours: animal-girl in jeans and stained white T-shirt, sun glinting off her pale hair—
>
> He thought: *No.*
>
> And the girl stood in front of him.
>
> Smiling.

What she does after that smile is pretty gruesome, but the suspenseful buildup, though quick, still lets the reader feel unnerved first.

Even if you don't write horror, challenging a protagonist's sense of normalcy is a useful suspense-building technique. Notice how the way she moves on all fours, like a crab, is creepy and unnatural, and makes the reader—as well as the character—look twice. You can challenge normalcy in many ways. For instance, you might confuse your protagonist. Not quite trusting one's eyes can lead to suspense: Was that man in black following him or just walking down the same streets? Did he actually see his dead wife in the crowd? You might also use bad weather, loud noises, fatigue, or physical illness to play with your protagonist's (and thus your reader's) sense of reality.

ENDING A SUSPENSE SCENE

Eventually, you must end the suspense, even if only temporarily. Sometimes one kind of suspense can lead to another. For instance, in *The Book of Illusions*, at the final moment of the scene after the suspense has mounted to a terrifying crescendo, David pulls the trigger, and this is what happens:

> I finally saw what the trouble was. The safety catch was on. She hadn't remembered to release it. If not for that mistake, one of those bullets would have been in my head.

The suspense doesn't end when the gun fails to go off; it ends when David reflects on the fact that he just survived his own death through a fluke (which also inserts a powerful symmetry into the subtext when you consider that his wife and sons did not have any luck on their side during their plane crash). You might notice the urge to take a breath here, now that the sense of imminent danger is over. To break the suspense, you must conclude the action and offer a pause—either a literal one or one of reflection from the character's point of view. For all the reader knows, Alma pulls out another gun in the next scene, but the reader isn't there yet—she's basking in a moment of relief. To conclude suspense, you finally give the reader what you've been withholding throughout the scene.

You can also end a scene of this type by maintaining the suspense right up to the end, leaving the scene in a state of limbo. In *BloodAngel*, the suspense persists:

> And in the moment before he blacked out, Lucas Maddox seized on the impossible fact that this was not a dream, not a drug.
> She had come for him.

By having a character lose consciousness, you end the scene but maintain the feeling of danger or trouble (hence, suspense).

If you leave your scene on a suspenseful ridge like that, however, you have to pick that dangling thread back up in the next scene, which means your next scene will have to open suspensefully, too—so consider whether that is what you want to do. This is one of the details about scene building that is so important to remember: You must always consider how the current scene will set up the scene that follows it.

One last caveat about suspense scenes: Too many of them in a row can take a toll on the reader. There's no perfect formula, but more than three suspense scenes in a row without relief is going to push the reader toward exhaustion. You might want to throw in a contemplative scene, or even just a dramatic but suspenseless scene, to temper the intensity.

SUSPENSE SCENE MUSE POINTS

- Open your scene in an uneasy or anxiety-provoking way.
- Throw your protagonist quickly into trouble.
- Add emotional intensity to the scene.
- Use sensory imagery to evoke a suspenseful mood.
- Let events or an antagonist add pressure to your protagonist through opposition.
- Delay conclusions to scene events and thwart character intentions.
- Either break the suspense at the scene's end or end on a cliff-hanger.

DIALOGUE SCENES

Dialogue is one of the most versatile elements of fiction writing. When done well, dialogue can even be a scene stealer—most of the great lines in literature were *spoken* by characters, not narrated. This chapter will focus on scenes that are composed primarily of dialogue, not those with the occasional line of dialogue tossed in.

Dialogue scenes find their way into narratives of all genre types because of the flexibility of conversation, so undoubtedly you'll wind up using these scenes. When dialogue is done right, it tends to move quickly, and therefore it can be used to pick up the pace and propel your plot and characters forward. Dialogue is a great conflict builder, too, as characters can argue, fight, and profess sentiments in words. It's also a wonderful medium for building tension, as characters jockey for power, love, and understanding.

OPENING A DIALOGUE SCENE

Before you start the scene, you'll want to decide if you're going to use dialogue to convey action or to reveal character, plot, or backstory information (or some combination of these things). One of the most common errors writers make is the use of dialogue as filler, with characters discussing the time or the weather, or dumping too much information on the reader at once. Don't assume that dialogue scenes need to open in the middle of a conversation to bypass pleasantries, either—in fact, this is often a confusing way to open a scene. A dialogue scene can open with one of the elements discussed in chapter two—for instance, you can use a scenic launch, or a narrative, action, or character launch—but then move quickly into dialogue. Here are some essential guidelines for opening a dialogue scene:

- Ground the reader in the setting before the conversation begins.
- Let the conversation begin within the first couple of paragraphs.
- Involve your protagonist in the conversation.
- Make it clear who is speaking to whom.
- Infuse conflict or opposition into the dialogue.

Interrogation and police interview scenes in fiction are almost always dialogue scenes. In fact, they rely heavily upon a whiplike energy that passes between the characters, back and forth, putting pressure on a suspect or trying to shake free a witness's memory. In Tana French's mystery novel *The Secret Place*, murder detectives Moran and Conway are sent to St. Kilda's private school for girls to speak to the students on a tip that one of them, or perhaps several of them, know who killed a teenage boy whose case has gone cold. The detectives begin the methodical process of interviewing these not-always-forthcoming teenage girls in dialogue scenes and meet their toughest nut to crack yet:

> Julia Harte. Conway didn't brief me on her, not after how Rebecca had gone, but I knew as soon as Julia walked in the door she was the boss of that outfit. ...
>
> "Detective Conway," she said. Nice voice, deeper than most girls', more controlled. Made her sound older. "Did you miss us that much?"
>
> A smart-arse. That can work for us, work nicely. Smart-arses talk when they shouldn't, say anything as long as it'll come out good and snappy. ...
>
> I said, "I'm Stephan Moran. Julia Harte, right?"
>
> "At your service. What can I do for you?"
>
> Smart-arses want a chance to be smart. "You tell me. Anything you think I should know?"
>
> "About what?"
>
> "You pick." And I grinned at her, like we were old sparring partners who'd missed each other.

Julia grinned back. "Don't eat the yellow snow. Never play leapfrog with a unicorn."

Notice how the scene meets all the criteria laid out above: We get just enough on the physical aspects of Julia to help ground us in the scene and, since the detectives are still doing what they did in the last scene—interrogating students—we know where they are. The dialogue in these interrogations establishes details about the key suspects, drops new plot information, and reveals the detectives' characters, as each girl tests them in a different way. This dialogue scene establishes that Julia the "smart-arse" is not going to give up any information easily; she's going to play the detectives and make their job harder.

Though you want to get into the dialogue fairly quickly, you don't necessarily have to do so in the first sentence—it may even start a few paragraphs in. Remember, grounding the reader in physical details is important to prevent confusion, and the details can also reinforce qualities about the protagonist.

DIALOGUE AND BIG REVEALS

Dialogue is a wonderful technique for giving the reader necessary information without resorting to exposition. Through dialogue, you can show the reader who your protagonist is, reveal the effect the protagonist has on other characters, and introduce new plot information that drives the narrative forward.

Revealing Character

One of the best ways to express your protagonist's personality, feelings, and perceptions is through his own words. Doing so allows the reader to feel as though he is right there in the same place as the character, getting to know him through direct experience. When the purpose of a dialogue scene is to reveal character, it should do the following:

- Show the character speaking under pressure or in conflict. Always avoid mundane conversation.

- Let your protagonist's true nature come through in words. Is she brave? Then show her speaking words of hope and courage. Is he seductive? Let him pull out all verbal stops to seduce every woman he meets.
- Show her expressing her feelings or thoughts about the significant situation or the most recent plot events. Whether through the character's internal or external dialogue.

In Truman Capote's brilliant novella *Breakfast at Tiffany's*, his main character, Holly Golightly, is revealed to the reader through memorable dialogue. Holly is rash and bold and sexy and girlish all at once, and this is conveyed every time she opens her mouth or appears in a scene.

The first time the narrator meets Holly, it's via an exchange she has with a neighbor:

> The voice that came back, welling up from the bottom of the stairs, was silly-young and self-amused. "Oh darling, I am sorry. I lost the goddamn key."
>
> "You cannot go on ringing my bell. You must please, please have yourself a key made."
>
> "But I lose them all."
>
> "I work. I have to sleep." Mr. Yunioshi shouted. "But always you are ringing my bell. ..."
>
> "Oh, *don't* be angry, you *dear* little man: I won't do it again. And if you promise not to be angry"—her voice was coming nearer, she was climbing the stairs—"I might let you take those pictures we mentioned."

Though the phrase "silly-young and self-amused" tells us about Holly's tone, her words speak for themselves. If she is sorry, as she claims, then why does she refer to it as the "goddamn key"? Clearly, in her worldview, the key is at fault; she is not. She calls her neighbor *darling* and *dear* to soften him up, and then promises him a few lines later that if he lets her off the hook she might in turn let him "take those pictures we mentioned."

We suspect that Holly is used to manipulating with her charm and beauty to get her way. Just a few paragraphs into the scene, Holly Golightly has made an impression and demonstrated her personality.

When you use dialogue to reveal character, the dialogue should be stylized and suited specifically to the character. An educated person speaks differently from someone who never learned grammar. A rude person will say rude things and insult people with her words.

Revealing Plot Information

One of the most important uses of dialogue—and the most necessary in a plot-driven narrative—is to reveal plot-pertinent information that changes your protagonist, creates conflict, or leads the protagonist toward an epiphany. I like to think of this as the "Luke, I am your father" technique. Darth Vader tells Luke that he is not only Luke's sworn nemesis, but also his father, creating an iconic turning point in the movie's plot and in the development of Luke's character. This moment forces Luke to choose between good and evil, and tests his ability to resist his own destruction. Now, not all reveals are this epic, but dialogue is one of the best ways to drop these emotional bombs and drive the plot forward.

When using dialogue to reveal plot information, consider the following:

- **THE INFORMATION MUST BE EARNED.** Avoid the use of a *deus ex machina*. (This term, which translates to "god from the machine," comes from the Greek dramatic technique of literally dropping a god from above into a play, usually without foreshadowing the god's involvement, to solve difficult entanglements. In fiction, it refers to any overly simple or convenient action or character that solves difficult problems without any effort on the part of the main characters.)
- **YOU NEED TO SHOW YOUR PROTAGONIST'S EMOTIONAL REACTION TO THE NEW INFORMATION.** The reader needs to see the character exclaim, gasp, shout, speak a word of surprise.
- **THE INFORMATION SHOULD DROP IN THE MIDDLE OR AT THE END OF THE SCENE TO ACHIEVE THE GREATEST EMOTIONAL IMPACT.** This helps to create a sense of urgency in the reader.

Here's an example of a big revelation from Maryanne Stahl's novel *Forgive the Moon* that both reveals character and drives the plot forward. Amanda Kincaid comes to a Long Island beach resort for an annual family vacation. Her oldest daughter has left for college; her husband is involved with another woman, and their twenty-year marriage is crumbling; and her mother, who suffered from schizophrenia, has recently died in an accident.

The scene opens with Amanda's new lover coming to the door while her father is visiting her cottage. Her father doesn't know who the man is, but from the opening of the scene there's discord, a feeling that something is going to come to a head. And it does, but not in one fell swoop—the scene builds slowly and plausibly toward the revelation.

In the exchange of dialogue below, which falls in the middle of the scene, Amanda and her father—who have never been close—begin talking about mundane details, like Amanda's childhood fear of lightning, and segue to more serious topics of the past, such as her mother's illness, and then to Amanda's accusation that her father retreated not only from his ill wife, but from his children as well. At first her father is shocked, but then he asks her a question that begins the process of his revelation about her piano teacher:

> "Were you angry, Amanda, about my relationship with Gloria?"
>
> "What?" Gloria Price had taught me to play the piano, redirecting my adolescent pain and fueling the fire of my nascent passion for music. Eventually, she'd moved away, but not before she'd made me promise to pursue my talent.
>
> Gloria's voice was the first auditory hallucination my mother had ever described to me.
>
> "Gloria," I repeated.
>
> Suddenly, as though I'd been physically struck, I realized what my father was saying. "What do you mean?"
>
> His fingers rubbed the bridge of his nose beneath his glasses, lifting them till I thought they would fall off, but they stayed. He dropped his hands to his lap.
>
> "Gloria and I," he said softly.
>
> My stomach quivered, as though the low, rolling thunder outside had slipped in through the screen and become particles of air. My mouth grew watery, a sign I was going to vomit. I moved to lean toward the sink and as I did, sugar spilled out of the torn packet, pouring across one of my father's shoes. ...
>
> "Amanda," he began, reaching his hand around to my forehead. I slipped away from him.
>
> "It's the tea," I said without looking at him. "The acid."

My father retreated toward the table and sat back in his chair. He began again. "Your mother and I never discussed Gloria," he said, picking up his spoon and dropping it into his empty mug. "Not in any rational way."

I recalled my mother's accusations. Gloria was her enemy, trying to harm her, trying to steal her children: all said to be hallucinations, all dismissed as evidence of illness. Now it turned out my mother had been right after all. She'd been right and she'd been ill, both at the same time.

No one had believed her.

The revelation of her father's affair is doubly devastating as Amanda realizes that, due to her mother's illness, they thought she was just being paranoid. There are a number of elements in this revelatory scene that any writer can learn from. First, Stahl starts the scene with her protagonist caught in an unbalanced situation: Amanda is reluctantly spending time with her father when her lover comes to the door. She uses subtext to create foreshadowing: The lover's appearance points toward the other affair—her father's—that the scene reveals. Then, she uses segues, small transitions between related topics, to create a sense of conversation and a realistically measured pace. The conversation feels natural, like how people really talk. She uses her setting very well, too: Jamming two family members into a small space creates a sense of tension, of something waiting to explode. And then there is the weather. In the opening pages of the scene, Amanda's lover says to her, "Feels like a storm," and the author continues to pepper in details about the weather. (Of course, the real storm coming is an emotional one.) There's also the element of opposition: Amanda has a feeling that her father wants to talk, but she doesn't want to, so she tries a few unsuccessful strategies to urge her father to go to bed, building the tension. And finally—yes, there's more—the author shows how this information affects the protagonist: Not only does Amanda become physically ill, she curses at her father and then walks down the hallway, where she kicks his shoe in anger.

Revelations are best when they are complex and built toward slowly, so that they are not just two people standing in a room shouting words at each other. Use as many of the core scene elements as you can. Once the revelation comes, it should alter your protagonist in some way; whether her plot changes, or just her feelings, revelations should lead to some kind of shift.

INFUSING YOUR DIALOGUE SCENES WITH TENSION AND SUBTEXT

Now that we've looked at how to use a dialogue scene to reveal important character and plot information, let's look at how to build tension through opposition and how to use subtext to keep even your most heated exchanges from turning into meaningless shouting matches or unrealistic melodrama, as discussed in chapter ten. No matter what you want to reveal through your dialogue, infusing it with additional elements ensures a richer, more layered scene.

Creating Tension Through Tug-of-War Exchanges

In a strong fiction narrative, characters should want things from each other—information, affection, favors, material goods, and so on. The act of *wanting* powers both conflict and drama. When there's something desired, there is the potential for loss and gain—the essence of good drama. Dialogue should be, on some level, an act of bartering, which keeps tension alive during the course of the scene. I call this technique tug-of-war. And it doesn't just apply when characters are on opposite sides of a conflict; even allies and loved ones should speak as though they are continually passing a hot potato back and forth. To use this approach in dialogue, think of each character as both asking for something and withholding something at the same time. Use dialogue tug-of-war when you need to demonstrate differing points of view or to illustrate the dynamics of a relationship. This approach also works when your characters are doing the following:

- Exchanging insults or arguing over something
- Trying to manipulate another character
- Trying to seduce another character, or resist seduction
- Attempting to convince another character of a painful truth
- Fending off untrue or unjust accusations

Here's an example from Alice Hoffman's novel *The Ice Queen*, in which the unnamed narrator is weighing whether or not to tell her brother, Ned, a shocking secret she has turned up about his wife. What the conversation reveals is that Ned has a secret too, but to learn each other's secrets, they would have to give up their own first, and neither character is willing to do that yet:

> "So are you sure you don't want to know any secrets?"
> "Do you?"
> "You have secrets?" I was surprised. ...
> "Unknown truths," my brother joked. "At least to you. Known to me, of course. At least in theory. What I know and what I don't know, I'm not sure I can be the judge of that."
> "Oh forget it." I was annoyed.

The tug-of-war style of conversation delays the reader's access to Ned's secret (a piece of plot information, incidentally), thus building tension. Then the tension mounts even more when the narrator continues to keep *her* secret a little longer. The scene shows the reader that both characters have an investment in keeping secrets, so the reader has to keep going to find out how these secrets will converge and what effect they'll have when brought to light.

Here's another tug-of-war example, from J.M. Coetzee's Nobel Prize–winning novel, *Disgrace*. In apartheid-fueled South Africa, white professor David Lurie has come to stay with his estranged daughter, Lucy, to flee scrutiny after a scandal involving an affair with one of his college students. In trying to escape one terrible event, however, he becomes a part of another; he and his daughter are attacked in her home by local men as a territorial act. David was badly burned, and Lucy was raped—but David doesn't know this for sure since he was not in the room with her and she won't tell him what happened. Even so, he quickly urges Lucy to press charges against the boy, but Lucy has her own political and personal reasons for not wanting to do so. And there is the other, unspoken subtext that reminds us he wouldn't have been there for her at all if not for his own bad deeds. Notice the feeling of tug-of-war between them—how they both want something and are resisting something at the same time:

Sitting across the table from him, Lucy draws a deep breath, gathers herself, then breathes out again and shakes her head.

"Can I guess?" he says. "Are you trying to remind me of something?"

"Am I trying to remind you of what?"

"Of what women undergo at the hands of men?"

"Nothing could be farther from my thoughts. This has nothing to do with you, David. You want to know why I have not laid a particular charge with the police? I will tell you, as long as you agree not to raise the subject again. The reason is that, as far as I am concerned, what happened to me is a purely private matter. In another time, in another place it might be held to a public matter. But in this place, at this time, it is not. It is my business, mine alone."

"This place being what?"

"This place being South Africa."

"I don't agree. I don't agree with what you are doing. Do you think that by meekly accepting what happened to you, you can set yourself apart from farmers like Ettinger? Do you think what happened here was an exam: if you come through, you get a diploma and safe conduct into the future, or a sign to paint on the door lintel that will make the plague pass you by? That is not how vengeance works, Lucy. Vengeance is like a fire. The more it devours, the hungrier it gets."

"Stop it, David! I don't want to hear this talk of plagues and fires. I am not just trying to save my skin. If that is what you think, you miss the point entirely."

Notice in both of the previous examples how there's a sense of movement, of action, even though the authors don't provide the reader with any actual physical movements. This has to do with the pace of conversations—the tug-of-war approach gives the exchanges the quality of movement by infusing them with emotional energy. The respective conversations bounce back and forth between characters and carry with them a sense of change.

Playing Up Subtext

While the tug-of-war technique is excellent for increasing the tension in a dialogue scene, you don't want your exchanges to become a meaningless volley of words. What is the key to keeping that from happening? Subtext. People don't always say what they really mean; they withhold information and feelings, use language to manipulate and barter and hint. Because of this, you have a lot of opportunity to play with your subtext.

Here's an example of a powerful subtext at work in a conversation from David Guterson's novel *Snow Falling on Cedars*. Ishmael Chambers grew up on San Piedro Island, Washington, where as a young teenager he had a brief love affair with a Japanese girl named Hatsue. Their relationship was cut short, however, when Hatsue and her family and many more Japanese residents of the island were moved to the internment camp Manzanar after the attack on Pearl Harbor.

Now, years later, Ishmael is back in town to write about a trial in which Hatsue's husband is accused of murdering a local fisherman. Hatsue and Ishmael have not spoken in all these years, and there is lingering resentment and desire between them. In this instance, the subtext comes from their history, which is shown in flashback scenes throughout the book. That history informs every scene in the present moment:

> "It's all unfair," she told him bitterly. "Kabuo didn't kill anyone. It isn't in his heart to kill anyone. They brought in that sergeant to say he's a killer—that was just prejudice. Did you hear the things that man was saying? How Kabuo had it in his heart to kill? How horrible he is, a killer? Put it in your paper, about that man's testimony, how all of it was unfair. How the whole trial is unfair."
>
> "I understand what you mean," answered Ishmael. "But I'm not a legal expert. I don't know if the judge should have suppressed Sergeant Maples' testimony. But I hope the jury comes in with the right verdict. I could write a column about that, maybe. How we all hope the justice system does its job. How we hope for an honest result."
>
> "There shouldn't even be a trial," said Hatsue. "The whole thing is wrong, it's wrong."
>
> "I'm bothered, too, when things are unfair," Ishmael said to her. "But sometimes I wonder if unfairness isn't … part of things. I wonder if we should even expect fairness, if we should assume we have some sort of right to it. Or if——"
>
> "I'm not talking about the whole universe," cut in Hatsue. "I'm talking about people—the sheriff, that prosecutor, that judge, you. People who can do things because they run newspapers or arrest people or convict them or decide about their lives."

There is no way to talk about unfairness without conjuring the fact that Ishmael—who is white—has had a much easier life than Hatsue, who was punished merely for being Japanese. Yet Ishmael has suffered too because he has lost her love, and so both characters feel that they have been unfairly treated. This subtext makes their dialogue that much more charged and interesting than it would otherwise be.

When trying to play up subtext in your dialogue scene, you can draw upon historical events, as in the example we just saw, or you might try one of these techniques:

- Use body language to say what isn't being spoken in words.
- Use setting details and objects to elicit references to past events.
- Zoom in on symbolic or suggestive objects in the setting.
- Let the conversation dance around an unspoken topic.

To the last point, let's look at an example from Ernest Hemingway's story "Hills Like White Elephants." The story takes place in a bar and features two characters who don't ever leave their seats. Through the course of the conversation, the reader develops a slow, painful realization of what the couple is discussing. Without the dialogue, the story has almost no action.

Hemingway opens with a quick brush of setting describing the hills of the valley, as well as the American and the girl sitting at the bar. Then, within a few more lines, the dialogue begins. Notice how the conversation feels like action because of its quick back-and-forth movement between these two characters:

> "And if I do it you'll be happy and things will be like they were and you'll love me?"
>
> "I love you now. You know I love you."
>
> "I know. But if I do it, then it will be nice again if I say things are like white elephants, and you'll like it?"
>
> "I'll love it. I love it now but I just can't think about it. You know how I get when I worry."
>
> "If I do it you won't ever worry?"
>
> "I won't worry about that because it's perfectly simple."

Even though ninety-nine percent of this story is dialogue, the subtext-laden nature of their tug-of-war exchange creates a sense of movement, of action throughout, allowing the reader to feel as though he is experiencing the events of a narrative himself, while the swiftness of the exchanges allows for emotional distance from the heavy topic of abortion. And even though the characters aren't engaged in a loud argument, even though there is no hot emotional intensity, the tension is palpable. There's real energy here; the reader sees the dynamics of the couple through their strained dance around a topic neither wishes to name outright.

ENDING A DIALOGUE SCENE

A strong dialogue scene includes information that either deepens the reader's understanding of the characters or explains a plot element (thus the big reveals we talked about earlier). In one way or another, dialogue scenes should offer characters a chance to reveal things, but these revelations must be well-timed. If you give away the information at the beginning of the scene—say one character tells her married boyfriend that she's pregnant—in the rest of the scene you will use the dialogue to work out their immediate feelings, motivations, fears, and reactions to that information.

But a particularly effective technique is to drop a revelation toward the end of the chapter. This will either force the reader to continue to the next chapter or leave the reader with a powerful experience to mull over.

Here's an example of a revelation that comes at the end of a dialogue scene, from Richard Russo's novel *Empire Falls*. In this exchange between protagonist Miles and his curmudgeonly screwup of a father, Max, a piece of information is revealed that tells the reader a lot about the characters and affects the plot.

Miles has never understood why his father didn't protest his mother's affair with one of the town's wealthy founders, Charlie Whiting—whose family Miles is still in service to as a result. Max has gone missing, disappearing from town with a mentally addled priest and some church funds, and he calls his son on the phone from Florida to let him know he's okay. Max and Miles quickly get into one of their customary arguments, but this time the argument comes with a revelation:

Why shouldn't he have a little fun? was what Max wanted to know, since they were asking questions. "Old men like to have fun too, you know. Down here, people like old men."

"Why?"

"They don't say," Max admitted. "Tom hears confessions every afternoon at the end of the bar. You should see it."

"That's terrible, Dad."

"Why? Think about it."

"It's sacrilegious."

"Your mother really messed you up, you know that?"

And that was all it took, just the one mention of Grace, and suddenly the question was out before Miles could consider the wisdom of asking it. "How come you never told me about Mom and Charlie Whiting, Dad?"

Max reacted as if he'd been expecting the question for years. "How come you never told *me*, son?"

The spoken revelation here is that not only did Max know about his wife's affair, he knew that Miles also knew. The implications, however, are far greater than a simple revelation of information. Miles has always blamed his father and held a grudge against him for being gone more than he was around. Yet here the reader learns that Miles took his mother's side against his father all those years ago, even knowing his mother was cheating. This exchange helps Miles realize that he has blamed the wrong parent, thus consigning himself to his fate of running the Empire Grill under the iron fist of Mrs. Whiting.

By letting this come at the end of the scene, Russo not only catches the reader off guard, he creates a powerful resting place. The next scene picks up in another character's point of view (the novel is co-narrated by multiple protagonists), so the reader is left mulling over how this information is going to affect Miles, and if it will help him to change his behavior and stop the cycle of guilt his mother started.

Some dialogue scenes will end just like that, on a *kerplunk*, with the final spoken word in the scene. If the revelation came earlier, however, the ending should still reflect whatever took place in the scene: The revelation should have a visible, dramatic impact on the character.

In the scene from *Disgrace*, the tug-of-war conversation reveals that Lucy, despite being raped, doesn't see herself as a victim; and yet David—who *elected* to have an affair with his student—*does* see himself as a victim. Coetzee ends the scene with one reflective line of David's thoughts:

Never yet have they been so far and so bitterly apart. He is shaken.

This is an uneasy, destabilized state to leave David in. Since David hasn't been terribly shaken by anything he's done yet, this signals to the reader for the first time that he may be able to change after all.

When it comes time to end a dialogue scene, you'll want to leave your protagonist in one of the following places:

- On the final words of a spoken revelation
- Emotionally, mentally, or spiritually destabilized in some way
- Poised to take an action based on what was revealed
- Caught in a reflective space to muse on what was revealed

Remember that dialogue should never be used to discuss mundane or banal topics, but always to reveal new information about plot and character. Dialogue can be stylized to match the personality of a character and should sound realistic.

Finally, be careful not to use too many back-to-back dialogue scenes. Remember that dialogue feels like action to the reader, so you can break up action by following a dialogue-heavy scene with a suspenseful scene, a contemplative scene, or an epiphany scene. Even within a single scene, a lot of dialogue can start to feel rushed after a while and should be grounded with physical gestures, setting details, or other brief snippets of exposition.

DIALOGUE SCENE MUSE POINTS

- Always reveal new information about either the characters or the plot in the dialogue.
- Add energy to an otherwise slower-paced scene by using dialogue, which feels like action to the reader.

- Balance a dialogue scene with setting details to create foreshadowing, build subtext, and keep the pace even.
- Use dialogue to reveal plot information in a realistic way.
- Reveal a character's intentions through her speech.
- Use opposing forces, or tug-of-war, in dialogue to keep tension alive.

FLASHBACK SCENES

Beneath any narrative runs a deep seam of history that informs your characters' lives, motivations, emotions, and much more. This rich seam is backstory, so named because it takes place behind or before the front of your plot, where the reader's attention will be primarily focused. The front plot, or front story, begins the moment of your inciting incident. If the plot begins when your protagonist finds his wife murdered on a Wednesday afternoon in 2001, then anything that came before that moment is backstory (though you are allowed some establishing scenes at the beginning of a novel).

Backstory is often most effective when revealed in the form of a flashback scene, where it can be made vivid and allow the reader to participate in it; otherwise, if written in an expository manner, it might drag the pace down to a crawl. A flashback scene still contains all the elements of a scene—setting, action, characters, plot information, dramatic tension—and differs from other kinds of scenes in only one major way: It takes place in the past.

Flashback scenes should do the following:

- Illustrate or explain a plot or character element in the front story
- Focus on action, information, and character interactions
- Be lean on setting and sensory details, which slow down the pace
- Enrich the reader's understanding of the protagonist

Note that just because you *can* write flashback scenes does not mean that you should. Flashbacks, even in the form of a well-constructed scene, still draw the reader away from the front story and run the risk of distracting her. Use flashbacks judiciously, even sparingly. If you use them early in your narrative, be sure to keep them short and fast paced. You may want to drop one into a contemplative scene or use one to heighten the tension in a suspense scene. I find that they can get in the way of a dramatic scene—which is all about character interactions in the present—so keep that in mind when writing flashbacks.

TRANSITIONING INTO THE PAST

A flashback is just another kind of scene, but it's especially important to consider how you transition into and out of them to create a seamless movement for the reader from the present narrative into the past. Detours into the past must be constructed carefully if they are to hold the reader's attention and avoid becoming narratively dense. Here are some quick and easy tricks for transitioning:

- **USE THE PAST TENSE.** Flashbacks often begin with words that conjure the idea of the past or indicate the past through a change in verb tense. Here are a few examples of transitional sentences that let the reader know she is stepping into the past.
  From the story "Mothers" by Sylvia Plath:

  A few days after they had moved into the house, Tom called her downstairs for a visitor.

From there, Plath quickly drops into a scene where the character Esther meets a Kenyan professor who has an affect on her religious decision. And from Neil Gaiman's novel *Anansi Boys*:

He had spoken to Mrs. Higgler several years earlier, when his mother was dying.

This memory comes in the middle of a scene in which the protagonist, Fat Charlie, is trying to explain to his fiancée why he doesn't want his father to come to their wedding.

- **USE A SPECIFIC DATE OR INCIDENT TO REFER TO THE PAST.** There's no more direct way to transition into the past than by referring to a time or date that the reader knows has already passed. Using a date is a nice, sturdy way to transition, especially if the date has significance to the protagonist, like in the story "Police Dreams" by Richard Bausch:

> On the morning of the day she left, he woke to find her sitting at her dressing table, staring at herself.

The reader already knows that the narrator is divorced in the front story. By leading the reader directly back to "the morning of the day she left," the author clearly signals that he is now moving into the past.

- **USE REITERATION.** Sometimes you can set up the reader by having a character tell him directly that you will be moving into the past, as in this example from the novel *Carolina Moon* by Jill McCorkle:

> "Anyway, that old Barry just wouldn't let it rest and kept right on talking; I'll do my best to re-create his exact words. ..."

The reader knows that the speaker is about to move into the past because she's referring to a conversation that has already taken place, thus the need to "re-create" his words.

- **USE REMEMBRANCES.** Some writers make it very obvious that a detour into the past is imminent by using specific phrases like "I remembered when" or "She remembered the day." This technique leaves no question that the character is stepping back in time, but it is a little less elegant than some of the techniques discussed above.

Using the past tense and providing just one transitional sentence between the scene at hand and the flashback is one of the most effective ways to dip into the past without jarring the reader too far out of the present narrative.

HOW TO USE FLASHBACK SCENES

A flashback is still a scene, for all practical purposes, but since the scene has already happened, it does not need to do quite as much as, and can be a great deal shorter than, a typical scene. You don't need to do nearly as much work with the setting, for instance, because setting details slow the pace and distract the reader from the flashback's purpose; with a flashback, you want to focus on action, information, and character interactions. In all essential ways, however, you structure a flashback like any other type of scene.

Flashbacks may be used when the past is directly responsible for present plot. In some narratives, the inciting incident of the plot may stem directly from something that happened in the past, and that past event may need to be reopened for the reader to understand what happened. In such a case, flashback scenes are the most direct way to convey the necessary information.

A good example of this comes from Elizabeth Kostova's sprawling gothic novel, *The Historian*, about a father's legacy to his daughter, linked to the existence of the real Dracula. The inciting incident occurs when the daughter finds a strange book in her father's study, along with an unusual note. When she asks him about it, he tells her about the night when he first found the book:

> You already know, my father said, that before you were born I was a professor at an American university. Before that, I studied for many years to become a professor. At first I thought I would study literature. Then, however, I realized I loved true stories even better than imaginary ones.

What is masterful about Kostova's transitions into the past is that they are elegant and subtle, so the reader never feels herself moving through time. The scene above opens with the narrator's father talking in the front story to his daughter. Then, slowly, as you will see in the next example, she shifts out of the front story. With the use of the phrase "one spring night," the scene slides into the past, and then very quickly she sets the scene of flashback with the words "I was in my carrel" so quietly that the reader doesn't think about the movement through time—the reader is just immediately drawn there. It's a brilliant technique:

> One spring night when I was still a graduate student, I was in my carrel at the university library, sitting alone very late among rows and rows of books. Looking up from my work, I suddenly realized that someone had left a book whose spine I had never seen before among my own textbooks,

which sat on a shelf above my desk. The spine of this new book showed an elegant little dragon, green on pale leather.

I didn't remember ever having seen the book there or anywhere else, so I took it down and looked through it without really thinking. The binding was soft, faded leather, and the pages inside appeared to be quite old. It opened easily to the very center. Across those two pages I saw a great woodcut of a dragon with spread wings and a long looped tail, a beast unfurled and raging, claws outstretched. In the dragon's claws hung a banner on which ran a single word in Gothic lettering: DRAKULYA.

Even though the flashback scene takes place before the inciting incident and the beginning of the narrator's storyline, it still meets the criteria of a full scene: There is setting, action, a protagonist, dramatic tension, suspense, and most important, a sense of relevance to the narrator's plotline.

The Historian is built on a weaving of past and present, and eventually the two storylines merge. The past catches up with the narrator's father in her present. When the narrator's father goes missing, she becomes involved in a search for him, Dracula, and the mother she never knew. The flashback scenes prepare the reader for this plot direction.

This type of structure works well when you intend to merge the past with present events—that is, when the events of the past will come into play in your protagonist's life in the present storyline. This is why the flashbacks in *The Historian* begin early in the narrative—they continue, becoming more and more recent, until the past and the present merge.

If you're only going to use flashbacks to illustrate or deepen the reader's understanding of a character, you may want to let a bit more action unfold and move further into the plot before throwing in a flashback, as flashbacks in the first part of your narrative can slow the pace and lose the reader's interest.

You might also use a flashback if you need to create a more suspenseful plot. When you want to use the past to build suspense in your plot, then you will absolutely need to use flashback scenes to let the reader see the events of the past in limited bites.

For example, in Mary Doria Russell's bold science fiction novel *The Sparrow*, Jesuit priest Emilio Sandoz returns in 2059 as the sole survivor of a mission sent to the planet Rhakat more than seventeen years before in the hope of making contact with the first-known sentient alien life. All the reader knows early on in the narrative is that Emilio Sandoz—once a respected Jesuit priest—behaved in such a way while on Rhakat that he is now referred to as a "whore" and "child killer." Emilio's hands have also been mutilated beyond use, and he is too traumatized to discuss anything at first.

The front storyline revolves around Emilio's interrogation by his superiors, who need to decide what to do with him and how to punish him. The reputation of the Jesuit priesthood rests heavily on their decision, since media attention is focused on his story.

Through careful flashback scenes of the actual mission in Emilio's point of view, Russell builds suspense as she slowly dips back in time, showing us a man who does not seem capable of being a "child killer." Here's an excerpt of a scene in which the reader gets to see Sandoz in the past firsthand:

> Then a juvenile, much smaller than anyone who'd spoken earlier, came forward with another adult, who spoke reassuringly before gently urging the little one to approach Emilio alone.
>
> She was a weedy child, spindly and unpromising. Seeing her advance, scared but determined, Emilio slowly dropped to his knees, so he would not loom over her, as the adult had loomed over him. They were, for the moment, all alone together, the others of their kinds forgotten, their whole attention absorbed. As the little one came closer, Emilio held out one hand, palm up, and said, "Hello."

This Emilio seems like a thoughtful man, and suspense is built in the disparity between what his superiors believe of him in the front story and what the reader actually sees in the flashbacks.

To use flashback scenes to build suspense, you need to dole out plot information slowly and be sure that each flashback provides a new piece of information. In Emilio's case, the reader sees that Emilio is a man who can be patient and kind to a child, which contrasts starkly with being a "child killer." But this is not the end of his story—it's only about halfway through the novel—so there is still a note of uncertainty about what kind of man Emilio is and how events might have changed him. The reader has to keep reading! Withholding crucial plot details keeps the reader engaged and reading on.

Flashbacks can also convey character depth and *death*. There are plenty of instances in fiction when a character who has had an effect on the protagonist is now either dead or not present in the front story. Yet you still want to show the effect this absent character has had on your protagonist. Narrative summary just doesn't cut it when it comes to understanding character depth and motivation. You'll need to use a flashback scene to render the effects visible to readers.

In Gaiman's fantasy novel *Anansi Boys*, protagonist Fat Charlie is planning a wedding with his fiancée, Rosie. In an early scene, they have a conversation about how she wants him to invite his estranged father to the wedding, and Fat Charlie wants nothing of the sort. He explains to Rosie that his father was a man who constantly embarrassed him at the most inappropriate times. There is no reason to doubt Fat Charlie, but the reader doesn't really relate to his feelings yet, either, creating a need for proof of how embarrassing his father really was. So Gaiman takes the reader back in time to offer an experience of Fat Charlie's father. In the excerpt below, Charlie's mother is in the hospital for cancer treatment, and his father shows up out of the blue to visit her in a most unusual manner:

> Coming down the hospital corridor, ignoring the protests of nurses, the stares of patients in pajamas and of their families, was what appeared to be a very small New Orleans jazz band. There was a saxophone and a sousaphone and a trumpet. There was an enormous man with what looked like a double bass strung around his neck. There was a man with a bass drum, which he banged. And at the head of the pack, in a smart checked suit, wearing a fedora hat and lemon yellow gloves, came Fat Charlie's father. He played no instrument but was doing a soft-shoe-shuffle along the polished linoleum of the hospital floor, lifting his hat to each of the medical staff in turn, shaking hands with anyone who got close enough to talk or attempt to complain.

Fat Charlie bit his lip, and prayed to anyone who might be listening that the earth would open and swallow him up or, failing that, that he might suffer a brief, merciful and entirely fatal heart attack. No such luck. He remained among the living, the brass band kept coming, his father kept dancing and shaking hands and smiling. ...

"Fat Charlie," he said, loudly enough that everyone in the ward—on that floor—in the hospital—was able to comprehend that this was someone who knew Fat Charlie, "Fat Charlie, get out of the way. Your father is here."

Fat Charlie got out of the way.

The band, led by Fat Charlie's father, snaked their way through the ward to Fat Charlie's mother's bed. She looked up at them as they approached, and she smiled.

The flashback offers insight into Charlie's father, who is not present in the real-time scene, and who, Charlie learns when he tries to track him down, is recently deceased. Without this insight, Charlie's resistance to having his father come to the wedding would not have any impact, and the reader would not believe him.

What's crucial about this flashback is its economical length. When writing flashbacks, you should strive to make yours brief as well. Gaiman hones in on the memory for not much more than a page and then returns to the present. Remember to keep your flashbacks short, or at least fast paced, so they hold the reader's attention.

Similarly, when a character has a distinct and vivid personality—perhaps he's shy, overly strict, can't speak, or cruel—you may decide to go back in time through a flashback and offer some perspective on this character so he doesn't seem one-dimensional. For example, to understand why Darth Vader was so starkly evil, George Lucas went back in time in his later movies and *showed* young Anakin Skywalker before he became Darth Vader. By witnessing Anakin's pain and loss, the viewers understand him better and develop compassion and sympathy for the character.

When you use a flashback for either of these reasons, be sure to keep the flashbacks short—their purpose is supportive, so you don't want to venture too far from the front story.

PARALLEL STORIES

Another common use of the flashback is what I call "parallel stories," where you run two stories side by side that eventually merge in the present. Your protagonist inhabits the front story, while other characters inhabit the flashback scenes—perhaps ancestors, villains, or other important characters whose stories came before the front story. In Erika Swyler's novel *The Book of Speculation*, protagonist Simon Watson, a young librarian who lives in the near-crumbling remains of his childhood home on Long Island Sound, receives a rare and unusual book that seems tied to the mystery of why all the women in his family have drowned on the same date. The novel is split between Simon's chapters and chapters from the book, which tell the tale of his ancestors who lived with a traveling sideshow.

Simon's scenes, in first person, read like so:

> It's an absurd hour for a phone call, but the more absurd the hour, the more likely someone is to be home. Though the sun is barely up over the water, Martin Churchwarry sounds as though he's been awake for hours.
>
> "Mr. Churchwarry? I'm so glad to reach you. This is Simon Watson. You sent me a book."
>
> "Oh, Mr. Watson," he says. "I'm delighted to hear it arrived in one piece." He sounds excited, almost breathy. "It's rather fantastic, isn't it? I'm only sorry that I wasn't able to hang on to it myself, but Marie would have killed me if I'd brought home another stray."

Then, in the flashback scenes, we drop into the strange book, which is written in an omniscient POV that can move between all the characters in Hermelius Peabody's sideshow:

> Hermelius Peabody's back was pressed against a wall shelf while his throat was half crushed by the forearm of a surprisingly strong Russian

crone. His initial response to Madame Ryzhkova's request had been negative, but he was rapidly becoming amenable to her position.

"An apprentice?" He coughed. "Madame, Amos is the most profitable Wild Boy I've encountered, not to mention that he is without speech. How precisely would you work with him?"

Ryzhkova made a noise that fell between snarl and squawk. "We will work well. The cards say it will be so."

In this novel, the chapters alternate—one in the present, one in the past, and so on—so there is never any confusion as to where we are in time. And the past story eventually catches up to the present, providing answers that Simon sorely needs. If you choose this technique for your narrative, you are essentially running two stories side by side, using the flashbacks to build toward a truth that will have to be addressed, answered, and realized in the front story.

ENDING THE FLASHBACK SCENE

When you end a flashback scene, either transition back to the present so the reader is brought full circle to the point where the flashback started or leave the flashback on a note that will force the reader to keep reading.

In *The Historian*, the goal of the first flashback is to set the plot in forward motion. The story piques the narrator's curiosity such that she begins her own investigation into the mysterious Vlad Dracula and her father's past. The flashback also offers insight into the character of her father, who has always been a bit reserved, and hints at details about her absent mother.

The flashback ends by coming back to the present:

"Good Lord," my father said suddenly, looking at his watch. "Why didn't you tell me? It's almost seven o'clock."

I put my cold hands inside my navy jacket. "I didn't know," I said. "But please don't stop the story. Please don't stop there."

The reader shares the narrator's attitude and doesn't want him to stop either—he wants to know what happened next. In this case, since the backstory has a direct effect on the front story, the reader and the narrator both have gained new insight that will compel the reader to go forward.

Bringing your flashback back to the present allows the reader to feel as though he has literally traveled back in time and has gained a fuller understanding of where he is going.

In the example from Gaiman's *Anansi Boys*, the flashback ends when Charlie's fiancée, Rosie, with whom he was arguing when he first slipped into the memory, calls his attention back to the present:

> "So," said Rosie, draining her Chardonnay, "you'll call your Mrs. Higgler and give her my mobile number. Tell her about the wedding and the date. ..."

The flashback achieves two crucial functions. First, it shows the reader what Fat Charlie considers embarrassing and inappropriate behavior. He sees his father as a fair-weather man—Charlie resented the fact that his father could just swoop in at the last minute and make his mother happy. (Some might argue that the flashback shows Charlie as selfish, not caring about his mother's happiness, only caring about himself.) Second, it reveals plot information, as the flashback moves to the day of his mother's funeral, where Charlie spotted a stranger who will play a very significant role in the future plot; but the character is merely dropped there as a hint, a piece of foreshadowing.

Structurally, this sort of flashback acts as a detour from the scene at hand, like an image from years passed slipped into a collection from a recent vacation. This is a very good use of the flashback for your consideration—it's brief, it adds to the reader's understanding of the characters, and it provides a hint of future plot events.

Flashbacks need to be purposeful or readers will feel as if you've departed from your story. Use them as strategically as possible. They should be vividly written and quickly paced, and they should leave the reader with the feeling that he has learned something important that he needs to know.

FLASHBACK SCENE MUSE POINTS

- Focus the flashback on all of the following: action, information, and character interaction.
- Make sure the information contained in the flashback has some bearing on the front story.
- Always use flashbacks judiciously so the reader doesn't lose track of the front story.
- Use flashbacks when the past directly affects the front plot.
- Use flashbacks when you want to use some element of the past to create suspense in the present.
- Use flashbacks to deepen the reader's understanding of a character.

CLIMACTIC SCENES

In fiction, the climax—which Martha Alderson and I call The Triumph in *Writing Deep Scenes*—is the high point of all the action and drama in your narrative. It's where the events that began with the inciting incident come to a roiling, intense head, a clash of forces between protagonist and antagonist. The results of these climax events will have the most dramatic impact on your character and point you toward the ending (often called the denouement) of your narrative. A climactic scene will be one of the most, if not *the* most, intense, dramatic, powerful scenes in your entire narrative.

Unless you have multiple narrators who each have their own Triumph to undergo, you should have only one *major* climactic scene in your narrative where the protagonist finally reigns victorious over the antagonist. Even if you have multiple protagonists, you may want them to undergo the same climactic event and simplify by choosing one person's point of view through which to reveal it. However, you may draw upon the elements of climactic scenes for other big scenes in the novel in which something dramatic takes place.

A successful climactic scene is characterized by the following:

- **THE COLLISION OF OPPOSING FORCES.** Most often these are your protagonist and antagonist (whether person, natural disaster, or other), but the protagonist could face the main antagonist's henchman, secondary characters who betray the protagonist, or even well-meaning characters who make bad or foolish choices.

- **A BUILDING OF ENERGY TO AN INTENSE CRESCENDO.** The energy of the scene rises and rises, as do your characters' emotions until the scene leads to a point of great intensity.
- **A CONFRONTATION AT THE CENTER OF THE SCENE.** Your protagonist must confront something or someone (possibly an inner confrontation in a more literary novel) so he can change or be changed.
- **HIGH STAKES.** Life and death, ties about to be severed, kingdoms on the verge of being lost—whatever is at stake, the characters must have a lot to lose.
- **A SWIFT PACE THAT STILL ALLOWS ROOM FOR EMOTIONAL CONTENT.**
- **A MOMENT OF REALIZATION.** The protagonist should finally see strengths and resources that have been hidden from her up to now.

Remember that The Triumph is something of a mirror to the Point of No Return, which comes at the beginning of your story. Once your protagonist arrives here, there is no turning back; character and plot will be changed permanently—hopefully for the better, and not without an incredible output of energy. After the climax, there is a lot less to do (for you and your protagonist); therefore, a climactic scene signals the beginning of the end of your narrative. In a literary novel, an epiphany scene can serve as the climactic scene—a character's epiphany may be big enough to carry a climax, although the narrative will feel less urgent, less intense to the reader as you work to tie up remaining threads. In most other kinds of stories, the climactic scene will involve more action.

SETTING UP A CLIMACTIC SCENE

A climactic scene should not come as a total surprise to the reader. If anything, it may come as a relief because prior scenes have increased in tension and become more emotionally dramatic for your protagonist in preparation for a terrible collision (literal or figurative). If you have created more consequences for your protagonist in the middle of your narrative, he should be under a great deal of obvious stress, and knee-deep in conflict, by the time the climactic scene arrives.

You want your climactic scene to open with a clear sense of action and drama about to unfold, and one very powerful way to do that is to leave the scene before it on a note of suspense to suggest conflict is coming.

Robert Heinlein's astonishing science fiction novel *Stranger in a Strange Land* tells the story of Valentine Michael Smith, a human child born on Mars and raised by Martians. When he is brought back to Earth, he has a transformative effect on everyone and eventually becomes the ringleader of a cult in which everyone is taught to see themselves as God, and jealousy, competition, and ambition are abolished. This leads to a blissful communal living situation, which, naturally, threatens "civilized" society. Michael's goal is to introduce all of humanity to this way of being, but the forces of humanity work against him. Ironically, his peaceful lifestyle eventually leads to violence.

At the end of the contemplative scene prior to the climactic scene, Michael—who has been meditating for a long time on how to handle the fact that humans, en masse, don't take too kindly to ideals he wants to teach them and consequently want him dead—comes to a decision point:

> Then Mike's eyes opened, he grinned merrily. "You've got me all squared away, Father. I'm ready to show them now—I grok the fullness." The Man from Mars stood up. "Waiting is ended."

While the reader doesn't know exactly *what* he's going to do, his words signal that action is coming in the next scene and that it will be big. And so it is. In the next scene, Mike leaves "the Nest"—the place where his group of followers lives—and goes out into the stormy lynch mob of a crowd that is waiting for him. They stone him and call him names, but he speaks his truth, even though he knows that they want to kill him:

> "*Blasphemer!*" A rock caught him over his left eye and blood welled forth. Mike said calmly, "In fighting me, you fight yourself ... for Thou Art God ... and I am God ... and all that groks is God—there is no other."

We'll talk more about how this scene unfolds further in the chapter. First, though, we'll look at two scene endings leading up to the climactic scene of *Geek Love* by Katherine Dunn, one of the most wonderfully weird, dark, yet human novels I've ever read. This discussion should help you think about how to set up your climactic scene a few scenes in advance.

In *Geek Love*, the Binewskis are a carnival family. To secure their livelihood, parents Al and Lily make sure their offspring are suitably carnival worthy by experimenting with chemicals and drugs during each pregnancy. They wind up with a set of Siamese twins, Elly and Iphy; Arturo the "Aqua Boy," who has flippers instead of limbs; Olympia, or "Oly," a "hunchback albino" dwarf; and Chick, who has telekinetic powers and can make people think whatever he chooses. The novel is written as Oly's memoir—though most of the time, the scenes are so vivid the reader forgets that all that is happening has, in essence, already happened.

Despite the horrific and absurd nature of the premise, *Geek Love* is a serious book in which serious things happen to the characters. As the family of freaks grows up, Arturo—who has long been the star of the show—develops a megalomaniacal need for attention and power. He exerts more and more control over his family members, as it becomes clear that there would be no show without him, and accumulates a following of people who worship him, using Chick's powers to get these people to do as he wants.

At the end of the chapter that precedes the climactic scene, protagonist Oly has been forced to give away her infant daughter, Miranda, because her brother Arty feels she is a "norm" who can't contribute to their act. Because Oly is afraid of him and afraid for her daughter, she does as she is told, but not without resentment. Here is how the scene ends, setting the reader up for the climax that comes two scenes later:

> My job was to come back directly, with nothing leaking from beneath my dark glasses, to give Arty his rubdown and then paint him for the next show, nodding cheerfully all the while, never showing anything but attentive care for his muscular wonderfulness. Because he could have killed you. He could have cut off the money that schooled and fed you. He could have erased you so entirely that I never would have had those letters and report cards and photos, or your crayon pictures, or the chance to spy on you, and to love you secretly when everything else was gone.

The statement "when everything else was gone" is the reader's first clue that bad things are coming in the next scene, which takes place a year later in time, though it doesn't feel like it. That next scene is very short and shows Arty at his narcissistic height, with Oly still tending to him in her fear. It ends with this strangely foreboding image of Arty:

> When it was set, the final greasing had a sheen of its own and kept the white on even through the final hour under water with Arty squirming his wildest. The white tipping and streaking were new touches. Arty examined himself in the mirror and his wide mouth wriggled from corner to corner.

You get the feeling that this is the last close-up of Arty the reader is going to get. This is Arty at his pinnacle, blind to what is about to happen. There's something about the line "Arty squirming his wildest" that perhaps suggests death throes. And anytime you end a scene with a narcissistic character admiring himself in the mirror, you're setting up the reader to knock him off his throne. The scene nicely sets the stage for the climax that follows later in the same chapter.

Setting up your climax requires that you lace the ending of the prior scene or two with a sense of impending doom and instability. It needs to be clear to the reader, whether through simple interior monologue or by some combination of setting detail and action, that change is coming.

THE CLIMACTIC EVENT

The actual opening of your climactic scene can be handled in many ways. Most climactic scenes get quickly to the action—after all, you've held the reader off for a long time already. Don't waste too much time setting up the opening; let things build fast. The nature of a climactic scene is that it builds quickly and steadily toward the climax with the pacing of an action scene. This is not a scene where you want to linger in a lot of exposition, as a climactic event should happen too fast to be stopped.

All the elements are present and working together in the best climactic scenes:

- Specific action
- Dialogue rather than interior monologue to convey what's happening

- Setting details to balance the action and to build atmosphere for the climactic event—details are good in a climactic scene because so much is at stake that you don't want the reader to feel he missed anything
- Emotional content—the protagonist's feelings should be conveyed in some way, from fear to relief

Let's look at how these details play out in the *Stranger in a Strange Land* climactic scene. Remember, it opened with Michael walking out to face his foes and being attacked. As the scene progresses, the crowd gets more aggressive, but Michael doggedly continues to speak his message of love:

> "God damn it—let's stop this taking the Name of the Lord in vain!"—"Come on men! Let's finish him!" [*Dramatic tension.*] The mob surged forward, led by one bold with a club; they were on him with rocks and fists, and then with feet as he went down. [*Action.*] He went on talking while they kicked his ribs in and smashed his golden body, broke his bones and tore an ear loose. [*Very specific details.*] At last someone called out, "Back away so we can get the gasoline can on him." [*Dialogue.*]
>
> The mob opened up a little at that warning and the camera zoomed to pick up his face and shoulders. The Man from Mars smiled at his brothers, said once more, softly and clearly, "I love you." [*Emotional content.*] An incautious grasshopper came whirring to a landing on the grass a few inches from his face [*Lovely details deliver a momentary pause before the finale.*]; Mike turned his head, looked at it as it stared back at him. "Thou art God," he said happily and discorporated.

(*Discorporated*, for those who haven't read the book, means that his soul has left his body.)

Notice that the pace is quick due to the action and dialogue, yet through the use of focused details, like the camera zooming in on him and the landing of the little grasshopper, the pace slows just enough so that the action doesn't overwhelm the impact of what is happening. The statements "I love you" and "Thou art God" convey an emotional tone—and in contrast to the mob that is tearing him apart, despite that this is his death, Valentine Michael Smith seems at peace. This is a more emotional climactic event.

You may choose an emotional climactic event when the content of your narrative has dealt with relationships, inner conflict, or any kind of powerful emotional content.

In *Geek Love*'s climactic event, Dunn also utilizes all the elements of a scene for a complex, emotional, detailed, and powerful climax. Unlike Heinlein, she strings together a series of small, terrible events that build more action and intensity into the final moment—there's not a lot of time for the reader to feel anything but a mounting sense of horror. First, Iphy kills her Siamese twin, Elly (a murder and a suicide, as they share organ systems), claiming that Elly killed her baby, Mumpo, by smothering him. That's three tragedies right there in a row. Chick and Oly rush in. Chick, who was devoted to the twins, tries to use his mental power to bring them back to life and is devastated when he fails; he decides that it is all Arty's fault and, in a brilliant stroke of character, the normally calm, sweet, devoted young man finally blows—literally—with this climactic event, exploding the entire tent and the people within it with the power of his mind.

> It came billowing, scorching toward us, and Chick, in his pain, could not hold himself but reached. I felt him rush through me like a current of love to my cross points, and then draw back. I, with my arms lifted, felt his eyes open into me, and felt their blue flicker of recognition. Then he drew back. … The flames spouted from him—pale as light—bursting outward from his belly. He did not scream or move but he spread, and my world exploded with him, and I, watching, bit down—bit down and knew it—bit down with a sense of enormous relief, and ground my teeth to powdered shards—and stood singed and grinding at the stumps as they died—my roses—Arty and Al and Chick and the twins—gone dustward as the coals rid themselves of that terrible heat.

Here the climactic event is a kind of relief for Oly, who never felt that she had any control over what was happening to her. It reveals to her that she *was* powerless, and now it's over before she can stop it.

The goal of the climactic event is to bring the inciting incident and the resulting plot consequences to a head so that there's some kind of transformation in your protagonist's life or struggle. The climax is the moment where the protagonist is tested, tried, and permanently altered by whatever happens.

A climactic event does not have to be subtle—you can launch into your climax in no uncertain terms. The only real goal is that the events of the action bring your inciting incident to a logical head that allows your protagonist either a victory or a better path forward.

This next example is from Sara Gruen's novel *Water for Elephants*, which is set in the prohibition era of the United States and stars Jacob Janowski, a young man whose dreams of taking over his father's veterinary business are dashed when his parents are killed in a car accident. To escape his grief, he jumps on a random train one night only to find himself an unwitting new player in the Benzini Brothers Circus come morning.

Jacob quickly falls in love with Marlena, the acrobatic star of the circus, who is married to the tempestuous August, a man who takes out his anger on the animals—in particular, on a new addition, an elephant named Rosie, who quickly tires of her abuse.

For pages, the tension builds between August and Jacob, as well as among the disgruntled circus employees and their employer, "Uncle Al," who often withholds their pay. These many tensions build for the entire novel until a bunch of men who were "red lighted" (thrown off the train overnight) come back for revenge during a performance with the intention of ruining the circus. Gruen signals the climactic event in a cacophonous way:

> I reach for it, but before I can pick it up the music crashes to a halt. There's an ungodly collision of brass that finishes with a cymbal's hollow clang. It wavers out of the big top and across the lot, leaving nothing in its wake.
>
> Grady freezes, crouched over his burger.
>
> I look from left to right. No one moves a muscle—all eyes point at the big top. A few wisps of hay swirl lazily across the hard dirt.
>
> "What is it? What's going on?" I ask.
>
> "*Shh*," Grady says sharply.
>
> The band starts up again, this time playing "Stars and Stripes Forever."
>
> "Oh Christ. Oh shit," Grady jumps up and backward, knocking over the bench.
>
> "What? What is it?"
>
> "The Disaster March!" he shouts, turning and bolting.

The climactic event gets underway with a literal crash of cymbals, and what happens from there is mayhem and chaos—animals and circus go-ers fleeing and screaming, people being run over and attacked, all leading up to the penultimate moment (I won't give it away completely, but you'll get the feeling of what's to come):

> My eyes sweep the tent, desperate to the point of panic. *Where are you? Where are you? Where the hell are you?*
>
> I catch sight of pink sequins and my head jerks around. When I see Marlena standing beside Rosie, I cry out in relief.
>
> August is in front of them—of course he is, where else would he be? Marlena's hands cover her mouth. She hasn't seen me yet, but Rosie has. She stares at me long and hard, and something about her expression stops me cold. August is oblivious—red-faced and bellowing, flapping his arms and swinging his cane. His top hat lies in the straw beside him, punctured as though he'd put a foot through it.
>
> Rosie stretches out her trunk, reaching for something.

In this climax, the opposite forces—the innocent elephant and the bru-tal animal trainer—clash, and the result changes Jacob and Marlena, and even Rosie, for good.

All climactic scenes should test your protagonist directly: He will rise to the challenge and prove himself worthy of something—he *will* deliver that ring to the fires of Mordor; he will vanquish evil; she will help the rebellion succeed. Either way, climactic scenes, like epiphanies, are about change, but climactic scenes are about more permanent change. A pro-tagonist can come to an epiphany without reaching the ultimate event of the narrative. But once you arrive at the climactic event, nothing will be the same.

POST-CLIMACTIC EVENT

When the climactic scene is over, your work changes. No longer do you have an imperative to drop in new plot information or create suspense. The scenes that follow a climactic one are about resolutions, sorting through the aftermath of the event and determining where to go next, showing that your protagonist has changed. You do want to be sure that all plot and character questions are answered, however.

In *Stranger in a Strange Land*, Michael's death gives his followers motivation to keep up his work—to turn the world into a better place. In *Geek Love*, the loss of Olympia's family and her livelihood forces her to finally become her own person, and it allows her to tell her daughter, Miranda, the truth of her origins. While the climax leads to loss, it also leads to a better future for Miranda. In *Water for Elephants*, Jacob and Marlena can now create a different kind of life for themselves, and those who suffered under brutality of one sort or another are able to get free of it.

Your climactic scene is a big one—it is, in essence, the point that the entire narrative has been driving toward, the realization of everything your protagonist has been after throughout the narrative, and it should be written with care.

CLIMACTIC SCENE MUSE POINTS

- Build a well-rounded, complex climactic event by using as many of the elements of a scene as possible: action, dialogue, setting details, emotional content, dramatic tension.
- Your protagonist and, if you have them, co-protagonists all should meet in one big climax.
- Make sure the climax event is directly related to the inciting incident.
- Make sure your protagonist permanently changes in some way.
- Keep the stakes high.
- Write the climactic scene as the high point of action and drama—all scenes that follow it will be slower, more reflective, and contain less action.

20

EPIPHANY SCENES

Epiphany is synonymous with change when it comes to character development. An epiphany is a moment when awareness or a sharp insight dawns suddenly on your protagonist as a result of events and interactions that have driven him to this moment. Very often epiphanies come with a cost—characters can be very attached to their perceptions of things and people, and it often hurts when they finally gain awareness. But epiphanies can also bring resurgence in hope or faith that the protagonist believed was lost. By introducing an epiphany, you provide your protagonist with an opportunity to grow, to learn, and to transform.

Epiphany scenes are more versatile than other scenes in that a character can have an epiphany in more than one type of scene—for instance, suspense and drama can build to an epiphany, or an epiphany can also be earned at the end of a contemplative scene. No matter what type of scene leads up to an epiphany, however, that moment of realization changes the final impact of the scene. The following happens in an epiphany scene:

- Your protagonist gains surprising new insight or breaks through denial.
- The epiphany comes at some kind of cost, or it renews hope or faith, or both.
- The epiphany rises out of plot events and information—it does not come out of the blue.
- As a result of the epiphany, the protagonist is forced to make some sort of choice or change.

Because epiphanies have a pivotal effect on characters, you don't need to have one in every scene. In fact, one major epiphany in each of the three main sections—beginning, middle, and end—would be plenty. Epiphanies shouldn't happen too early in a narrative either, as they require events, circumstances, and emotional information to drive them into being. People don't usually just wake up with insight—it is earned through experience.

TYPES OF EPIPHANIES

When you write an epiphany scene, you need to take stock of who your character is before the epiphany, what kind of change she needs to undergo, and how you will lead her to this change. Let's look at the kinds of epiphanies a character can undergo.

- **REMOVING THE BLINDERS.** This is when a character has been in denial but through an act of will decides to learn the truth.
- **REALIZING A SUPPRESSED DESIRE.** This is when a character who has lived his life in a limited way realizes what it is he really wants to do or be—the lawyer who realizes he really wants to work with children; the failed artist who realizes he was only acting out against his parents' plans for him. These are powerful and usually suggest that the character will leave one way of life for another.
- **ACCEPTING THE LIMITATIONS OF ONESELF OR OTHERS.** Many times a character must realize that the abusive spouse is not going to change; the dead-end job is not going to improve; and that any transformations she craves will have to be an inside job that nobody else can facilitate.
- **EXPERIENCING IDENTITY EPIPHANIES.** These kinds of epiphanies are fairly specific and limited. This is when a person realizes something essential to his being—that she is a lesbian after all; that he wants to embrace his father's African-American culture rather than his mother's Caucasian background; that it's time to convert to Judaism. A character's decision to claim an identity that he had been resisting or denying can come as the result of an epiphany.
- **UNDERGOING A RUDE AWAKENING.** Sometimes a character needs to be forced to change by circumstances out of his control. His friends

stage an intervention for his drinking; his wife confesses she doesn't really love him.

OPENING AN EPIPHANY SCENE

Now that you have a feeling for the kinds of categories that epiphanies fall into, let's talk about how to open one. What is most important about the opening is that you show the character in some kind of conflict, under pressure, or in some way destabilized. This is the scene in which his old façade is crumbling (or about to), and you want the reader to know that change is on the horizon. Epiphany openings work best when you've set the stage:

- The protagonist is afraid or anxious about the future.
- The protagonist is under pressure or stress.
- The protagonist takes an unusual action or behaves oddly.
- The protagonist expresses conflicted feelings about a given plot event or relationship.
- Your setting details or images are symbolic and hint at the kind of epiphany that is to come.

Let's take a look at a few examples of epiphany scenes that show the protagonist unbalanced or en route to an epiphany at the very opening of the scene.

In Michael Cunningham's Pulitzer Prize–winning novel *The Hours*, Laura Brown is a housewife in 1949 with a "perfect" life—a husband with a good job, a healthy son, and a second child on the way. She has a nice house and all the material things she could possibly want, but her true self is stifled; she wants to be more than a mother and a wife, yet there is no way for her to express this in her current life.

In the earlier scenes, the reader sees Laura repress desire, resentment, and her own creative spark, so there's a feeling that some kind of change in her life is on its way, but they don't yet know what it will be (and neither, it seems, does Laura). Two major factors begin to push Laura toward her epiphany. The first is reading Virginia Woolf's book *Mrs. Dalloway*, which boldly emphasizes a woman's right to her feelings. The second is the example of her neighbor, Kitty, who seems, without any angst, to be able to balance all the demands that Laura cannot. One day, she and Kitty kiss—and though this kiss happens with no premeditation on Laura's part, it further awakens in her a terrible hunger and desire. After that, she has more trouble dealing with the status quo of her life, and she finds her son's and husband's demands incredibly oppressive.

The epiphany scene opens with her reality in the process of shifting:

> As she pilots her Chevrolet along the Pasadena Freeway, among hills still scorched in places from last year's fire, she feels as if she's dreaming or, more precisely, as if she's remembering this drive from a dream long ago. Everything she sees feels as if it's pinned to the day the way etherized butterflies are pinned to a board.

There are a number of cues that something is different here. The way she feels "as if she's dreaming" and the eerie details of everything feeling "pinned" to the day like "etherized butterflies" are not typical reflections for Laura. The reader feels the tide of change coming, which prepares him for the reveal that she left her son with a neighbor in a moment of panic and is on her way to rent a motel room. Will she kill herself, take a lover, or make some kind of decision about her future and her feelings?

Opening an epiphany scene with a character behaving oddly or under stress or pressure is a very effective technique. It sets the reader up from the get-go to know that, in this scene, your protagonist is emotionally volatile—like a fragile chemistry experiment that can all too easily blow up. If you don't open the scene with your protagonist under stress, however, you must put pressure on him before too long.

Though character openings are a strong way to begin an epiphany scene, you can also open with strategically chosen setting details or images that foreshadow or set the mood for the epiphany to come. Such is the case in an upcoming example from Janet Fitch's novel *White Oleander*.

Seventeen-year-old Astrid—whose poet mother, Ingrid, has been in prison for six years for murdering her lover—has lived through a series of dysfunctional foster homes and undergone terrible traumas. All she has ever wanted was her mother's devoted, unconditional love, which Ingrid has withheld, claiming it is in favor of building Astrid's character (though the reader only experiences it as cruelty). In this scene, Astrid is coming to see her mother after a long absence; her mother is finally up for trial, and Astrid is the only witness whose testimony could free her. The scene opens with metaphor-laced setting details about fire season in southern California, which suggest the trial by fire that Astrid is about to undergo when she sees her mother:

> September came with its skirts of fire. Fire up on the Angeles Crest. Fire in Malibu, Altadena. Fire all along the San Gabriels, in the San Gorgonio wilderness, fire was a flaming hoop the city would have to jump through to reach the blues of October.
>
> It was in the furnace of oleander time that Susan finally called. "I had a trial," she explained. "But we're back on track. I've scheduled you a visit, day after tomorrow."
>
> I was tempted to balk, tell her I wasn't available, make things difficult, but in the end I agreed. I was as ready as I would ever be.

The symbolic image of fire is very powerful here, setting up the idea of someone getting (emotionally) burned in the scene to come. There's also the tension of Astrid considering, for the first time, not going to see her mother—which is a little flash of her steadily growing autonomy. She is "tempted to balk" but ultimately she acquiesces with the line "I was as ready as I would ever be" (suggesting she really won't ever be ready, but it's a "flaming hoop" she has to jump through to reach the other side). The reader knows that there is a great deal at stake for Astrid in this scene, and the rest of the scene (which we'll discuss later on) delivers.

DRIVING YOUR CHARACTER TOWARD EPIPHANY

Once you've set up the scene in which your character is unbalanced and worried about the future, you'll need to up the ante on your character to drive him toward that epiphany. Every character will have a unique set of circumstances that add up to epiphany.

Keep in mind that the intention to change or see the unvarnished truth will rarely be part of that setup. Think about how difficult it is to get a person to change a habit like keeping a messy room or smoking cigarettes, much less a deeper, more internal behavior or belief. Though you'll have done some of this work toward epiphany already by raising the stakes in previous scenes and complicating your protagonist's life and plot, this scene is the one in which the dam must finally break.

Since epiphanies do not come easily, you will have to exert stress, pressure, and tension upon your protagonist to get him there. Here are some forms of pressure:

- **THREAT OF LOSS.** The possibility of losing something or someone your protagonist holds dear is a powerfully motivating force for awareness to come in.
- **INCONTROVERTIBLE EVIDENCE.** When a character has been in denial and is finally faced with hard evidence of the truth—a photograph proving that her husband really is cheating, for example—the foundation of denial will often crack and let an epiphany shine through.
- **INJURING A LOVED ONE.** You'd be amazed at the kind of epiphany your protagonist can come to when confronted with the damage he has unintentionally caused others through his actions.
- **DANGER.** Threat is a powerful agent of change. Confronted with either death or bodily harm, characters often face their most basic and unvarnished feelings. Your protagonist might suddenly realize the error of her ways and wish for a second chance, for example, or be surprised to realize that there is only one person she really hopes to see again before she dies.

However you choose to push your protagonist into his epiphany, you must be realistic, and you must utilize dramatic tension. Remember that your protagonist must resist the awareness or change just a little, and the epiphany must come with an emotional, physical, or spiritual cost. The goal of an epiphany is to force your character to change, and change isn't something that comes easily.

THE MOMENT OF EPIPHANY

While you may stress and pressure your protagonist for the entire scene, if you like, I recommend saving the actual moment of epiphany for near the end of a scene. It's good to leave the reader and the protagonist not too long after this sudden dawning of insight. Most people don't take a sudden, spontaneous action after an epiphany; they let it sink in, and so should you. Pausing will also relieve you of the need to try to explain away any tension or emotional weight that the epiphany brought.

In *The Hours*, the moment of epiphany comes for Laura once she is alone in a room with nothing but Virginia Woolf's strong voice. It's there that her own silenced desires finally have space to rise into her thoughts. With time to herself, she is able to realize her epiphany:

> It is possible to die. Laura thinks, suddenly, of how she—how anyone—can make a choice like that. It is a reckless, vertiginous thought, slightly disembodied—it announces itself inside her head, faintly but distinctly, like a voice crackling from a distant radio station. She could decide to die. It is an abstract, shimmering notion, not particularly morbid. Hotel rooms are where people do things like that, aren't they? It's possible—perhaps even likely—that someone has ended his or her life right here, in this room, on this bed. Someone said, Enough, no more; someone looked for the last time at these white walls, this smooth white ceiling. By going to a hotel, she sees, you leave the particulars of your own life and enter a neutral zone, a clean white room, where dying does not seem quite so strange.

Laura's epiphany falls into the category of realization of a suppressed desire. She has lived her life in a limited way, and suddenly, this epiphany that she could free herself from her unhappiness through death jars her into a new way of thinking. The epiphany is handled through interior monologue—the reader enters into her thoughts and directly learns of the epiphany. In many cases, revealing an epiphany through interior monologue is necessary, as it is hard to demonstrate an epiphany through behavior. Even dialogue can be a stretch because epiphanies are usually quiet, intimate affairs. Laura's epiphany does, in fact, lead to a major change.

In *White Oleander*, Astrid's epiphany is more directly elicited. In her meeting with her mother, Astrid takes a courageous leap and asks something of her mother—challenging her mother's all-powerful hold over her and begging for some tenderness in the process:

She shook her head, gazed down at her bare tanned feet. "If I could take it all back, I would, Astrid." She lifted her eyes to mine. "You've got to believe me." Her eyes, glinting in the sun, were exactly the color of the pool we swam in together the summer she was arrested. I wanted to swim there again, to submerge myself in them.

"Then tell me you don't want me to testify," I said. "Tell me you don't want me like this. Tell me you would sacrifice the rest of your life to have me back the way I was."

The reader aches for Astrid as she waits to hear what her mother will say, but at the same time, the reader fears Astrid is about to get burned, as the opening of the scene suggested. Her mother does not reply automatically, which already tells Astrid something—and in the time that she waits for her mother to show up for her, Astrid has her epiphany:

And suddenly I felt panic. I'd made a mistake, like when I'd played chess with Ray and I knew a second too late I'd made the wrong move. I had asked a question I couldn't afford to know the answer to. It was the thing I didn't want to know. The rock that never should be turned over. I knew what was under there. I didn't need to see it, the hideous eyeless albino creature that lived underneath.

"Listen, forget it. A deal's a deal. Let's leave it at that."

Astrid realizes in that moment, in a removing-the-blinders style of epiphany, that she has lived in terror of learning that her mother doesn't really love her in the unconditional way that allows a mother to put her child first. Her whole life she has lived with this fear, and now here it is—she knows her mother won't suddenly change. This kind of epiphany usually comes with a kind of resignation for the character—on some level she has known all along who her mother is but has willed herself not to see it.

The scene doesn't end there, however. By taking the responsibility out of her mother's hands, by agreeing to the deal, Astrid gets the *result* she wants—her mother tells her that she does not have to testify and that she would do anything to have her daughter "partway back." But this all comes at a cost for Astrid because it was not offered unconditionally. Also, though Astrid is happy to hear those words, the reader still mistrusts Ingrid and isn't sure she means it. By the epiphany's end, Astrid's blinders are fully removed. She sees her mother as she truly is and doesn't have to try to please her anymore.

When you reach it, the moment of epiphany should come with great emotional consequences that either make things better for your protagonist or present him with a difficult emotional choice. An epiphany can free the protagonist, or it can bind him to a terrible decision. You want to demonstrate the cost of the epiphany—whether through a brief passage of interior monologue or through an action he takes that clearly stems from the epiphany.

The post-epiphany work of resolving and concluding the effects of the epiphany will take place in the next scene or scenes. I encourage you to resist using narrative summary or too much interior monologue to deal with the changes wrought by the epiphany. Character changes are best demonstrated. If your character's epiphany was an identity epiphany, in which he realized that he could not be a doormat any longer, then you will want him to take actions that show him improving upon his self-esteem and confronting people who have treated him carelessly. Epiphanies mark a change of direction and path for your protagonist, and from the point of epiphany on you will want to show how that realization has changed him. You may refer back to chapter eight for help charting your character's emotional journey.

EPIPHANY SCENE MUSE POINTS

- Use an epiphany to cause a protagonist to change.
- Open this type of scene with your character anxious about the future or under stress.
- Exert pressure and generally up the ante on your protagonist midscene to drive him toward epiphany.
- End your scene just after the epiphany to give the reader and the protagonist time to digest it.
- Own the change in the protagonist's outlook and direction by having the protagonist demonstrate the change in future scenes.

THE FINAL SCENE

All good things must end. But, as the aphorism goes, the end of one thing is also the beginning of another. Final scenes, then, are the end of one chapter in a protagonist's life. A rare few protagonists will actually die at the end of a narrative, but in general your final scene is the conclusion of the events of your inciting incident. However, the final scene need not feel completely conclusive. In fact, a final scene may very well feel like a new beginning. This scene should do the following:

- Provide a snapshot of where your protagonist is after the conclusion of your plot
- Be reflective in tone
- Bring matters full circle by recalling the inciting incident
- Move at a slower pace
- Include one last surprise, answer, or insight (this is optional)

Though the final scene marks the end of your narrative, in the reader's mind your characters and settings hopefully will live on, so you want to put as much work into creating a memorable ending as you put into your captivating beginning.

LEADING UP TO THE FINAL SCENE

Before we go on to look at the structure and content of your final scene, let's discuss the final *scenes*—yes, that's plural—that come before the last scene of your narrative. The three to five scenes that come between the climax and the very last scene have the job of supplying answers to outstanding questions that your plot has raised (see chapter eight). This is where you solve the crime, return the kidnapped child, or bring the lovers back together, thus tying up your plot, decreasing tension, and bringing a sense of resolution to your narrative. The job of the *true* final scene is to show the reader where your protagonist is now, how he has changed, and what he thinks or feels as a result of the consequences of your inciting incident.

Showing Character Transformation

The final scene is the last impression your protagonist will make upon the reader. Unless you have a very, *very* good reason for your protagonist not to have changed (if, for instance, the plot of your novel involved people trying to change her through brainwashing, cult activities, or some other form of coercion, and a successful arc would demonstrate your character *resisting* change), your protagonist should not be the same person she was when she started out. The principle areas where your character is most likely to reflect change are in her attitude, job, relationships, and location. Whether she has a new outlook, a new lifestyle, a new love, or a new sense of self, character change is the defining factor of your final scene.

Concluding the Inciting Incident

As a result of your narrative's inciting incident, a world of consequences has unraveled for your protagonist, taking him on a complex and interesting journey. That journey eventually has to conclude in a way that ties up the storyline: If the story is a murder investigation, the reader must learn whodunit by the end; if it's a romance, the reader should glimpse the happily ever after. You get the idea. The final scene of your narrative will signal the conclusion of the inciting incident, even if it leaves room for further possibilities to spin off in a new book.

The final scene is the place where your protagonist reflects upon, deals with, or accepts the consequences of your inciting incident.

Final scenes often (but not always) have a contemplative air about them and may be shorter than most other scenes because there's no need to introduce elaborate new actions or plot situations. The final scene should offer just a glimpse of where your protagonist finds himself at the end of his journey. Most tension and drama should be concluded or winding down by then. (You rarely leave a narrative on a suspenseful note unless there's *definitely* a sequel coming.) The ending is a place of reflection and, right from the launch of your final scene, you want to make this clear by slowing down the pace and providing room for reflection or interior monologue.

FINAL SCENES VS. EPILOGUES

Just as there is a difference between a first scene and a prologue, a final scene is not the same as an epilogue. The reason you will not find a chapter devoted to epilogues in this book is because I am not a fan of them. (Much of the time, an epilogue allows you to be lazy about completing your character's journey and transformation in the final scenes. Without one, you must do the work and come to a satisfying end point.) But many, many writers choose to write them, and they do so quite well. I have read some very successful epilogues. In some books, I'll concede that they are even necessary; and you are certainly free to write one. Keep in mind that an epilogue is a scene, or a reflection, that comes sometime in the future after the narrative has concluded, which means that your epilogue is never your final scene. It is a scene that comes *after* your final scene. Here are a few books that are enhanced through the inclusion of an epilogue:

- The epilogue for *Life of Pi* by Yann Martel works because Pi's story—of being trapped with a Bengal tiger in a tiny boat and surviving on the ocean for 227 days—is so wild and fantastical that the epilogue, which takes place outside of Pi's point of view, offers insight the reader could never have gotten from Pi himself.
- The epilogue of *Lolita* by Vladimir Nabokov explains why Humbert Humbert, who had no intention of having his behavior toward Lolita discovered, is confessing. It turns out to be a suggestion

his lawyer made, a tactic to make him seem more sympathetic in court.

- The epilogue of *Sleep, Pale Sister* by Joanne Harris works because it allows the reader to see what became of Henry Chester—a character who gets away with some pretty awful behavior toward his wife throughout the narrative. Harris gives the reader a satisfying peek into how he gets his comeuppance.

OPENING YOUR FINAL SCENE

Counterpoints and reflective exposition are two popular techniques for kicking off your final scene because both methods allow you the opportunity to fully illustrate to the reader just how much the events of the story have changed your character.

Counterpoints

A fantastic way to provide your reader with direct and specific cues that your character has changed as a result of your inciting incident is to open the final scene with a counterpoint to the first scene. What this means is that you set up your final scene to resemble your first, but you change the details to reflect the kind of change your character has undergone.

For example, in Kate Atkinson's literary mystery novel *Case Histories*, cop-turned-private-investigator Jackson Brodie's final scene opens with a distinctly lighthearted tone, with the words (in French) "goodbye sadness." He has solved his case, accepted that his ex-wife will never take him back, and found himself attracted to Julia, the quirky woman he met while investigating her sister's death. There's a carefree tone and mood to the scene. He's driving in his convertible, playing music on the radio, and wishing he could get rid of Julia's dull sister Amelia so he can flirt with Julia more effectively:

> *Au revoir tristesse.* Jackson drove with the top down, the Dixie Chicks playing loudly on the car stereo. He picked them up at Montpellier Airport. They were dressed ready for the convertible, in chiffon head scarves and sunglasses, so that Julia looked like a fifties movie star and Amelia

didn't. Julia had said on the phone that Amelia was a lot more cheerful these days, but if she was then she was keeping it to herself, sitting in the backseat of his new BMW M3, harrumphing and grunting at everything that Julia said. Jackson suddenly regretted not buying the two-seater BMW Z8 instead—then they could have put Amelia in the boot.

Now contrast that with the Jackson Brodie the reader met at the beginning of the narrative, who was struggling to quit smoking, dealing with car and work troubles, and fighting with his ex-wife:

> Jackson switched on the radio and listened to the reassuring voice of Jenni Murray on *Woman's Hour.* He lit a new cigarette from the stub of the old one because he had run out of matches, and faced with a choice between chain-smoking or abstinence, he'd taken the former option because it felt like there was enough abstinence in his life already. If he got the cigarette lighter on the dashboard fixed he wouldn't have to smoke his way through the packet, but there were a lot of other things that needed fixing on the car and the cigarette lighter wasn't high on the list. Jackson drove a black Alfa Romeo 156 that he'd bought secondhand four years ago for £13,000 and that was now probably worth less than the Emmelle Freedom mountain bike he had just given his daughter for her eighth birthday (on the proviso that she didn't cycle on the road until she was at least forty).

Notice how in both scenes he's driving in a car and listening to the radio, yet the feeling of the first scene is tense and cranky, while the final scene is relaxed and free. In the final scene, he's driving a new BMW, not a lemon of an Alfa Romeo. He's not worrying about his ex-wife or his daughter and, whereas in the first scene he had "enough abstinence in his life," now he's got the prospect of a new relationship.

Counterpointing your first scene with your final scene is a wonderful way to provide a definitive sense of closure and change to your narrative. Look back at your first scene and see how you can set up a similar one using setting and other small details, while changing the tone, pace, and interior monologue to show that your protagonist is clearly in a different place from where he started.

Reflective Exposition

Reflective exposition is another strong way to kick off your concluding scene. Since the final scene is a time for reflection—after all, you've just devoted a full novel or story to dealing with actions and interactions, putting your protagonist in conflict and danger, and keeping tension and drama alive—interior monologue and exposition can be a natural fit here.

By the end of Janet Fitch's *Paint It Black*, protagonist Josie Tyrell has finally gotten a glimpse into the life and mind of her boyfriend, Michael, who committed suicide at the start of the book. She has driven to the hotel where he did it, read the journal entry he made just before, and come to understand the family he came from. Now she's left to pick up the pieces of her life and carry on:

> Josie sat on the bed in number 4, smoking a ciggie. The sunlight shone bright and cold through the open door. She knew it was time to leave. There was nothing else to do but pack up and head home. And yet, how could she leave this place where he'd made his end? She sat up against the rickety headboard and picked cholla spines out of the bedspread, flicking them into the ashtray. Maybe she should take up knitting. Something quiet and productive. She didn't want to go back home, back to the empty house, as if Michael had fallen through a hole in the ice and just disappeared. But she couldn't drag his raw death through her days like this, like a giant bleeding moose head.

When you open with interior monologue, you can drop the reader directly into the mood, emotion, or thematic state you want him to be in for the finale. Final scenes should not often be very long—they are merely the closing bookend to your protagonist's journey. If you want to set the stage for redemption, forgiveness, acceptance, or any of the common large themes of literature, interior monologue and exposition allow you to do this quickly.

THE PACE OF A FINAL SCENE

Your final scene does not need to have the same dramatic structure as the rest. Your inciting incident is now resolved, and your protagonist has undergone his changes. Your final scene does not require you to set a new intention that must be carried out. It is the place to let your protagonist rest and reflect, and for you to convey a feeling, an image, or a sense of theme to the reader. Therefore, the pace tends to be slower. Actions are small and few, with attention to details that convey your character's inner life and attitudes, hopes, and feelings.

Let's look at a few excerpts from the middles of final scenes. Notice their pacing—how they feel slower, quieter, and more reflective than many of the excerpts we've seen throughout this book.

Author Louise Erdrich uses setting details to bring her pace down in the final scene of her novel *The Painted Drum*. Protagonist Faye Travers, whose sister died young, has just been through an intense relationship with a local sculptor whose teenage daughter was killed. The novel has spent a lot of time focusing on the loss of children and on dealing with grief—and Faye herself had pushed much of her own grief away. By the end, however, her experiences have softened her, and she's ready to face things as they are. In the final scene she goes to visit her sister's grave:

> My sister's stone marker is very distinctive. It's a carved angel that our mother bought from a church about to be demolished and had engraved with the date and name. Perhaps because the angel was not meant as a memorial in the first place, there is something stealthily alive about her—wings that flare instead of droop, an alert and outwardly directed expression, a hand clutched to her breast not as a gesture of reverence or sorrow, but, I think, breathless delight.

There is little action in this scene—the most Faye does is clear away the debris that has piled up on her sister's headstone—because actions are not necessary. Notice, too, that despite being in a cemetery, at her sister's grave, Faye seems optimistic. You can feel her grief lifting in the way she describes the angel on her sister's marker as being "stealthily alive" and clutching her breast with "breathless delight." This final scene is pointing toward positive change. Faye is freed from her grief, which is demonstrated to us in the details.

Setting details are powerful when you want to slow the pace and convey mood. In your final scene, ask yourself how you can direct the reader's focus onto small details in a way that also hits the right note. For example, if your story were about a criminal who finds redemption, in the final scene you could use images that convey freedom and forgiveness—like a bird flying across the expanse of the Grand Canyon or another character offering your protagonist his hand. The close focus on these images will help you to bring your pace down to reflect the tone of your narrative.

You can also slow your pacing down in the final scene by dropping into the realm of metaphors, which have a timeless quality. In Margaret Atwood's novel *The Robber Bride*, three women—Tony, Roz, and Charis—have been personally injured by another woman, Zenia, whom they all met in college. Zenia is a masterful manipulator who has always selfishly put herself before others, and who even manages to fake her death and stage a funeral. But she is not dead at all, and she continues to wreak injustice on the three friends until, finally, the women stop her for good.

In the final scene, Tony reflects upon what has happened and who Zenia was in a series of metaphoric reflections that slow the pace and aim for an emotional finish:

> No flowers grow in the furrows of the lake, none in the fields of asphalt. Tony needs a flower, however. A common weed, because wherever else Zenia had been in her life, she had also been at war. An unofficial war, a guerilla war, a war she may not have known she was waging, but a war nevertheless.
>
> Who was the enemy? What past wrong was she seeking to avenge? Where was her battlefield? Not in any one place. It was in the air all around, it was in the texture of the world itself; or it was nowhere visible, it was in among the neurons, the tiny incandescent fires of the brain that flash up and burn out. An electric flower would be the right kind for Zenia, a bright, lethal flower like a short circuit, a thistle of molten steel going to seed in a burst of sparks.

There are images of war and of flowers—two very powerful contrasting metaphors that sum up the themes of the novel nicely. Metaphors often show up in literary novels, but you'll find them even in genre works because they say so much with so few words.

THE FINAL SENTENCES

In the final scene, the last two to three sentences (and especially the last one) are like DNA—they carry some piece of the entire novel with them, even beyond your narrative. They should leave an emotional flavor that speaks to the entire journey your protagonist has undergone. Here we'll look at final sentences that end with action, reflection, and images.

Final Actions

The reader likes to know that the characters she's come to love will live on. Actions have a way of continuing the motion of characters' lives even after the book or story is over. So you may decide to end your final scene with your protagonist taking a symbolic action or gesture. I stress *symbolic*. If you end on an action, it should suggest something larger than the mundane—it should conjure a sense of the trajectory the protagonist is taking in her life.

In *The Robber Bride*, for instance, the action doesn't come until the final sentence. In much of the final scene Tony is outside reflecting on the damage Zenia wrought—she caused her to mistrust other women, even to hate them at times. The final paragraphs show Tony outside staring at a pottery statue of Zenia, thinking, and then being drawn to the sounds of her friends inside. The scene could easily end at the finish of these reflective paragraphs:

> Tony picks her up and turns her over, probes and questions, but the woman with her glazed pottery face does nothing but smile.
>
> From the kitchen she hears laughter, and the clatter of dishes. Charis is setting out the food, Roz is telling a story. That's what they will do, increasingly in their lives: tell stories. Tonight their stories will be about Zenia.
>
> Was she in any way like us? thinks Tony. Or, to put it another way around: Are we in any way like her?

But Atwood has Tony make one last action, a symbolic one:

> Then she opens the door, and goes in to join the others.

For Tony, rejoining her friends is an important action that suggests she is ready to reopen herself to friendship and connection. That final action crystallizes all of Tony's thoughts and tells the reader that Tony has healed.

Final actions should speak to how your protagonist is going to behave differently in the world now that he has survived the trials of your narrative. Think symbolically. Ask yourself how a small action can convey a larger meaning. At the end of a narrative in which your protagonist has been afraid to make choices, for example, he could be staring down a dirt road. As his final action, he can walk down the unknown road. Symbolic actions carry weight at the end of a narrative and will give your final scene a feeling that there is more to come for your protagonist.

Final Reflections and Thoughts

By the end of the narrative, the reader should be able to tell how the protagonist has changed, but it may still be unclear how the protagonist feels about his changes or about something that took place in the narrative. In this case, a direct expression of feelings is needed.

In Chuck Palahniuk's novel *Invisible Monsters*, a novel about identity and learning to accept oneself in whatever way possible, the narrator—Shannon, a former fashion model—is shot in the face early in the narrative and must undergo massive facial reconstruction, losing her beauty entirely. While in the hospital, she meets Brandy Alexander, a transgender woman preparing for sex reassignment surgery. Brandy's female form looks uncannily similar to how Shannon looked before her accident. At the end of the novel, the reader isn't quite sure how Shannon feels about herself now that her beauty is gone. What the reader knows is that she has made some sort of peace with the past and found friendship in an unlikely source—Brandy. The final sentences convey Shannon's feelings on her identity:

> Completely and totally, permanently and without hope, forever and ever I love Brandy Alexander.
> And that's enough.

Brandy represents the self she used to hate, who was pretty on the outside but tortured within. By admitting her love for Brandy, she does in effect admit to loving herself.

A summary thought or reflection on your narrative works best when it is unclear how the narrator feels at the end, or if there has been some gray area or waffling about feelings. A final thought sums it up so the reader can rest with a sense of understanding.

Final Images

Images resonate with the reader more than actions or interior monologue because they speak the language of the subconscious—they directly trigger emotional responses without an intellectual interpretation.

In Richard Lewis's novel *The Killing Sea*, two teens in Indonesia are affected by the cataclysmic tsunami of 2004. The life of Sarah, an American girl on vacation with her parents and brother, is changed drastically when her mother is killed in the tsunami strike and her father disappears. In the aftermath of the crisis, struggling to get back to a place where she and her brother can get help, she meets Ruslan, an Indonesian boy, and winds up helping him to find his missing father. All throughout the narrative, Sarah's grief for her mother is tangled. She has always believed that her mother didn't want to have her, and this thought haunts her. In the final scene, Ruslan draws Sarah a picture of her mother as he imagines her:

> And in the simple, graceful lines of her gently smiling face, in the eyes that looked right into her, Sarah saw all the love that her mother had always had for her, and how absolutely, utterly wrong she'd been to ever have doubted it.

While that is a lovely sentiment, the final sentence is the most powerful because it plants an image in the reader's mind that conjures not only tears, but also the waters of the tsunami itself that took her mother and father away:

> Something gave way within her, and the raw waters of grief came rushing in.

I am a fan of images that symbolically and metaphorically speak to the journey the protagonist has undergone. Think about the themes of your narrative. Is it about loss, healing, faith, forgiveness? It helps to make a list of images that come to mind for whatever your themes are, and then from that list selecting or creating a final image that especially speaks to your protagonist's personal journey.

FINAL SCENE MUSE POINTS

- The final scene is a snapshot of your protagonist in the aftermath or at the very end of the inciting incident.
- Final scenes should reveal that your protagonist has changed.
- Final scenes are slower and more reflective.
- Final scenes do not require much action.

PART IV

OTHER SCENE CONSIDERATIONS

" The writing of a novel is taking life as it already exists, not to report it but to make an object, toward the end that the finished work might contain this life inside it and offer it to the reader. The essence will not be, of course, the same thing as the raw material; it is not even of the same family of things. The novel is something that never was before and will not be again. "

—EUDORA WELTY

POINT OF VIEW

In fiction, point of view (POV) is the camera through which the reader enters your protagonist's world, sees what he sees, and shares in his feelings and perceptions. It is also the entry point into character development, and therefore worthy of careful consideration before you set out. POV has a direct influence on the tone, mood, energy, and pace of a scene (not to mention your overall narrative).

To master POV from one scene to the next, you must use it with integrity and consistency—by which I mean that the reader should feel expertly guided through your scenes at all times and never confused about whose POV is being presented. If you've shown the scene of a murder through a shocked widow's eyes, for example, you don't want to suddenly leap into the point of view of the vigilante detective who is hunting down the murderer without legitimate reason and careful transition. Haphazard shifts in POV will leave your story feeling amateurish and your reader feeling like she has whiplash.

In this chapter, we'll examine the different kinds of POV in relation to their effects. We'll also talk about how to make POV leaps and transitions within and between, so that whatever POV you choose to use works for your scenes, not against them.

CHOOSING YOUR CAMERA

POV is not only the camera that shows the reader what your characters see; it is the mechanism that determines how close the reader can get to your characters. The distance between your characters and the reader determines what I call in my book *Writing the Intimate Character* the *intimacy* of the scene or story. The more intimate, or "internal," the POV, the more the reader feels as if he is personally experiencing what the character is. The more distant, or external, the POV, the more the reader feels like an objective observer, a witness looking on from the sidelines. Your material will motivate your choice of intimacy. Use this next section to choose the degree of intimacy you want, and the level of objectivity you need, to tell your story.

First Person

First-person POV reaches out and grabs the reader, like a small child standing in a room screaming "Me, me, me!" You can't help but turn to look. The "I" pronoun is very immediate, and it draws the reader directly into the characters' emotional experience.

The following example comes from Kaitlyn Greenidge's novel, *We Love You, Charlie Freeman*. In the novel, a black family is invited to a heavily white community in rural Massachusetts to take care of a young chimpanzee as part of a research experiment. All of the chapters are in first-person POV, but each one is related by a different character. Here is a snippet of the first chapter, narrated by protagonist Charlotte, where the family meets Charlie the chimpanzee:

> Then it was my turn.
>
> I reached out my hand to touch him. I thought he would be bristly and sharp, like a cat, but his hair was fine, so soft it was almost unbearable. I could feel, at its downy ends, the heat spreading up from his skin beneath. I pulled my hand away quickly. The scent of him stayed on my fingers, old and sharp, like a bottle of witch hazel. ...
>
> My mother was the last to hold him. She was crying and she said through her tears, her hands shaking as she reached out to touch him, "Isn't he beautiful?"

> I wanted to say something snide. I wanted to say what I had been telling her since she told us about this crazy experiment: that this was crazy, that she was crazy, that it would never work. I wanted to sign *bullshit*.

If it's intimacy you strive for in creating characters, you can't get much closer than first person. You are literally inside the protagonist's head, which is very useful when you want to put the reader directly into your characters' shoes. We know what Charlotte thinks, how she feels, because we get all the sensory experiences and physical actions directly through her POV.

On the same note, the problem with first person is that if your character undergoes tremendous suffering, physical pain, or crisis, first person might be too immediate and difficult. To provide objectivity and pull back from the intensity, you can use third-person limited, which we'll look at shortly.

Also, because first person is so immediate, your verb tenses have much more power than in other points of view. The present tense, when conjoined with first person, is probably the most immediate experience you can give the reader: "I hold the gun up to Max's head." Whew! That gun is liable to go off, and poor Max may have only moments left. Compare the past tense: "I held the gun up to Max's head." Do you see how the past tense offers a tiny beat of distance?

Second Person

Second person is a narrative version of self-talk. The "you" pronoun is coming from the character, aimed back to himself. It is first person turned even more deeply intimate; the reader is not only inside the character's mind and thoughts, he essentially *becomes* the character.

Here's an example from Aimee Bender's story "The Bowl" in her collection of short stories, *The Girl in the Flammable Skirt*:

> When you open the wrapping (there's no card), you find a bowl, a green bowl with a white interior, a bowl for fruit or mixing. You're puzzled, but obediently put four bananas inside and then go back to whatever you were doing before: a crossword puzzle. You wonder and hope this is from a secret admirer, but if so, you think, why a bowl? What are you to learn and gain from a green and white fruit bowl?

This POV is hyperintimate in this usage—the character is narrating to herself. This form of second-person intimate is best used when the intention of the scene is to explore a character's feelings or attitude, or to draw the reader in incredibly close, but not so effective when you have a lot of action or character interaction unfolding in the scene at hand. The "you" second-person point of view plants the reader deeper inside the character's experience until the line between reader and character is blurred.

Second person can seem slightly humorous, even when the subject matter is not, because it's not a tense that we use in actual conversation unless we're asking questions or providing directions. In fact, using second person may make the reader feel that they are being given a sequence of directives that includes everything from what they should do to what they should think and feel about what they do. Second person is an exquisitely self-conscious point of view, which can be fascinating and fun when the subject matter or the protagonist is quirky or the style is experimental; otherwise, second person feels as if the reader has just opened a window on a character's mind in the middle of a deeply personal thought process. As a result, it's more often used in asides throughout a novel to drop into a universal experience or in short stories, where it doesn't need to be sustained for a long period of time.

Third Person

You'll recognize third person by the use of pronouns "she" and "he." There are two main forms of the third-person point of view—third-person omniscient, which is more distant, and third-person limited, which I call third-person intimate. I find that writers have a tendency to interchange the two in confusing ways, so it's best to draw a definite line between them and decide ahead of time which you plan to use throughout.

Third-Person Intimate

Third-person intimate is one of the most straightforward and practical of all points of view. Here you use "he" and "she" pronouns, which provides enough distance that the reader is not riding piggyback with the characters and allows you to develop one character at a time so that you never confuse the reader. When in the third-person intimate, the reader only knows, hears, and sees what the focus character does—you can't slip outside the character and provide information that a second character knows or understands (unless it's spoken aloud). There is no guesswork or moving between characters' thoughts.

The main thing to avoid when using third-person intimate is providing information that your focus character could not know. For example, you might write, "John was unaware of the black van lurking around the corner." If John is unaware, then you're slipping into the omniscient, or "all knowing," and must correct this. Simply wait until John does notice the van, or falls victim to the consequences of whoever is in the van, to reveal his awareness of it.

Third-Person Omniscient

In the third-person omniscient POV, the camera can move wherever it needs to, into any character's head, to look out upon any facet of the scene at hand. The camera can drop into any character's inner landscape, then just as quickly move back out and look at the character from afar. This flexibility offers more options for drama and conflict, and is often employed in an epic or historical novel, where important information needs to be communicated outside of a character's perspective.

Omniscient Continuous

When you can see inside the head of more than one character and hear multiple characters' thoughts in a back-and-forth kind of fashion throughout the story, you're in the omniscient continuous, as I like to call it. When the camera pans from Snow White to Dopey, Grumpy, and then Doc, and you can hear the thoughts and opinions of each one without breaking into a new scene as they discuss what to do about the nasty old witch, you're smack-dab in omniscient continuous.

When you employ omniscient continuous, it creates a sense of movement in your scenes because you jump from character to character, but it also creates emotional distance. While it may be useful to dance back and forth between characters' thoughts when a scene involves multiple characters, the narrative does not stick closely to any specific character when you do so. Because of this, omniscient continuous is often not the best choice if you want to explore the complexity and development of characters' psychologies in your novel.

Omniscient Instants

Omniscient instants, on the other hand, are bits of information inserted into third-person limited POV that offer up information in the scene that the characters can't know but that helps clarify details for the reader.

Here's an example in Ingrid Hill's novel of ancestors, *Ursula, Under*, which is a series of linked historical stories that trace back the lineage of Ursula, a child who has slipped down a mine shaft and is awaiting rescue.

> [Rene Josserand's skull] is still there today, undiscovered, four and a half feet into the rich earth, beneath leaves, grass, and clay, never touched by a gravedigger's hand. There are local post cards, but none of them says, "Paradise, Michigan, home of the tomahawked skull of Rene Josserand," because no one knows.

Since Rene Josserand—one of Ursula's ancestors—is long dead, and "no one knows" about his existence, technically there isn't a single person in the narrative who could deliver that information to the reader. Yet Hill chooses to tell it to us, since his story is integral to the life of the protagonist, Ursula, and this information ties up his storyline for us as best as she can.

Keep in mind that too many omniscient leaps will inevitably pull the reader out of the continuity of his reading. He might stop to ponder, "Hey, I'm not really supposed to know that," or even, "Who exactly is telling me this?"—and you don't want too much of that to happen in your book.

USING MULTIPLE POINTS OF VIEW WITHIN A SCENE

POV is the camera through which you show the reader the character's perceptions of events in each scene. If you choose a limited POV and have one protagonist only, then that is the character who gets the camera. If you have an omniscient narrator, the narrator gets the camera. Use the POV descriptions in this chapter to decide what kind of effect you want to achieve, and choose your POV accordingly.

Choosing POV gets trickier when you have multiple protagonists. If you elect to use a limited POV, you will never have to worry about jumping from head to head within a given scene; your biggest concern will be when and where to switch from narrator to narrator. But if you *do* want to be able to pan the camera through the thoughts of characters A, B, and C as event X unfolds, pay attention to this next part.

Changing POV Within a Scene

If you have multiple characters whose points of view are relevant within a single scene —meaning you want to get inside their heads, not just have them speak or act in ways the other characters can see—then you'll need to use the omniscient POV. When your narrative tackles large issues—war, culture, race, identity—in which a complex or comprehensive look at a situation is required, omniscient POV may be a good choice. Omniscient allows you to go beyond the personal—beyond the intimate experience of a small handful of characters—to include more history, details, or perspectives that still add up to a cohesive look at a subject.

Omniscient is also useful when you need to show more than one side of a story—and need to be able to jump back and forth between characters to offer alternate takes on events as they're happening, rather than later on in reflection.

However, you must make an omniscient POV clear right away, from the first paragraph in the first scene. If the reader believes that he is *only* able to see inside character A's head, and then you suddenly leap into character B's head, the reader will feel confused and possibly irritated. And a word of warning: Too much jumping back and forth—or between more than three or four people in a given scene—*will* create confusion.

Here's an example of omniscient POV from the novel *Rosie* by Anne Lamott—the story of a single mother, Elizabeth, raising her daughter after her husband's death. From the first scene in the book, Lamott shows the reader that she is in the omniscient by providing information that comes from a godlike, all-knowing source:

> There were many things about Elizabeth that the people of Bayview disliked. They thought her tall, too thin, too aloof. Her neck was too long

and her breasts were too big. The men, who could have lived with the size of her breasts, found her unwilling to flirt and labeled her cold. The women were jealous of how well her clothes hung on her.

Since this information is not delivered through the lens of any one character, the reader understands immediately that it is omniscient—the camera can move wherever it needs to go. Lamott maintains this POV throughout all the scenes, dancing effortlessly into the thoughts and feelings of her protagonists, Elizabeth and Rosie. In one paragraph she is in Rosie's POV:

> Rosie Ferguson was four when her father died. As she sat on her mother's lap at the crowded Episcopal service, she knew that her father was dead but kept waiting for him to join them in the first pew, wondering what he would bring her.

Then, in the next paragraph in the same scene, we're in Elizabeth's POV:

> Elizabeth held Rosie on her lap, dimly aware that her daughter was trying to take care of her—Rosie kept patting her and smiling bravely—but Elizabeth couldn't concentrate on what was happening. It was too surreal. ...

Once you choose omniscient, you have to commit to it—you can't back down from it within the scene. Notice, too, that Lamott lets each character have a good paragraph of her own—the minimum amount of space I recommend you give each character if you're going to hop from head to head. Starting a new paragraph is a good way to signal to the reader that you're moving the camera again. Along those same lines, keep in mind the following:

- To promote a sense of cohesiveness, change POV at the end of action, not in the middle.
- Change POV at the end of a line of dialogue—do not try to weave one character's thoughts into another character's speech.
- Change POV when you want to offer another character's reaction to an event in the scene.

A word of warning: Even though you're in the omniscient and can move into any character's head, be selective. The reader doesn't need to hear the thoughts or know the opinions of all minor characters. Stick to the points of view of characters who can contribute plot information or deepen the reader's understanding of your protagonists.

Changing POV from Scene to Scene

Remember that, unless characters are in a moving vehicle or taking a stroll, a scene should take place largely in one location. Therefore, if you've got a chapter-long scene—that is, you're writing one scene per chapter—you automatically limit the physical location of the chapter.

When you have multiple scenes within a chapter, try to think of each as a separate square of a quilt, or a piece of a puzzle, that must add up to some sort of whole or understanding within the chapter. It's best to use multiple scenes in a given chapter when you want to achieve the following:

- Look at one issue or topic from multiple angles.
- Switch to multiple physical locations or in and out of present time.
- Build up new plot information that the current scene won't allow, but that needs to come at that juncture in the story.
- Introduce another character.

Author Jodi Picoult includes multiple scenes per chapter in her books because she writes about subjects that can be viewed from many different angles: suicide, rape, motherhood. In any given chapter, when addressing a specific plot event, she'll often give multiple characters a scene of their own, allowing her to shed light on numerous perspectives on one subject.

For instance, her novel *Second Glance* is about Comtosook, a Vermont town where paranormal events occur when a developer threatens to build on sacred land, and where a long-hidden 1920s eugenics program designed to weed out "undesirable genes" is revealed. The novel features multiple viewpoints. Each chapter is broken into a series of short scenes told from the points of view of as many as ten different characters who are affected by strange events. Note that although there are multiple scenes per chapter, each scene has only one point of view. To show that she's beginning a new scene, Picoult uses a visual cue—a break of four lines (sometimes called a soft hiatus) or symbols like * * * —and identifies the point-of-view character within the first couple of lines. These scenes offer different pieces of insight into the plot event that is being explored at that particular juncture. Here are three samples of scene launches that all appear within chapter two, in which people are trying to determine whether Angel Quarry is haunted or someone is pulling a prank:

> Ross didn't know whom he blamed more: Ethan, for planting this seed in his mind; or himself, for bothering to listen. Angel Quarry is haunted, his nephew had said, everyone says so. ...

> "What do you make of it?" Winks Smiling Fox asked, grunting as he moved the drum a few feet to the left. Where they'd been sitting, the ground beneath their feet was icy. Yet over here, there were dandelions growing. ...

> "Ethan?"
> From his vantage point beneath the blackout shades, Ethan froze at the sound of his mother's voice. He whipped his body back so that it wasn't pressed against the warm glass windowpane. ...

Each scene may be its own unit, but the multiple scenes within the chapter all play off each other and add up to form the reader's own image of Angel Quarry. By the end of the chapter, the reader is pretty sure that, yes, Angel Quarry is haunted.

Using multiple scenes within a given chapter is a common and effective way to create a mosaic of little parts that add up to form a larger, more comprehensive whole. But it comes with a caveat: When you have multiple scenes within a chapter, you will serve the reader best if each of those scenes has only one viewpoint—and not an omniscient one—since you're already forcing the reader to move around.

Changing POV from Chapter to Chapter

In many narratives, one chapter can be its own long scene. The benefit of this construction is that you don't have to create boundaries to clarify a complicated POV structure. One scene per chapter is undoubtedly the simplest and clearest structure to work with, and if you are new to writing, I recommend that you stick with this structure until you've mastered scenes and can confidently move on to more complex structures. When your whole chapter is one long scene, you can focus on the protagonist's scene intention, decide what kind of scene it's going to be (see chapters twelve through twenty-one), and use your core elements, one chapter at a time. This structure requires less work of you, and it allows the reader to stay in one place and time per chapter. This structure will feel more straightforward to the reader, and perhaps also less textured or layered, but you can guarantee that you will tell a simple, clear story by using this method. One scene per chapter is an ideal structure in the following instances:

- When you want to keep your characters in a unified time and place
- When you're writing a dialogue scene, as dialogue takes up a lot of room
- When you're writing a suspense scene, as building tension requires that actions be drawn out
- When your narrative has a linear chronology—it doesn't flash back in time
- When you want to switch to a different type of point of view to achieve a different effect for another protagonist—for instance, protagonist A is narrated in the first person, but protagonist B is better served by third-person limited

When a chapter is one long scene, you have time to devote to each protagonist. If you use a limited POV, by nature of the length of a chapter, you have more page time to delve into one protagonist's experience and reveal it to the reader.

THE STORY ARC OF MULTIPLE CO-PROTAGONISTS

If you decide to give POV scenes and chapters to multiple protagonists, you allow yourself some freedom to play with different personalities and worldviews, but you also create an additional challenge for yourself: You are burdened with giving each character a narrative arc—each must undergo change and be connected to the inciting incident—and eventually you must merge the separate plotlines in order for the narrative to work.

This means that, following the instructions in chapter twenty-three, each of your characters has several imperatives they must address:

- Responding to the inciting incident (your work will be a lot more cohesive if they all share the same inciting incident)
- Engaging in consequences stemming from the inciting incident
- Changing as a result of the inciting incident
- Merging her individual storyline with those of the other protagonists by narrative's end

Ultimately, you want to select points of view that will convey the intimacy or distance appropriate to your narrative, offer consistency to the reader so that there is no confusion over whose POV you are in, and devote equal stage time to each of the protagonists who star in your narrative.

The following books successfully merge two or more protagonists' storylines: *The Girl with All the Gifts* by M.R. Carey; *Truly Madly Guilty* by Liane Moriarty; *My Sister's Keeper* by Jodi Picoult; and The Passage trilogy by Justin Cronin.

DEVOTING EQUAL TIME TO CO-PROTAGONISTS

Now that we've covered the idea of using multiple points of view, it's important to discuss how to let your narrators share the time on the page. The most definitive way to signal that you have more than one protagonist is to give each protagonist equal time in your narrative, whether you split time based on the number of scenes or the number of individual chapters.

A lot of authors adopt a simple formula: Each POV character narrates one chapter or scene, taking turns in order. Character A goes first, then B, then C. Then you repeat that pattern: ABC, ABC, ABC. In other words, you give each character a chance to narrate, then you start all over again. You may find the need for variations on this pattern: AAA, BBB, CCC, for instance, or AA, BB, CC, so long as the time each protagonist gets is as close to equal as you can make it.

SECONDARY AND MINOR CHARACTERS

As the creator of all the wily and fascinating characters in your fiction, it can be difficult to assign levels of importance to them at first; after all, they're all wonderful to you, even the evil ones. Yet, when it comes to how your characters contribute to each scene and to the overall journey of your narrative, you do, in fact, need to develop a hierarchy. Even though this is a chapter on the role of minor characters, let's quickly review the role of the protagonists before moving on.

Most important to any narrative is your protagonist—the character around whom your inciting incident revolves and who is most challenged and tested in your narrative. Depending on your narrative, you might have more than one protagonist. The protagonists are the headliners of your story, and they do the most work and get the most lines; their emotional and spiritual conflicts are of central interest to the reader. In limited POV chapters, each protagonist narrates his own scenes. It's not as common to show the points of view of secondary or minor characters unless you're writing from an omniscient POV, and even then you want to give those lesser characters far less stage time.

SECONDARY CHARACTERS

A secondary character's job is to affect your protagonist in meaningful ways, exerting change and conflict, offering support and sympathy, and enriching your narrative. True secondary characters are not the stars, but neither are they minor players; secondary characters have important roles that affect the narrative arc of your protagonist. But if one should die or disappear, the story should be able to go on without her (though her loss will have an impact on the protagonist, of course!).

Here we'll look at the roles of the two main types of secondary characters: antagonists and allies. Neither type of character should get his own point-of-view chapters (you will find books where this rule is beautifully broken, but it's not the norm) or, if you've written in omniscient POV, too many paragraphs or pages inside his head. The reader will perceive who your protagonists are by how much time is spent telling the story from their points of view, so if you do include the perspectives of secondary characters, do so sparingly. Main characters get more time on the page, and the reader sees through the protagonist's lens more than through the perspectives of any other characters.

Antagonists

The antagonist is the person or the group of people whose objective is to thwart the goals of your protagonist. Often called "villains," antagonists should cause conflict and pile on the emotional pressure. (An antagonist can also be a force of nature or some other means of thwarting your protagonist, but for this chapter we're specifically going to talk about antagonists as people.)

While the antagonist does not have to appear in every scene, every scene should convey a sense of pressure, menace, or uncertainty as a result of her presence within the story itself. The antagonist needs to be developed well enough that you can understand how she thinks and what motivates her, but she doesn't need to have the full character arc of a protagonist.

With an antagonist, you really only need to know the following:

- What the antagonist's motivation is for trying to thwart your protagonist in the first place
- What the antagonist expects to gain or seeks to obtain by thwarting your protagonist
- What the antagonist stands to lose if he does not attain his goal

Unlike the protagonist, who must undergo some kind of transformation in the narrative, antagonists don't need to be developed too fully. They can start out evil and stay evil (though try to stay away from "caricature" villains—those who are bad beyond belief). The most character work you'll need to do with an antagonist is to show why and how she came to be the way she is, uncovering her motivations so that the reader understands why she is causing so much trouble for your protagonist. Is it pure evil, greed, lust, or fear? All great villains have a motivation, and the top motivator is often revenge. She was slighted, injured, thwarted, or insulted, and she is out to set things straight.

Even though readers should be aware of your antagonist's motivations, however, what makes him important to your narrative is not his own individual story so much as how he affects your protagonist and acts as a catalyst for change. Here are some ways that antagonists force protagonists to change or act:

- **BY PROVIDING AN IMMEDIATE LOOMING THREAT.** The antagonist has threatened your protagonist with an imminent consequence if the protagonist does not prevent it. This creates urgency as well as suspense.
- **BY PROMPTING A COURSE OF ACTION MOTIVATED BY FEAR.** The protagonist behaves or takes a particular action out of fear of the antagonist.
- **BY PROMPTING A DEFENSIVE OR COURAGEOUS COURSE OF ACTION.** The protagonist takes an action to defend himself or a loved one, or demonstrates an act of sheer courage that is specifically inspired by the antagonist.

Though you are not required to include any change for the antagonist outside of her defeat, you may choose to redeem your antagonist by the end of your narrative so that after her downfall, or at the precipice of it, she decides to help rather than hinder the protagonist. This is a challenging feat to pull off, and it generally works only when the antagonist has already demonstrated the potential for duality early on. For instance, a Nazi soldier who earlier hesitated to follow an order may have a sudden fit of conscience and help a Jewish person escape. You are just as free to have your antagonist meet her demise and never be thought of again.

Allies

The other main type of secondary character is the protagonist's friend, ally, or loved one (we'll lump them all under the category of allies for ease of discussion). Again, these characters most likely don't need to be given their own POV scenes or chapters because the story does not require that an ally undergo a dramatic personal transformation. The ally's actions are meant to support the protagonist and make it possible for him to succeed and face his challenges. Your ally may simply be a love interest in whom the protagonist has faith and who keeps him grounded when everything is going wrong. Or your ally might be a companion on a long journey who keeps your protagonist on her toes and rallies her to keep up her strength to reach her goal.

Though these allies do not need to have a complex character arc, most often they *will* have to rise to some kind of challenge to support your protagonist. Allies often must undergo an act of courage or selflessness on behalf of the protagonist—remember, however, the goal is not for the ally to change, but for the protagonist to. Allies will achieve these feats in one of a few different ways:

- **SACRIFICE.** It's very common for an ally to sacrifice himself in a narrative so that your protagonist can carry on with his task. All great epic stories have a sacrifice of this kind. One of my favorite fantasy series, by Robin Hobb, begins with *Assassin's Apprentice* and continues on for a total of nine interlinked books. The series is rich with wonderful allies who sacrifice themselves in many different ways for the protagonists. Hobb is a master of character development, and I recommend her books to anyone who struggles to build characters of any type.
- **FINDING SURPRISING STRENGTH OR COURAGE.** Another wonderful way to use your ally is to have him rally strength or courage nobody

knew he was capable of just when the protagonist needs it most. Think Neville Longbottom, who finds his power just in time to support Harry Potter in a big fight. There's nothing more dramatic than a scared ally exhibiting sudden courage, conscience, or strength in the face of danger.

- **RALLYING LARGER SUPPORT GROUPS.** Sometimes your protagonist must go it alone for one reason or another. Secondary characters can rally support on the protagonist's behalf without her knowing and show up at the scene of her drama with reinforcements that she did not expect. This might take the form of a group of activists who descend upon their cause at the last minute, like a group of suffragettes in a historical novel all showing up to fight for their right to vote.

Allies should be vivid and memorable, but they should also function under this main imperative: to support, bolster, and serve the protagonist. If your secondary character doesn't do one of those three things, you have either a superfluous character who should be cut or an antagonist in disguise.

MINOR CHARACTERS

Finally we come to the last set of characters that will appear in your fiction: minor characters. Their job is to add spice and realism. These are the store clerks, passersby, phone operators, plane stewards, waitresses, strangers on a train, movie ushers, etc., who provide small opportunities for interactions and challenges to your main characters. They can be both disposable or essential, depending on your needs. You will know minor characters by the fact that they do not make frequent appearances in scenes as protagonists or secondary characters—they pretty much appear as needed, which might be once in the entire narrative.

Think of the munchkins in *The Wizard of Oz*, who turn up only to give Dorothy pointers on finding the yellow brick road. Or think even more minor, like one of the nameless "floaters" in the Murder squad in Tana French's mystery novels. Minor characters do not need to be complex. This flat quality works because minor characters exist as foils for your protagonists. In fact, I like to think of them as chemicals that cause reactions in a solution. By that, I mean they are there for protagonists to bounce ideas off of, get into brief fights with, and gain tiny pearls of wisdom from in passing scenes. They don't need to be present in as many scenes as your main characters, and they don't need to be complex. However, many successful minor characters have some vivid quality that the protagonist will react to, such as a cashier who loudly (and annoyingly) pops her gum.

You most definitely don't have to worry about whether these characters will change. You don't have to give them a love interest or a childhood.

Here's a list of good uses for minor characters in scenes:

- **OFFER OR CONNECT A PIECE OF PLOT INFORMATION.** This should be information that the protagonist needs to know and couldn't access alone.
- **ACT AS A WITNESS TO MAJOR PLOT EVENTS, HELPING TO TIE THREADS TOGETHER.** This may be the witness to a murder, the child who speaks up in his parents' vitriolic divorce, the silent neighbor who reveals the husband's betrayal when the protagonist needs to know.
- **PROVIDE A TEMPERING FORCE OF BEHAVIOR.** Your protagonist is fiery and rash, but a call from a friend or acquaintance can act as a calm conscience.
- **ADD A TOUCH OF REALISM.** Most of us live near, and interact with, other people on a daily basis in nearly everything we do, so your characters are bound to encounter others, from close friends to clerks at the grocery store. In fact, if your character does not meet people at some point in your narrative, you'd better have a good reason for that—incarceration or a case of agoraphobia, for example.
- **ADD COMIC RELIEF.** A wisecracking joker can be a great addition to balance intense scenes.
- **ACT AS A TROUBLEMAKER.** A minor character can exist merely to add trouble and conflict to your characters' lives: an ex-girlfriend who has a habit of turning up each time your protagonist starts dating a girl he really likes, or a hostile relative who steals from your protagonist's house.
- **FUNCTION AS A DISTRACTION.** A minor character can be a red herring to distract the reader from a plot twist you plan to throw into an end

scene. The serial killer might be someone the reader comes to think is a pretty nice guy, so you throw in a minor character who looks pretty bad—a history of drugs and violence, say—and lead the reader away from your real killer long enough for the truth to come as a surprise.

As the above list implies, minor characters are almost a part of the setting. You don't need to develop them deeply; you simply need to make them useful.

HOW TO KEEP YOUR CHARACTERS IN THEIR PLACES

I'd like to mention that secondary and minor characters can be seductive. You can find them saying a bit too much or showing up in more scenes than is useful. Let's refer back to Harry Potter. Though Harry has many friends and comrades, and meets many interesting wizards and compelling creatures (without whom he never would have made it through seven books of adventures), the reader is not going to waste much time worrying about what happens to Madam Rosmerta, the pub proprietor, or Argus Filch, the Hogwarts caretaker. (It's also worth mentioning that, though Hermione Granger and Ron Weasley, Harry's two best friends, are well developed and undergo some change, they are still secondary characters. Ultimately, it is Harry's journey and story, and he is the character who must undergo a dramatic transformation. As allies, Ron and Hermione exhibit courage and strength, sacrifice and support, but if one of them had been killed off [horror!] the story would have continued.) While your minor characters are important, remember that they will stay minor only as long as they follow these guides:

- Make infrequent appearances—they should not appear in every scene
- Demonstrate little or no internal reflection
- Are not emotionally complex
- Demonstrate a behavior or personality that challenges or supports your character
- Act as a catalyst to stimulate change or reaction in your protagonist

If you've got one secondary or minor character present in nearly every scene, the reader will start to think that maybe this character isn't so minor anymore, and then she will begin to expect more from that character—which means more from you. Secondary characters can certainly show up in a number of scenes with your protagonist, but again, the focus must remain on your protagonist, and these secondary characters must be there to serve, support, or thwart the protagonist in some way.

Promoting Secondary Characters

From time to time you may discover that someone you intended to be a secondary character is rich and vivid, and fits into your plot so well that you want to bump up his status to co-protagonist—which means that he now needs to get POV time equal with any other protagonists currently in your narrative, or he may make a better protagonist than the one you've chosen. These thoughts might crop up in revision. Pay attention to how you feel when writing a secondary character. He may be more major than you realized if he does any of the following:

- Appears in all or most scenes
- Begins to undergo an emotional transformation separate from that of your existing protagonist
- Becomes so integral to the plot that it falls apart or becomes confusing without him

If he starts to take over the story, or you find that he is more compelling than you first thought, you might consider whether he's been given too low a status in your narrative and needs to be promoted.

Secondary characters thwart or support your main character: They are either allies or antagonists. They are memorable and vivid, but come with no imperative for dramatic transformation. Minor characters are almost a part of the scenery, acting as simple catalysts to get your protagonist moving on to the next aspect of his plot, and don't require as much detail or backstory. These characters have no imperative to change whatsoever.

Together these kinds of characters will create a rich, vivid cast you can call on in your scenes to provide many challenges and situations under which your protagonist can transform.

SCENE TRANSITIONS

So far we have talked about the construction of individual scenes, which is the most important subject of this book and will more than prepare you to begin writing a manuscript. Yet a bunch of scenes stacked one after the other doesn't automatically equal a narrative. Now we'll look at ways to link individual scenes together to compose a strong, vivid storyline.

It's useful to think of your scenes as the cells that make up a body. Each type is distinct and individual, performing a different role, but they all must work together or you won't have a cohesive narrative. The simplest way to link scenes is through transitions, passages of text at the beginning or ending of a scene, where you condense and shift time, space, point of view, and many other details to create a sense of flow and bypass mundane or nondramatic moments in your characters' lives.

That last point is very important: Fiction is a *simulation* of real life; your goal is to offer only the most meaningful, relevant, and dramatic moments, and to bypass the moments that don't contribute to your narrative. Remember this!

Transitions are most noticeable at the beginning of a scene—this is where the reader will make the mental leaps you need: "Oh, I see, he's not on the farm anymore, he's in an airplane!" "Oh, it's not early morning anymore; it's nighttime!" So we'll focus first on how to make your transitions clear at the beginning of a new scene. We've already covered how to set up the various scene types at the end of the prior scene, but we'll talk briefly about keeping the next scene in mind here as well.

The reader doesn't like to be jarred every time you begin a new scene, and since a narrative is composed of many scenes, sometimes hundreds, you'll need to make sure that each successive scene feels connected to or derived from the one that preceded it. Chapters are also breaks in your story's action, whether a chapter is composed of one or ten scenes. Chapter transitions need to be smooth as well.

The end of a scene or chapter is a note to the reader that you are concluding something, at least temporarily—offering a break from the preceding events to change, refresh, or throw a twist into character or plot details. You might change something minor, such as physical location, or the next scene might take place years down the road. Either way, at the beginning of a scene, you are, first and foremost, signaling that changes have taken place.

SIGNALING A SCENE CHANGE

When you open a new scene, your first job is to orient the reader as to where the protagonist and other characters are in relationship to the scene (or scenes) before. You start, as the writer, by asking: What has changed? Where and when are my characters now? How can I make this clear to the reader?

Time of Day, or Day of the Week, Month, or Year

At the beginning of a scene, it's likely you'll have to somehow make clear to the reader that time—minutes, days, or years—has passed. Condensing time is a handy trick for covering only the interesting points of a character's life and story. Here are two different examples of leaps in time. The first is from Chris Bohjalian's *Midwives*, and the second is from Caleb Carr's *The Alienist*. Notice how they both rely on simple expository descriptions, which I've italicized to make them stand out:

> *At some point soon* after my mother started to speak, Corporal Richard Tilley began taking notes. He wrote fast to keep up with my mother, and

the few questions his partner asked usually began, "Could you repeat that please, Mrs. Danforth?"

What has been condensed is the time between Mrs. Danforth's arrest and when she is questioned.

> *I got to Kreizler's house*, at 283 East Seventeenth Street, a few minutes early, white-tied and caped and not at all sure of the conspiracy I'd entered into with Sara—a conspiracy that for better or worse would now play out.

Here Carr condenses a few hours, and he also condenses the journey from point A to point B. The reader doesn't see the character's entire walk from his office up to East Seventeenth Street because there is nothing significant to the plot in that journey. Carr simply gets his character to the next place with a few words: "I got to Kreizler's house."

When you want to condense time, you can use one of the following tools:

- **NARRATIVE SUMMARY.** A few months later, they stood on the same stoop where they had first met.
- **DIALOGUE.** "I haven't seen you since Matt's wild kegger gone bad!"
- **SETTING.** The young sapling she had planted when she left was now a full-grown tree.

I do want to add a note of caution here. You should condense time only when you need to condense short periods of time, and then only specifically to bypass mundane and irrelevant information. Be aware that large leaps—like many years, or from one plot event to another—undertaken without making sure the plot keeps pace with these leaps in between to make them plausible will only get you into trouble with your reader. If you feel the need to condense large periods of time frequently, or find that you jump too freely from one event to another, you may need to renegotiate your plot and reconfigure the events so they result in a more plausible time line.

Location/Setting

Many times the reason for ending a scene is to move the characters to a new location, whether this is just down the street or involves putting the character on a steamship to a new country. If you have changed the setting from the last scene, you want to make this clear fairly quickly. Here is an excerpt from Chitra Banerjee Divakaruni's *The Vine of Desire*, in which the introduction of a new setting is used to launch the scene:

> Chopra's house is huge and pink, like a giant, lighted cake plopped down on a bald stretch of hillside. There's a uniformed white guard at the gate, to whom Sunil has to show his invitation, then a circular driveway with an illuminated fountain and Grecian-style statuary, mostly nymphs at various stages of undress, or plump, peeing cherubs.

This setting is most definitely not the "tiny apartment" that protagonist Anju and her husband, Sunil, live in, nor is it the university where Anju takes classes. The reader knows right away that these characters are not in any of their familiar locales. Here are some ways to make a setting shift:

- Select details carefully so that the setting description is engaging.
- Allow your protagonist to interact with the setting when possible.
- Allow your protagonist to have opinions about the setting.
- Allow the setting to reflect your protagonist's mood, feelings, or inner world in some way.

Ambiance and Atmosphere (Mood, Tone, and Weather Changes)

Not all scenes will require a shift in setting, so if your protagonist is in the same location he was in during the previous scene, but you want to demonstrate that something is different—that a new plot twist is coming, or that the character's attitude has changed—you can change the atmosphere or mood. Here's an example from Jean Hegland's novel *Windfalls*, about a struggling single mother, Cerise, who endures a terrible loss. Many of the scenes starring Cerise take place in her small trailer, where she lives with her teenage daughter and young son, but the reader is alerted by a literal change in atmosphere that this scene is going to be different from others:

> When the smoke first filtered into her sleep, her dreams recognized it. It was a nasty smoke, the smell of cheap things burning, and for a while her dreams engulfed it, offering weird dream-reasons to explain its presence.

> It was an explosion that finally woke her, a blast that left her unmoored in
> the darkness, adrenaline prickling her flesh, dread clinging to her bones.
> A bad dream, she told herself, as she struggled to find a way out of its grip.

The smell of smoke and the loud explosion are not normal occurrences in Cerise's trailer—the reader immediately knows something is wrong (and different from the last scene). These details pique the reader's curiosity and excite anxiety for the welfare of the characters, while also suggesting that something has changed from the last time the reader saw Cerise.

Atmosphere is closely connected with mood, as in this example from G.K. Chesterton's novel *The Man Who Was Thursday*, a sort of philosophical mystery. One night, the poet Gabriel Syme meets up with a mysterious stranger, Gregory, who initiates a debate about art and anarchy and convinces Syme to come along with him for a "very interesting evening." Syme is unwittingly drawn into a secret society and a mystery that will challenge his view of himself. From the pub—which has a kind of upbeat, jolly energy—where Gregory brought Syme, he is taken by boat on the English Channel to a new location. Notice how the mood immediately begins to turn mysterious and suspenseful with just a few details:

> At first the stone stair seemed to Syme as deserted as a pyramid; but
> before he reached the top he had realized that there was a man leaning
> over the parapet of the Embankment and looking out across the river.
> As a figure he was quite conventional, clad in a silk hat and frock coat of
> the more formal type of fashion; he had a red flower in his buttonhole.
> As Syme drew nearer to him, he did not even move a hair. …

There are many ways to signal shifts in mood or atmosphere:

- **THROUGH WEATHER.** Weather can be used to show that the scene opens in a different season or time of year, and can also reflect and mirror the changed inner world of your characters or the tone of the new scene. If the scene needs to feel eerie or suspenseful, dark clouds, low light, and other symbols of moodiness can convey this tone to the reader.
- **THROUGH SENSORY DETAILS.** Changes in the way things smell, sound, or feel are giveaways for scene changes. Sounds, for example, can be misconstrued; what sounds like a scream might turn out to be a laugh.

A character may step in a puddle of something sticky that wasn't in the house when they were there last and, in the dark, fear it is blood.

- **THROUGH UNUSUAL JUXTAPOSITIONS**. In the Chesterton example, the strange sight of a man dressed in silk and a frock coat on a parapet overlooking the embankment signals a new mood. You can use jarring, unusual, or just dissimilar images to signal that the tone is now shifting. The new mood doesn't have to be eerie; you can create comic, romantic, and happy juxtapositions, too.

A Shift in Point of View

Many narratives have co-protagonists who each get their own POV scenes or chapters. In order to show that you've moved into a new character's POV, you may need to use a few simple transitions.

Many authors dedicate an entire chapter to one character at a time, which is a very simple, direct way to communicate whose POV the scene is in (see chapter twenty-two). To keep the reader oriented, authors may use a header below the chapter title that gives the character's name:

Chapter 1	Chapter 2
Mary	Jack

However, if you don't want to use the character's name as a header, you must be sure to drop the character's name or some obvious detail about him into the opening couple of sentences in each scene or chapter devoted to that character, as in these examples from Michael Chabon's Pulitzer Prize–winning novel, *The Amazing Adventures of Kavalier & Clay*:

> Josef Kavalier's determination to storm the exclusive Hofzinser Club had reached its height one day back in 1935, over breakfast, when he choked on a mouthful of omelet with apricot preserves.

In a chapter that follows, he shifts to another point of view:

> When the alarm clock went off at six-thirty that Friday, Sammy awoke to find that Sky City, a chromium cocktail tray stocked with modern bottles, shakers, and swizzle sticks, was under massive attack.

In both cases, it's obvious whose point of view the reader is entering, and there's no room for confusion. Don't make the reader wade through a full page to figure out whose eyes he is looking through!

SIGNALING PLOT AND CHARACTER TRANSITIONS

Consider your character and her plot as you start each new scene. You do not need to drop the scene's new piece of plot information into the very opening of that scene, but your protagonist or another character could use words (dialogue or written text) to express that a transition has taken place. "You're not so powerful now," the villain might say to the superhero. Or a character might find a letter in place of his wife that reads, "I've left you."

Sometimes the shift in location or mood is enough to signal that something is coming later in the scene. But you do want to be sure that the opening sets up the scene for whatever you have in mind. So consider the following:

- **IS YOUR PLOT EVENT BASED, AND DOES AN IMPORTANT EVENT HAPPEN IN THE PRIOR SCENE?** Maybe a building exploded—where is your protagonist in relationship to that event now? On the phone with the cops, for instance, or hunting down the bomber?
- **IS YOUR CHARACTER PICKING UP FROM A CLIFFHANGER?** Perhaps your character is beginning an action after an epiphany ending; don't forget to conclude that action.
- **DOES YOUR CHARACTER NEED TO EXPRESS FEELINGS (INTERIOR MONOLOGUE) RELATED TO THE PLOT IN THE SCENE AFTER AN EVENT?** Is she afraid for her life, or refreshed after a long vacation? You might launch the next scene with a line of interior monologue that tells the reader how your protagonist's feelings are different from, or related to, the previous scene.

Transitions are the way you speed past the dull and the mundane, as well as condense time and space so that your characters can get right to the important work of the plot. What has taken place in the scene before is your clue to effectively linking to the scene that comes next.

25

SCENE ASSESSMENT
AND REVISION

So here you are, with a finished draft (or at least a finished scene) still smoking from the sheer effort of your labor. The next step? Put it aside. After some distance, maybe a week, maybe more, when your work is cool to the touch and you've had enough of a break, you're ready to tackle revising. There are many ways you can approach the process. A scene-by-scene revision is a good approach—it's a bit like unpacking the boxes full of interesting, but not necessarily organized, stuff in your garage and putting everything in order.

IDENTIFYING VIGNETTES

Anyone can learn to dance by following the footwork, but not everyone who learns to tango can actually perform for an audience with any grace or dramatic effect. This is true of scene writing. You can learn how to write a basic scene, yet still write scenes that don't do anything for your plot. This assessment chapter hopefully will prevent you from becoming a very competent vignette writer—that is to say, someone who is very good at writing scenes that don't contribute to your plot.

It's important that you can recognize when a scene is just a free-floating vignette that doesn't serve your narrative. There are multiple definitions of a vignette, but my favorite is "a small, graceful literary sketch."

To this, let us add "which does not necessarily relate to the plot and is therefore extraneous." Vignettes may be some of the most beautiful passages in your entire narrative, but if they are conspicuously lacking in plot context, missing an important scene element, or failing to reveal something new about the character, they aren't actually scenes. To determine whether your scene is actually a vignette, you must run it through another set of questions:

- Does the scene introduce new plot information?
- Does the scene relate to the inciting incident?
- Does the scene build upon the last scene?
- Does the scene involve, inform, or affect the protagonist?
- Does the scene make the reader feel smarter or more clued in?
- Does the scene move forward in time (even if only by seconds)?
- Does the scene create new consequences that require a next scene?

If the scene in question is relevant to your plot, the answer to every one of the above questions will be a resounding yes. If you answer no to *any* of those questions, you have a vignette, and it must be fleshed out into a proper scene or be cut.

A vignette is often a half-formed scene, missing just one of the core elements or lacking just one of the necessary parts of its structure (a launch, a middle, or an end). But vignettes often get written because the author is taken with language or finds a character's inner life compelling. Among my editing clients, vignettes often show up as tangents; the writer stumbled onto an inspiring idea or a description and ran with it. Unfortunately, vignettes usually please the writer far more than the reader.

Every scene is part of a larger matrix of scenes that add up to the outcome of your narrative. A vignette usually leaves the reader scratching his head, wondering why the scene was necessary. Ultimately, the most important question you can ask of a scene to determine whether it is a vignette, and thus whether it needs to be cut or transformed, is *Will my narrative still make sense and flow if I cut this scene?* If the answer is yes, you've got a vignette on your hands.

TRANSFORMING OR CUTTING VIGNETTES

If you've determined that your scene is *not* relevant to your plot or character development, and thus is a vignette, then you have two options: Cut it, or make it relevant. If you decide to make it relevant, your next step is to determine what's missing so you can add it in. Here are some common scene elements missing from vignettes:

- **CHARACTER MOTIVATION.** You have forgotten your character's motivations and relationship to the inciting incident of your plot, and you have had him behave in an unrealistic or unrelated way. **FIX:** Go back to your character sketch (or do a new one) and see what more you can learn about your character that will fill in the blanks. Don't drop into lengthy backstory exposition, however. Characters act out their backstory in words and deeds.
- **PERTINENT DIALOGUE.** You've written a scene full of dialogue that goes nowhere, is too mundane, or does not pertain to plot. **FIX:** Edit or cut dialogue, and look to the other methods included in this book for demonstrating character and revealing information.
- **SETTING.** You put your characters in a setting that does not make sense to your plot, or your setting is so vague that the reader can't connect to it. This situation results in "floating heads" syndrome—where the characters may as well be floating in space, untethered to a physical location. **FIX:** Ask yourself how important your setting is to your story. Determine if you have too much setting or not enough.
- **INFORMATION.** Nothing new is revealed, so the momentum peters out. **FIX:** Think about what happens next and how you can reveal it through your character's actions and dialogue.
- **ACTION.** Your scene lacks action, and the reader finds it boring or gets distracted. **FIX:** Remember to think about forward motion and increasing the stakes. Ask what action could get your plot or characters moving in the most complicated way.
- **CONFLICT.** There's not enough push-and-pull energy in the conflict; obstacles are too easily dealt with, and as a result, the reader's attention wanders. **FIX:** Consider the consequences. Refer back to your significant situation and make a list of all the consequences that have devel-

oped so far. Consider whether you have enough, and think about what else you can drum up that will make sense to your plot.

When it comes time to cut a vignette, you're likely to suffer a moment of doubt, or even panic. Always save your last draft of something before you revise, or save the excised pieces, so that you can reclaim them if you make a mistake and need to get them back. Generally, however, true vignettes will not be missed. In fact, you may feel a sense of clarity once they're gone because all they did was obscure the plot.

If you feel empty or your plot stops making sense after you cut a scene, then most likely that was a valuable scene, and you should put it back in and try to fix what rings false about it.

Additional options when cutting a scene:

- **SAVE A DETAIL FOR ANOTHER SCENE.** Remember that if a vignette isn't working, before you decide to just cut it, consider whether there is something crucial in it that can be woven into a later scene.
- **COMBINE SCENES.** I often find in my own work that I've written two scenes or vignettes that are both attempting to solve a plot or character issue halfheartedly. In these cases, two vignettes can be brought together into one working scene.

PARING DOWN NARRATIVE SUMMARY

If you find that you have trouble assessing how much narrative summary to snip out, ask yourself these questions:

- If I cut the narrated section in question, will the plot or characters suffer? If no, then it can go.
- Can the narrative summary—family history, backstory, lengthy explanations—be revealed through dialogue or action, or perhaps in a flashback scene? If no, ask whether it really has a place here or needs to be cut.
- Have I repeated this information in another scene? If so, it can go.

The following are checklists for you to run through when it comes time to assess individual scenes that don't feel quite right to you.

ASSESSING SCENE ARCHITECTURE

One of the most important questions to ask when you're revising is whether your scenes are cohesive in structure and if each one not only works as an individual unit, but also sets up the next scene. Does each scene:

- Have a beginning, a middle, and an end?
- Launch vividly and engage the reader?
- Have a rich subtext, with texture, themes, and imagery?
- Include complications that up the ante on the characters?
- Leave the reader hungry for more upon its ending?
- End in a logical way that leaves room for the next scene to launch?

ASSESSING CORE ELEMENTS

Because a scene is made up of so many core elements, you'll really want to take a solid look at each scene to see if it fulfills the goals of setting and the senses, if characters are well-developed, and if it contains enough tension to keep the reader's interest.

Visual and Sensual Details

Does each scene:

- Have an effective setting that is vivid but not overbearing?
- Reveal the time, place, and culture of your setting?
- Use objects to reveal details about plot and character?
- Engage the senses to create a sense of realism and authenticity? (Don't forget those seemingly mundane senses, like taste and hearing.)

Characters

Does each scene:

- Include a distinctive protagonist within the first two paragraphs?
- Feature useful minor characters as catalysts and antagonists?
- Use voice, dialogue, and behavior, rather than narrative summary, to reveal character?
- Keep consistent points of view?

- Offer your protagonist a chance to act or react?
- Force your protagonist to reevaluate or change?
- Engage your protagonist in the plot?

Plot

Does each scene:

- Introduce at least one new piece of information (who, what, where, when, how, or why)?
- Build upon the information revealed in the last scenes?
- Relate only information that ties directly to the significant situation and its consequences?
- Dole out plot information slowly, creating a sense of mystery?
- Use flashback scenes in place of backstory (where needed and possible)?

Dramatic Tension

Does each scene:

- Employ subtlety over melodrama?
- Create an emotional response in the reader, not just the characters?
- Create the feeling of potential conflict?
- Thwart your protagonist's goals, delaying satisfaction?
- Throw in unexpected changes without immediate explanation?
- Shift power back and forth?
- Pull the rug out—throw in a piece of plot information that changes or alters your protagonist in some way?
- Create a tense atmosphere through setting and senses?

ASSESSING SCENE TYPES

Remember that at the end of each scene-type chapter in this book, you will find a bulleted list of Muse Points. Refer to these when assessing a specific scene type.

. . .

All in all, if you've answered no to any of the questions on these lists, you now have an indication of where your scene needs to be strengthened.

When you assess individual scenes, you create a cohesive sense of integrity in your overall narrative because you assess each scene not only on its own merits, but also on its contribution to the adjacent scenes and to the storyline as a whole.

It is my hope that by the time you reach this final chapter, you will see scenes as dynamic, living, and integral parts of any narrative, which build upon each other and work together to tell a powerful story. By practicing each of the many elements separately and together, you have the power to transform an interesting idea into a compelling novel or story that your readers will be unable to put down.

INDEX

musings, philosophical, 36–38

Musk, Justine, 161–62, 162–63

Nabokov, Vladimir, 27, 30, 213–14

narrative arc, 234–35

narrative launches, 19–20

narrative summary, 7, 8, 11–12, 15, 17, 19–20, 77

   reflective, 216

   and tension, 99–102, 254

   used to condense time, 246

natural settings, 43–44, 47–48

Némirovsky, Irène, 61

objectivity, 226

objects

   purposeful placement of, 48–52

   significant, 50–51

   vague, 51–52

   withholding, 28

O'Brien, Tim, 52

omniscient POV, 37, 228–29, 230–31, 236

opposition, 66, 115–16, 170, 192–93. *See also* conflict

pace, 8, 12, 139, 141

   in climactic scenes, 193, 197

   in contemplative scenes, 151

   and dialogue, 164

   in final scenes, 216–18

   in first scenes, 135–37

   in suspense scenes, 155

Palahniuk, Chuck, 220–21

parallel stories, 188–89

past, transitioning into, 181–82

past tense, 181

Patchett, Anne, 74–75, 101

Percy, Walker, 146–47

philosophical musings, 36–38

Picoult, Jodi, 232–33

place, 75. *See also* setting

placement, purposeful, 48–52

Plath, Sylvia, 181

plot, 110

   assessing, 256

   and character, 70–71, 72–89, 129, 145–47

   defined, 72

   information about, 7, 9, 73–78, 168–71

   revealing, 168–71

   and scene, 73

   and setting, 53, 75

   structure, 79–88

   transitions, 250

plot-based intentions, 111–14

point of no return, 79–80, 193

point of view (POV), 7, 9, 10, 25, 224–35

   changing from chapter to chapter, 233–34

   changing from scene to scene, 232–33

   changing within a scene, 230–32

   and scene transitions, 249–50

   using multiple, 229–34

post-climactic event, 200–201

POV character, 125–26. *See also* protagonists

present tense, 226

pressure, emotional, 237

prologues, 121–27

props, placement of, 48–52

protagonists, 7, 66, 168. *See also* characters

   and antagonists, 238

   changes in, 154

   and climactic scenes, 200

   and conflict, 66, 82

   in dialogue scenes, 178

   and epiphany, 210

   introducing, 129–32

   ultiple, 234–35, 243, 249–50

   personal history, 66–67

   role of, 236

   and setting, 53

Proulx, Annie, 28–29

Printed in the United States
by Baker & Taylor Publisher Services